# Assessing the Implicit Personality Through Conditional Reasoning

# Assessing the Implicit Personality Through Conditional Reasoning

**Lawrence R. James
and James M. LeBreton**

American Psychological Association • Washington, DC

Published by
American Psychological Association
750 First Street, NE
Washington, DC 20002
www.apa.org

To order
APA Order Department
P.O. Box 92984
Washington, DC 20090-2984
Tel: (800) 374-2721; Direct: (202) 336-5510
Fax: (202) 336-5502; TDD/TTY: (202) 336-6123
Online: www.apa.org/pubs/books
E-mail: order@apa.org

In the U.K., Europe, Africa, and the Middle East, copies may be ordered from
American Psychological Association
3 Henrietta Street
Covent Garden, London
WC2E 8LU England

Typeset in Goudy by Circle Graphics, Inc., Columbia, MD

Printer: United Book Press, Baltimore, MD
Cover Designer: Mercury Publishing Services, Rockville, MD

The opinions and statements published are the responsibility of the authors, and such opinions and statements do not necessarily represent the policies of the American Psychological Association.

**Library of Congress Cataloging-in-Publication Data**

James, Lawrence R.
Assessing the implicit personality through conditional reasoning / Lawrence R. James and James M. LeBreton. — 1st ed.
    p. cm.
Includes bibliographical references and index.
ISBN-13: 978-1-4338-1057-2
ISBN-10: 1-4338-1057-3
1. Personality assessment. 2. Subconsciousness. I. LeBreton, James M. II. Title.

BF698.5.J34 2011
155.2'8—dc22

                                        2011015084

**British Library Cataloguing-in-Publication Data**

A CIP record is available from the British Library.

*Printed in the United States of America*
*First Edition*

DOI: 10.1037/13095-000

# CONTENTS

# LIST OF TABLES, FIGURES, AND EXHIBITS

## TABLES

## FIGURES

## EXHIBITS

# ACKNOWLEDGMENTS

*Assessing the Implicit Personality Through Conditional Reasoning* was made possible through the efforts of a number of very talented and dedicated graduate students, and Larry James would like to expresses his gratitude to them one and all. He is especially indebted to Michael McIntyre, who was there at the beginning and continues to contribute. He would also like to express his gratitude to his friends Larry Williams and Terry Mitchell, who graciously provided many hours of consultation and guidance. And he writes to Jack Feldman, "Let me say thanks for setting me on the path."

James LeBreton would like to thank his students for their hard work and hard questions. Interacting with them has been one of the great rewards of working in academia. He would also like to acknowledge the continued support of his wife, Beth, and the generosity and support of his parents, who first taught him the value of higher education.

Both authors would like to extend their sincere appreciation to Linda Malnasi McCarter and Peter Pavilionis in the Books department at the American Psychological Association. Their advice and guidance made this book possible.

# Assessing the Implicit Personality Through Conditional Reasoning

# 1

# INTRODUCTION: THE IMPLICIT AND EXPLICIT PERSONALITIES AND THE ISSUE OF THEIR ASSESSMENT

Although maintaining a consistently popular position in the psychological lexicon, the unconscious or *implicit* personality was abandoned by many in the academic community during the middle part of the last century. The implicit personality remained banished until it was discovered that implicit cognitions often have potent effects on how people reason (e.g., Nisbett & Wilson, 1977), what attitudes they have (e.g., Fiske & Taylor, 1984; Greenwald & Banaji, 1995), and why they behave as they do (e.g., McClelland, Koestner, & Weinberger, 1989; Westen, 1991). These discoveries served as catalysts for a renaissance of interest in many things implicit. Indeed, the rebirth triggered an "explosion of empirical studies" (Westen, 1998, p. 333) that were assisted by old techniques and the development of new techniques to measure the implicit personality (see Baumeister, Dale, & Sommer, 1998; Cramer, 2006; Fazio & Olson, 2003; Greenwald et al. 1998; James & Mazerolle, 2002; Westen, 1998).

Formally, we define *personality* as the dynamic mental structures (e.g., scripts, schemas, motives, needs) and associated mental processes (e.g., perceiving, framing, encoding, analyzing, inferring) that determine an individual's cognitive, affective, and behavioral adjustments to his or her environments (Allport, 1961; James & Mazerolle, 2002; Kelly, 1963; Mischel & Shoda, 1995). Such adjustments may include both specific responses to environmental

3

stimuli (e.g., retaliating against a neighbor, persisting on a task after meeting with initial failure) or decisions concerning which situations one selects into or out of (e.g., physically confronting a classmate, deciding to quit a safe and secure job to start a new business). The goal of personality psychologists is thus to identify stable differences between individuals in these mental structures and processes.

One group of psychologists has sought to identify and measure these differences by focusing on the *explicit* component of personality. *Explicit personality* refers to the dynamic mental structures and processes that influence an individual's behavioral adjustments to his or her environment *that are accessible via introspection*—although this introspective process may not necessarily result in veridical self-perceptions, as we discuss later in this book. The explicit personality refers to the aspect of personality about which an individual is conscious or aware; it consists primarily of self-ascribed dispositions to think, behave, or feel (see Allport, 1961; Bornstein, 2002; Hogan, 1991; McClelland et al., 1989). We note that some leading personality researchers who rely on self-report surveys in their assessments may question the belief that these items are necessarily capturing introspectively accurate self-perceptions. For example, Harrison Gough and Robert Hogan believe that self-deception is a normal (and at times healthy) aspect of personality (Hogar, 2006). Such scholars would not necessarily equate endorsing an item on a survey with veridical introspective insight. Nevertheless, for the purposes of this book, we have opted to classify variables assessed via self-report surveys as being reflective of the explicit personality (i.e., self-assessments—accurate or not—of one's general pattern of thinking, feeling, and behaving).

Psychologists interested in understanding individual differences in the explicit personality have most commonly relied on direct assessments such as self-report surveys or structured interviews. Such assessments ask individuals to respond to questions concerning the self-attributed aspects of personality as manifested in explicit needs, motives, values, and traits (cf. Allport, 1961; Cattell, 1957; Costa & McCrae, 1992; Edwards, 1959; Goldberg, 1993; Hogan, 1991; Hogan, Hogan, & Roberts, 1996; Jackson, 1984; Lanyon & Goodstein, 1997; McClelland et al., 1989; McCrae & Costa, 1997; Winter, John, Stewart, Klohnen, & Duncan, 1998). Exemplars of explicit measures include the Hogan Personality Inventory (Hogan & Hogan, 1995), NEO-PI-R (Costa & McCrae, 1992), and the Self-Report Psychopathy Scale (Paulhus & Williams, 2002).

A second group of psychologists has sought to identify and measure stable differences in personality by focusing on the implicit component of personality. *Implicit personality* refers to the dynamic mental structures and processes that influence an individual's behavioral adjustments to his or her environment *that are not accessible via introspection*. This definition emphasizes the often hidden or unconscious cognitive–affective systems and structures that engender explicit behavior. By definition, these underlying dimensions of personality are not available for social observation and/or introspection on the part of the individual. Researchers subscribing to this definition are often interested in measuring cognitive structures such as implicit needs and motives and cognitive processes such as defense mechanisms (cf. Allport, 1961; Brewin, 1989; Cramer, 1998, 2000, 2006; Epstein, 1994; Freud, 1959; Greenwald & Banaji, 1995; Hogan, 1991; James, 1998; Kihlstrom, 1987, 1999; Kihlstrom, Mulvaney, Tobias, & Tobis, 2000; McClelland et al., 1989; Millon, 1990; Mischel & Shoda, 1995; Murray, 1938; Nisbett & Wilson, 1977; Westen, 1991, 1998; Westen & Gabbard, 1999; Winter et al., 1998).

Because the implicit personality refers to events outside of conscious awareness, researchers must rely on indirect assessment techniques such as projective tests or response latency tests. Projective techniques ask individuals to respond to various stimuli (e.g., picture cards, inkblots). Responses are then interpreted by trained raters who draw inferences concerning the extent to which aspects of the implicit personality (e.g., defense mechanisms, latent motives) were instrumental in shaping individuals' reactions to the stimuli. Response latency tests presume that the speed with which individuals respond to various stimuli are indicative of implicit (unconscious) cognitive structures associated with personality (e.g., implicit personality-driven schema).

Historically, studies of implicit and explicit personality have proceeded relatively independently of each other. The result has been a dialectic in which the different camps of researchers attempt to defend or promote their preferred system of assessment while discounting alternative measurement systems. Tacit in this continuing debate is the assumption that one method of measurement is superior to others.

Perceptions of superiority are likely engendered by tradition and history (Frost, Ko, & James, 2007). For example, assessments of the explicit personality are grounded in the factor-analytic dominated psychometrics of Thurstone, Spearman, and Guilford, whereas assessment of the implicit personality is linked to the psychodynamic foundation established by Freud, Jung, and Murray (see Guilford, 1954). The dimensions of explicit personality come from the lexicon of laypeople and have the aura of directness and practicality (Block, 1995). The attributes associated with implicit personality emanate from the psychological theories of Jung, Rorschach, and Freud, and often seem dense and academic. Both camps are uncomfortable with the principal measurement technique for personality used by the alternative camp.

Nevertheless, the extant literature supports the idea that implicit and explicit personalities represent relatively independent aspects of personality (McClelland et al., 1989; Winter et al., 1998). This literature also suggests that these aspects of personality often predict different behaviors (see Chapter 4, this volume) and that it is possible to integrate the information obtained from implicit and explicit personality to maximize our understanding of behavior (see Chapter 5). Thus, we see no real debate regarding the "superiority" of implicit or explicit personality. Instead, we believe these aspects of personality work in a complementary manner. Consequently, measuring both aspects of personality is instrumental to developing a comprehensive understanding of the dispositional underpinnings of human behavior (see Bing, LeBreton, Migetz, Davison, & James, 2007; Bornstein, 1998, 2002; Brunstein & Maier, 2005; Frost, Ko, & James, 2007; James & Mazerolle, 2002; Langan-Fox, Canty, & Sankey, 2010; LeBreton, Binning, & Adorno, 2006; McClelland et al., 1989; Winter et al., 1998).

The primary purpose of our book is to introduce readers to a new indirect measurement system applicable to assessing implicit personality (Chapters 1–3). This measurement system was designed to address several of the limitations of existing implicit personality measures. A secondary purpose is to illustrate how the information obtained using this new measurement system complements the information obtained concerning the explicit personality (see Chapters 4 and 5). In this chapter, we review several of the more common measures of implicit personality and note both their strengths and limitations. We then describe the requisite features for a new measurement system assessing the implicit personality. Our review of alternative measurement systems is necessarily brief, for it serves only as a foundation for our primary objective, which is to introduce a new system of assessment. Readers interested in more comprehensive treatments of popular implicit assessments are directed to reviews by De Houwer, Teige-Mocigemba, Spruyt, and Moors (2009); Gawronski (2009); Lilienfeld, Wood, and Garb (2000); Nosek, Greenwald, and Banaji (2007); and Schultheiss (2008).

## COMMON MEASURES OF THE IMPLICIT PERSONALITY

### Projective Tests

*Projective tests* are designed to provide a context within which an individual's implicit personality may be mapped or projected into consciousness. The basic idea is that vague or ambiguous stimuli can be used to activate the implicit personality. Projective tests are designed to assess the implicit personality via indirect means. A measure is said to be *indirect* when the purpose of assessment is not disclosed and participants are not asked to self-report on the construct in question (Greenwald & Banaji, 1995). Allport (1961) suggested that projective techniques could be classified into one of three types: perceptive, apperceptive, and productive.

*Perceptive tests* ask respondents simply to describe various stimuli. A prototypical perceptive test is the Rorschach Inkblot Test (Rorschach, 1942). This test consists of 10 symmetric inkblot pictures presented on a white card (five use black ink, two use black and red ink, and three use multiple inks). Each card is presented to respondents, who are asked to describe what they see in the inkblot picture. All of the comments are recorded. These comments are then scored by one or more raters according to various categories or characteristics (e.g., does the respondent see moving or stationary objects, does the respondent note the colors in the cards, does the respondent rotate the cards). Various scoring systems have been developed for use with the Rorschach, with Exner's (1986) Comprehensive System being the most popular (Masling, 2002). Test administration typically takes 45 min with an additional 1 to 2 hr spent coding, scoring, and interpreting an individual's answers (Lilienfeld et al., 2000).

*Apperceptive tests* ask respondents to move beyond simple perception and to create a more sophisticated analysis of the stimuli. A prototypical apperceptive test is the Thematic Apperception Test (TAT; Murray, 1935). This test consists of 30 cards depicting ambiguous situations and one blank card. Different sets of cards are used, depending on what the psychologist hopes to assess. The test was originally developed to provide a tool for assessing the needs and presses identified by Henry Murray (e.g., Need for Achievement, Need for Aggression). Respondents are asked to generate a story that explains what is happening in the "snapshot" portrayed in each picture. The basic idea is that as a respondent (a) generates a story (what has happened up to this point, how do people in the picture feel, what is likely the resolution to the story, etc.), he or she is likely to (b) project his or her own fantasies, fears, needs, and goals into the story. As in the Rorschach test process, the stories are recorded and scored by one or more raters. And like the Rorschach, various scoring protocols have been developed (Vane, 1981), with each test taking roughly 1 to 2 hr to score and interpret (Lilienfeld et al., 2000).

Finally, *productive tests* ask respondents to generate or produce something, such as a drawing or painting. These tests differ appreciably from perceptive and apperceptive tests because they do not rely on verbal ability to communicate (project) the implicit personality. A prototypical productive test is the Draw-A-Person Test (Harris, 1963). This test asks the respondents, often children, to draw a person. The basic idea is that the choice concerning what is drawn (e.g., sex of person, size or content of the face, facial expressions, behavior of the person) is driven by the implicit personality. Unlike the Rorschach and TAT, the Draw-A-Person Test takes only 5 min to complete and another 5 min to be scored and interpreted (Lilienfeld et al., 2000).

*Strengths*

A large number of projective tests exist. The three aforementioned ones were selected because they are popular and representative of the various forms that projective tests may take. Because each test is different, it is difficult to draw global inferences concerning the strengths of projective tests. That said, we would like to note several features of projective tests that appear to make them particularly attractive tools for assessing the implicit personality:

- Projective tests are (relatively) indirect tests of personality, so they presumably neither inform the respondent about the specific construct being assessed nor require respondents to describe themselves on that construct. We describe these tests as "relatively" indirect tests because, although most respondents understand that aspects of their personality are being assessed, they are uncertain as to the particular construct or constructs under investigation.
- Measurement is based on multiple responses. Many projective tests rely on a diverse array of stimuli to evoke the implicit personality. As noted earlier, the Rorschach consists of 10 cards and the TAT consists of (some subset of) 31 cards. Thus, inferences concerning the implicit personality are not based on a single response to a single stimulus; instead, they are based on a pattern of responses across multiple, diverse stimuli.
- Most projective techniques are relatively uncorrelated with measures of the explicit personality. For example, McClelland et al. (1989) noted that the needs for achievement, power, and affiliation as assessed with the TAT were relatively uncorrelated with these same needs as self-reported, with correlations ranging from −.21 to .08. Such low correlations reinforce the notion that the implicit measures are capturing something different from what the explicit measures capture.
- Some of the projective tests permit psychologists to draw inferences that appear to have some degree of construct and criterion-related validity. For example, Lilienfeld et al. (2000) noted that "there is modest support for the construct validity of several TAT scoring schemes, particularly those assessing need for achievement and object relations" (p. 46). They also noted that meta-analyses "suggest that at least some of the Rorschach indexes possess above-

zero validity" (p. 38). In addition, meta-analyses of the TAT also support the predictive validity of the TAT when scored for the Need for Achievement (Spangler, 1992). Nevertheless, the criterion-related validity evidence of projective tests, while often nonzero, often fails to exceed the .30 barrier noted by Mischel (1968; see Garb, Florio, & Grove, 1998; James & Mazerolle, 2002; Lilienfeld et al., 2000; Spangler, 1992).

## Limitations

Like all measurement systems, projective tests are not without their limitations. Given the diversity of projective tests (and scoring systems), it is difficult to draw broad conclusions about all projective tests (or scoring protocols). However, we believe several issues are of concern in regard to some of the more popular projective techniques:

- There is some evidence that respondents are able to manipulate (fake) their answers to projective tests such as the TAT (Holmes, 1974; Kaplan & Eron, 1965; Orpen, 1978). Such faking seems to be less of a concern for the Rorschach (Ganellen, Wasyliw, Haywood, & Grossman, 1996; Meisner, 1988). Any new measures of implicit personality should be developed in a manner that minimizes the likelihood of such response distortion/faking.
- There is considerable controversy concerning the psychometric characteristics of many projective tests. The following quotations were extracted from a comprehensive review of several projective techniques conducted by Lilienfeld et al. (2000):

Despite its continued widespread use by clinicians, the Rorschach Inkblot Test remains a problematic instrument from a psychometric standpoint. (p. 38)

The CS [Comprehensive System scoring] norms for many Rorschach variables appear to have the effect of misclassifying normal individuals as pathological, the possibility of significant cultural bias in the CS has not been excluded, the inter-rater and test-retest reliabilities of many CS variables are either problematic or unknown, the factor structure of CS variables does not correspond to investigators' theoretical predictions, and the validities of most Rorschach indexes rest on a weak scientific foundation. (p. 38)

Even the few promising TAT scoring systems, however, are not yet appropriate for routine clinical use. For all of these systems, (a) adequate norms are not available, (b) test-retest reliability is either questionable or unknown, (c) field reliability is untested, and (d) there is almost no research to ensure that such systems are not biased against one or more cultural groups. (p. 48)

These quotes simply echo similar concerns raised by psychometricians concerning projective tests such as the TAT and Rorschach. Some of the more critical reviews include:

> Among their shortcomings are inadequacies of administration, scoring, and standardization. The lack of objectivity in scoring and the paucity and deficiency of representative normative data are particularly bothersome to specialists in psychometrics. (Aiken, 1994, quoted in James & Mazzerolle, 2002, p. 135)
>
> Many experts consider the TAT, like the Rorschach, to be psychometrically unsound. With the unstandardized procedures for administration, scoring, and interpretation it is easy to understand why psychometric evaluations have produced inconsistent, unclear, and conflicting findings. (Kaplan, 1982, quoted in James & Mazzerolle, 2002, p. 135)
>
> Aside from their questionable theoretical rationale, projective techniques are clearly found wanting with regard to standardization of administration and scoring procedures, adequacy of norms, reliability, and validity. (Anastasi, 1982, quoted in James & Mazzerolle, 2002, p. 135).

Progress has been made in the areas of standardization of testing and scoring protocols (Cramer, 2006). We anticipate greater emphasis in these areas, and in enhancing reliability and validity, as interest continues to grow in assessing the implicit personality.

### Response Latency/Implicit Association Tests

An alternative approach to assessing the psychological unconscious relies on response latency tests. Such tests are designed to measure the amount of time it takes an individual to respond to various stimuli. The most popular response latency measures are based on the Implicit Associate Test (IAT; Greenwald et al., 1998).

The IAT was originally developed for use in studying implicit attitudes, but its application has been recently extended to personality. For example, Greenwald and Farnham (2000) used the IAT to assess implicit self-esteem. In this study, respondents were asked to generate a set of "me" and "not me" items. The me items included things such as a first name, last name, state, address, etc. The not me items included things that were not self-identified. These items were used to distinguish the target concepts (i.e., self vs. not self). The assessment of implicit self-esteem proceeded by asking individuals to respond to pairings of the "target concepts" (me vs. not me) with "attribute dimensions" (positive vs. negative words). The basic idea is that the speed with which these associations are made should be reflective of the strength of the connections these concepts hold in the psychological unconscious.

The assessment process consists of crossing the stimuli representing the target concept (e.g., me vs. not-me words) with the attribute dimension (positive vs. negative words). Respondents are then asked to press keys on a computer whenever certain target concepts and attributes are paired (e.g., "Press the *f* key whenever you see a 'me' item or a positive word and press the *j* key whenever you see a 'not me' item or a negative word"). Respondents are exposed to all possible pairings of target concepts and attribute dimensions. Implicit self-esteem is then estimated by examining the latency (time lag) with which respondents make the various associations. For example, short lags when associating positive words with me items versus longer lags when associating negative words with these same items would be an indicator for positive implicit self-esteem.

*Strengths*

Similar to projective tests, response latency measures such as the IAT are applicable to the assessment of a wide range of personality traits. For example, researchers have expanded the IAT to the assessment of the Big Five personality traits (Grumm & von Collani, 2007), aggression (Richetin, Richardson, & Mason, 2010), and depression (Meites, Deveney, Steele, Holmes, & Pizzagalli, 2008). These and other studies have documented that scores on the implicit personality assessed via the IAT tend to be relatively uncorrelated with scores on self-report measures of explicit personality. In addition, like the projective tests, the IAT uses a large number of stimuli as the basis for drawing inferences about personality. By relying on such a large number of items and using updated scoring protocols, IATs are often able to achieve satisfactory levels of internal consistency reliability, which is atypical for latency measures (Nosek et al., 2007). Although the findings are somewhat mixed, in general the IAT appears to be relatively immune to concerns over faking or response distortion. This is especially true when only vague instructions are giving to respondents. However, as respondents gain experience taking IATs or more specific instructions are given to respondents concerning the testing process, faking appears to increase (Nosek et al., 2007).

*Limitations*

Like any other measurement system, the IAT is not without critics. Although IATs often obtain reasonable levels of internal consistency reliability for basic research purposes, higher estimates would be desirable for use in high-stakes testing (e.g., clinical diagnoses, employment selection).

In addition, some authors have noted other psychometric and substantive concerns/limitations:

- Test-retest reliabilities are often quite low (Nosek et al., 2007). Moreover, many replications/items are often needed in order to obtain reasonable internal consistency estimates. This is likely due to the fact that IAT reliability estimates are derived from difference scores, which can tend to be unreliable (Allen & Yen, 1979).
- Evidence for the predictive validity of IATs is limited but growing (Fazio & Olson, 2003). There is also an active debate about the strength of this validity evidence (cf. Blanton et al., 2009; Greenwald, Poehlman, Uhlmann, & Banaji, 2009; McConnell & Leibold, 2009; Ziegert & Hanges, 2009).
- In a related concern, some have argued that the IAT is based on questionable assumptions. For example, Blanton, Jaccard, Christie, and Gonzales (2007) questioned the appropriateness of combining two constructs (e.g., implicit attitude about the arts and implicit attitude about mathematics) into a singular construct (e.g., implicit attitude about math/arts). These and other concerns challenge the basic construct validity of the inferences being drawn from IATs (cf. Arkes & Tetlock, 2004; Blanton et al., 2007).
- Concerns have also been raised about the arbitrary nature of the scores on IATs. For example, Blanton and Jaccard (2006) urged researchers using the IAT technology to take more care in the development of nonarbitrary metrics. Such metrics should provide a psychometric bridge linking scores on the IAT to the underlying psychological construct and to meaningful behaviors (Blanton & Jaccard, 2006).
- Finally, questions persist about the mechanisms by which the IAT works (Fazio & Olson, 2003). That is, the theory linking exact psychological processes to underlying response latencies has yet to be satisfactorily mapped and tested (De Houwer et al., 2009).

In sum, the IAT has become a very popular vehicle for testing aspects of the psychological unconscious. This includes implicit attitudes and implicit personality. The "technology" for the IAT has been around for roughly 10 years. However, many of the IATs designed to assess personality have been in use for much less time. Consequently, the necessary psychometric and validity evidence is still being acquired. And what evidence exists seems to represent a combination of promise (Nosek et al., 2007) and concern (Blanton & Jaccard, 2006; Blanton et al., 2007).

# REQUIRED FEATURES FOR A NEW IMPLICIT PERSONALITY MEASUREMENT SYSTEM

We were struck by the fact that most of the common implicit personality measures appear to share several strengths. As we set out to develop a new technology for assessing implicit personality, we sought to retain as many of those strengths as possible. We identified three functions that were particularly important to include in developing a new measurement system, if possible:

- maintain (or enhance) the indirect nature of assessment,
- maintain the use of diverse evocative stimuli (items) as part of the assessment process, and
- maintain the independence of any new measure of implicit personality from existing explicit measures.

We also noted that each of the common implicit personality measures had limitations or concerns. Thus, we also sought to take proactive steps in our test development and validation process to address or circumvent these issues. Specifically, we sought to develop a measurement system that

- overcame the psychometric limitations noted previously (e.g., reliability, validity, factor structure);
- was relatively immune to issues associated with faking and response distortion;
- was amenable to the development of nonarbitrary metrics; and
- lent itself to standardized test administration, scoring, and interpretation.

Finally, we sought to build a measurement system that was consistent with Ozer's (1999) principles for personality assessment. Specifically, he identified four principles for an "ideal" measurement system, with three of the four being relevant for relatively new measures:

- the content of the instrument should relate rationally to a psychological theory;
- the item characteristics, scale characteristics, and factor structure of the instrument should be consistent with the psychological theory; and
- the instrument should possess demonstrably high validities for the most theoretically relevant inferences.

To these criteria we might add the three normative criteria identified by De Houwer et al. (2009) for an ideal implicit measure. Again, these are optimal standards that few (if any) implicit measures will ever fully satisfy. These include

- the *what* criterion, which stipulates that we should know the attributes causing variation in the measure (i.e., what construct is influencing scores on the implicit measure);
- the *how* criterion, which stipulates that we identify the psychological processes (e.g., defense mechanisms) through which the attribute (e.g., motive to aggress) causes variation in the measure; and
- the *implicitness* criterion, which stipulates that the processes occur automatically.

## AN OVERVIEW OF OUR BOOK

Our book is organized as follows. In Chapter 2, we lay out the logic and rationale for our new measurement system, denoted *conditional reasoning* (CR). We explain how CR is designed to capture stable individual differences in implicit processes (i.e., implicit cognitive biases) that are believed to be linked to implicit components of personality (i.e., implicit motives). The crucial role of implicit biases in reasoning, referred to as *justification mechanisms*, is explained. Chapter 3 explains how to measure implicit personality by capturing biases in framing, reasoning, and analysis. We introduce the reader to the CR problem, which is an inductive reasoning problem. Our problems differ from traditional reasoning problems in a number of important ways. For example, they have multiple correct solutions. One solution is designed to be attractive to individuals whose reasoning is unknowingly influenced by motive-based implicit biases (e.g., the hostile attribution bias). The other solution is designed to be attractive to individuals whose reasoning is impartial and unbiased (i.e., not shaped by motive-based implicit biases).

Chapter 3 gives considerable attention to explaining how to go about building CR problems. We delve into the nuances of inductive reasoning, formal and informal logic, and how these factors can be linked to personality-related unconscious cognitive biases. Our goal is to provide researchers and practitioners with the knowledge needed to begin developing and validating new CR tests.

Chapter 4 summarizes the validation efforts of our research team over the past 15 years. The emphasis of this chapter is on the Conditional Reasoning Test for Aggression, which has been the centerpiece of our research program. We also briefly review the validity evidence for the Conditional Reasoning Test for Relative Motive Strength, which is designed to assess implicit biases associated with the motive to achieve and the motive to avoid failure. This chapter reviews the psychometric, factor analytic, and validity evidence for these tests, including their relationships with explicit measures of personality.

Chapter 5 summarizes our efforts to integrate information about the implicit personality with information about the explicit personality. Following Winter et al. (1998)'s channeling hypothesis, we illustrate how integrating information about the implicit personality with information about the explicit personality yields enhanced prediction and explanation of important behaviors (above and beyond using either component of personality in isolation from the other component). We review both additive and interactive "integrative" models.

Finally, Chapter 6 represents a "new ideas" chapter. Specifically, we illustrate how one could begin developing tests to measure traits such as depression, addiction proneness, and toxic leadership. The purpose of our final chapter is not to review the validity evidence of new tests but, instead, to serve as a catalyst for psychologists to consider how the principles of CR may inform their research and practice. The information in this final chapter represents our latest thinking on possible constructs that lend themselves to our theory of implicit personality and our assessment technology.

# 2

# CONDITIONAL REASONING AND THE IMPLICIT PERSONALITY: CONCEPTS AND THEORETICAL FOUNDATIONS

Considerable progress has been made in recent years in understanding the implicit or unconscious personality. Psychology now has a much better idea of the defensive cognitive processes that people use to create an artificial sense of rationality for what, in truth, are desire-driven behaviors. This knowledge of defensive cognitive processes was used to design a new system for measuring the implicit personality. The new measurement system is based on a "cover" task in the form of an inductive reasoning problem. The use of reasoning to cover the measurement of personality is made possible because people use the illusion of rational analyses to justify their desire-driven behaviors. The measurement system builds on this process by constructing answers to inductive reasoning problems that are grounded in the same defensive thinking that people use to rationalize desire-driven behaviors. People with strong desires to engage in a behavior are drawn to these answers. This is because people who habitually create justifications for these behaviors find reasoning based on the same types of protective thinking to be logically compelling (James, 1998).

We propose that unseen biases in what people believe to be reasonable explanations for their behaviors reveal their implicit personalities. We propose further that these biases can be measured objectively and that the measurements can be used to make valid inferences about individuals' implicit motives and future behaviors. Measurement is based on the principle that people with a strong motive (desire) to engage in a behavior will develop biased (i.e., defensive) ways of reasoning that make the behavior seem rational and sensible as opposed to irrational and foolish. The biases in the ways of reasoning are referred to as *justification mechanisms* to indicate that they serve to enhance the rational appeal of behaviors that express a desire. People with contrasting motives and behaviors—for example, people with intense desires to achieve versus people with deeply seated desires to avoid failing (Atkinson, 1978)—tend to develop different sets of justification mechanisms. People with contrasting sets of justification mechanisms often differ in consistent and predictable ways in what they regard as reasonable behavior. We refer to reasoning that varies among individuals with contrasting motives and justification mechanisms as *conditional*—the term is meant to connote that what is considered reasonable behavior is provisional on the personality (i.e., motive and justification mechanisms) of the person doing the reasoning.

Conditional reasoning (CR) and justification mechanisms are the foundation for a new system of measurement for personality. The first application of this system focused on assessing the extent to which (a) people are implicitly or unconsciously disposed to approaching versus avoiding demanding tasks, irrespective of (b) what they explicitly or consciously believe to be their approach-versus-avoidance tendencies (James, 1998). Measurement is based on assessing the strength of the motive to achieve in relation to the strength of the motive to avoid failure. The relative strengths of these motives, or *relative motive strength*, have been shown to contribute to whether one is truly disposed to approach and to persevere on demanding tasks or to avoid them because one fears failing (Atkinson, 1957, 1964, 1978; McClelland, 1985).

It is possible to infer whether the motive to achieve is dominant or subordinate to the motive to avoid failure by assessing what a person consistently judges to be more logical over time and in various situations—reasoning that supports approach to achievement-oriented objectives or reasoning that defends avoidance of achievement-oriented objectives. If a person is consistently attracted to reasoning that defends approach over avoidance, then it is inferred that this person's motive to achieve dominates his or her motive to avoid failure. Conversely, if a person consistently favors reasoning that defends avoidance over approach, then it is inferred that the motive to avoid failure dominates the motive to achieve. A category also exists for cases in which neither type of reasoning or motive has a mandate.

The second application of CR focused on measuring the strength of the implicit component of the motive to aggress, which consists of a person's desire to harm others (see James & Mazerolle, 2002; James et al., 2005). Assessment of the desire to harm others is again based on the principle that aggressive people want to believe that their decisions to engage in aggressive behavior are justified. In attempts to justify their behaviors, aggressive people often use biases that allow them to disengage moral standards against aggression (Bandura, 1999), to neutralize societal norms that disapprove of aggressive behavior (Sykes & Matza, 1957), and to build illusory logical rationales (i.e., rationalizations) for harming others (Frost, Ko, & James, 2007). Again, we refer to these biases in reasoning as justification mechanisms. In the case of aggression, however, the term *justification mechanism* has a more defensive connotation. This is because the justification mechanisms are used to shape reasoning so as to create a self-deceptively rational excuse for releasing an antisocial motive, namely, a desire to harm others (James, 1998).

The basic premise of the measurement procedure for aggression is that (a) it is possible to infer whether the motive to harm others is dominant or subordinate to the motive to behave in socially adaptive ways by (b) assessing whether a person judges reasoning based on justification mechanisms for aggression or reasoning based on contrasting prosocial norms and ideologies to be more logical. If a person is consistently attracted to reasoning that defends aggression (e.g., retribution, preemptive attack) over prosocial behavior, then it is inferred that this person's motive to aggress dominates his or her motive to behave in socially adaptive ways. Conversely, if a person consistently attributes greater reasonableness to arguments that favor nonaggressive options to aggressiveness, then it is inferred that the motive to behave prosocially dominates the motive to aggress. Unclassified cases are placed in an intermediary category.

Our belief is that a person's latent desire to harm others is reflected in the scope and magnitude of his or her capacity to create seemingly rational excuses for aggression. In other words, how extensive and strong are his or her justification mechanisms for aggression? We argue that those with a weak or nonexistent desire to harm others have no need of justification mechanisms to rationalize aggressiveness. They will not, therefore, possess well-developed justification mechanisms for aggression. On the other hand, possession of an elaborate and cognitively accessible system of justification mechanisms for aggression indicates (a) a history of defending aggressive behaviors, and (b) preparation to defend these same types of behavior in the future. This in turn suggests that a strong implicit motive to harm others is a force in selecting and sustaining behaviors. Simply stated, a well-developed set of mechanisms for disengaging the moral standards that sanction aggression, for neutralizing societal norms against harming others, and for building illusory logical rationales for acting aggressively indicates a strong implicit motive to aggress (James & Mazerolle, 2002).

The type of reasoning that people find logically preferable is measured by means of a new type of inductive reasoning problem. We refer to these tasks as *conditional reasoning problems*. Two illustrative CR problems are presented in Exhibit 2.1. The first problem is designed to assess whether a respondent is logically attracted to reasoning (a) that could be used to justify approach to achievement-oriented objectives or (b) that could be used to justify avoidance of achievement-oriented objectives. The second problem measures whether a respondent logically prefers reasoning (a) that could be used to justify aggression to (b) a contrasting prosocial rational for engaging in nonaggressive behavior. Building and scoring CR problems are the themes for Chapter 3. The remainder of this chapter is devoted to a more thorough development of the theoretical foundation for CR.

This discussion of CR's theoretical foundation is organized around Ozer's (1999) principles for personality assessment. Ozer condensed an earlier attempt by Meehl (1972) to apply the basic standards for sound psychological test development to the assessment of personality. Ozer proposed that the

EXHIBIT 2.1
Illustrative Conditional Reasoning Problems

---

1. Problem for Relative Motive Strength

   Studies of the stress-related causes of heart attacks led to the identification of the Type A personality. Type A persons are motivated to achieve, involved in their jobs, competitive to the point of being aggressive, and impatient, wanting things completed quickly. Interestingly, these same characteristics are often used to describe the successful person in this country. This association logically suggests that

   a. striving for success increases the likelihood of having a heart attack,
   b. most successful people are prone to violence,
   c. few nonambitious people have heart attacks, and
   d. people often mistake enthusiasm and drive for aggressiveness and impatience.

2. Problem for Aggression

   A large number of business partnerships break up. One reason for this is that dissolving a partnership is quick and easy. If the partners can agree on how to split the assets of the partnership fairly, then they can break up simply by filling out the appropriate forms. They do not need to engage lawyers.

   Which of the following is the most reasonable conclusion based on the above?

   a. The longer a partnership has existed, the less likely it is to break up.
   b. If one's partner hires a lawyer, then he or she is not planning to play fairly.
   c. Partners might resolve their differences if breaking up was harder and took longer.
   d. The younger partner is more likely to initiate the breakup.

---

"ideal" personality instrument would satisfy four standards, which he referred to as *principles*. Three of these four principles apply to new instruments:

1. the content of the instrument should relate rationally to a psychological theory;
2. the item characteristics, scale characteristics, and factor structure of the instrument should be consistent with the psychological theory; and
3. the instrument should possess demonstrably high validities for the most theoretically relevant inferences.

New instruments seldom reach the lofty goal of ideal. However, it is reasonable to ask how we believe advances made to this point for CR stack up against Meehl and Ozer's exacting standards.

We begin by discussing the first principle in relation to the CR measures developed for aggression and relative motive strength. This principle asks for a "theory of the instrument" (Ozer, 1999, p. 672). That is, how this instrument is rooted in psychological theory needs to be specified. We begin this specification for the CR instrument for aggression because it has received the lion's share of our attention. We then turn to a theory of the instrument for the measure of relative motive strength before concluding with recommendations and guidelines for those who wish to design their own instruments.

The actual content of the measurement instrument is also a critical component of Ozer's first principle. The specific problems that constitute the CR tests for aggression and relative motive strength are presented and discussed in Chapter 3. Guidelines are then suggested for the development of new CR problems. Ozer's second and third principles pertain to empirical results, and they are the subjects of Chapter 4.

## THEORY OF THE INSTRUMENT FOR THE CONDITIONAL REASONING TEST FOR AGGRESSION

We use the illustration that follows to demonstrate how CR provides a means for understanding how and why aggressive and nonaggressive individuals frame the same events differently (James & Mazerolle, 2002). We then show how these differences in framing shape different inferences about why the events occurred and what additional events are likely to follow.

### Tom's Description of His Teacher and Classmates

Tom, a sophomore in a medium-size college, believes that he is being dominated and oppressed by Dr. Andrews, who teaches his world history class. What follows is Tom's description of the situation to a college counselor.

Dr. Andrews has an intense desire to be powerful. She runs her class in ways that highlight her dominant position as a professor and reinforce her entitlements (e.g., status, prestige) and superiority. My understanding is that professors are expected to use their authority and influence to promote cooperation among students, maintain order, develop their students, and enhance the overall quality of the education experience. In contrast, Dr. Andrews uses her authority and influence to personally dominate students, control behavior and thought, intimidate students, and assert her will. Using her authority in this manner is professionally unethical. We do work on world history, but it is always in a context of Dr. Andrews asserting her dominance over the students. What she wants from the students is deference to her ideas and opinions, which she describes as being socially aware and showing respect for people in authority.

Specific illustrations of her tyranny include a proclivity to administer tests that ask for subjective opinions of world events and then demean and criticize students for not doing well. "Not doing well" means that a student does not agree with her position on what caused an important world event, such as our entrance into the war with Iraq, or what the ramifications will be for China emerging as a superpower. Dr. Andrews also acts as a catalyst for conflict among the students. One of her favorite strategies is to split the students into different groups representing different perspectives on a world event (e.g., the best approach to dealing with global warming). She then has each group work together to build a case for the position she assigns them, which is followed by an in-class debate. These debates often evolve into open verbal conflict between the groups. Rather than end the conflict, Dr. Andrews allows it to escalate to a point where people are ridiculed and degraded by others. She seems to enjoy this.

I believe that Dr. Andrews's students, and especially me, are victims of oppression. We are treated unfairly and inequitably by an abusive, unethical, and untrustworthy instructor who likes to make us suffer if we do not conform totally to her will. I believe that in the interest of righting the many wrongs that have been done to us, we are justified in seeking retribution. We have a right to defend ourselves against Dr. Andrews's tyranny.

My fellow students are not of much assistance in defending against the domination of Dr. Andrews. They are afraid of her, which she undoubtedly sees as weakness. Indeed, their weakness and compliance invites more oppression by Dr. Andrews because it shows that they are willing to submit. I have been the only one to stand up to Dr. Andrews. I have had to fight fire with fire. She must learn that she cannot tyrannize people like me without fear of retaliation.

In regard to specifics, I make an effort to undermine Dr. Andrews's credibility. I frequently complain to the administration about her attempts to coerce and to intimidate me and the other students. So far this has had little effect, but I am hopeful the accumulating record of abuse will be useful in causing her problems in the future. In the classroom, I have found ways to resist Dr. Andrews. For example, I often challenge her interpretations of world history, showing where she is biased in her interpretations of events and attributions of cause and effect. I do just the minimum needed to pass the class, and I take as long as possible to do it. I ignore Dr. Andrews's e-mails to the class, often complaining that I did not receive the e-mails (trying to imply that she left me off the list of e-mails). I miss class as much as possible, come to class late, and text message others during class sessions. It's not much, but it's a start.

I resent the fact that other students in the class do not support me. Although none of them will say it, I believe that they respect me for being brave enough to stand up to Dr. Andrews. Through my efforts, they are able to regain some of the honor and respect they have lost by capitulating to her oppression. They do not openly appreciate me for this, however. In fact, I often sense that they are plotting against me in order to curry favor with Dr. Andrews. For me, this creates a sense of threat that the other students could stab me in the back, so to speak, while I am concentrating on Dr. Andrews. To counteract this threat, I protect myself by letting the other students know what I will do to them if they interfere with me while I am dealing with Dr. Andrews. Every once in a while I have to give one of them a preemptive object lesson. This seems to keep the others in line.

## View of Other Students in the Class

Suppose we ask the other students in Dr. Andrews's class to describe the same set of events described by Tom. If Tom's inferences and framing of the events are accurate, then we should hear similar sentiments about Dr. Andrews's oppression of students (James & Mazerolle, 2002). This, however, is not the case. Most of the other students give comments such as these:

Dr. Andrews can be a little demanding at times, but this is largely because she wants us to learn about world history and to use this knowledge to make informed decisions. Basically, most students believe that Dr. Andrews is a good professor. She serves as a catalyst for successful accomplishments by us. She willingly takes responsibility for directing us in the interest of seeing that we become proficient in world history.

Dr. Andrews is willing to commit intense effort, over long periods of time if necessary, to helping us accomplish this objective. For example, she conducts special study sections on weekends, she designs specific plans of study for students who are interested in a particular world event, and she organizes several field trips to famous museums and sites during the semester. She always treats us with respect, and tries to see that we treat each other with integrity, equity, and justice. Indeed, she is exemplary of the kind of instructor who willingly makes the commitments and sacrifices that a professor must make to promote cooperation among students, maintain order, avoid conflict, and develop her students.

Dr. Andrews is fair, objective, and equitable in describing world events. This does not stop Tom from criticizing her for favoritism for specific positions and opinions. We generally believe Tom never really attempts to understand points of view other than his own, which usually involve some form of attack and war. He seldom completes his homework and does poorly on tests. He is also disruptive during one of our favorite activities, which consists of in-class debates about how best to deal with world crises. Tom's aggressive positions are usually rejected by all sides of the debate, which results in his becoming verbally abusive to us and Dr. Andrews.

Tom has a history of problems with instructors. It seems that Tom is in competition with instructors for who will be the "alpha leader" of the class. It often appears to other students that Tom wants to engage in a personal and visceral form of conflict with his instructors. Dr. Andrews's class exemplifies this: Tom is grossly insubordinate to Dr. Andrews (e.g., talks back, is late for meetings, and then does not pay attention). He denounces her as a dictator behind her back. However, Tom is unsuccessful in his attempts to convince us that his belligerence toward Dr. Andrews is justified. We see none of the oppression and unfairness that Tom sees. Rather, we think that there is something wrong with Tom. We also resent Tom's attempts to bully other students. We have begun to worry about just how far Tom is willing to go in confronting Dr. Andrews. We are also concerned about Tom's attempts to intimidate us because we have not supported either his behaviors or his rationalizations. We fear Tom, and wish that he would just go away.

### Use of Personality Theory to Explain Differences in Framing and Analyses

How is it possible for Tom's framing and analysis of events to be so different from the framing and analyses of most of the other students in the class? Why does Tom see Dr. Andrews as a tyrant, whereas (most) other students see an empathic professor who volunteers extra assistance? Why does Tom see an interpersonal style that involves intentional attempts to demean and to dominate students, but others see a person who creates a nurturing class environment characterized by challenging but fair assignments? And why does Tom see himself as a victim of oppression who is performing justifiable acts of retribution, whereas other students see a belligerent, contentious, and obstreperous bully who might be dangerous?

Answers to these questions arise from the fact that Tom and the other students, or at least most of them, have different personalities (James & Mazerolle, 2002). The differences in personalities help shape, define, and sustain framing such as how Dr. Andrews is perceived as well as how Tom is perceived by himself and by his classmates. Differences in personalities also help shape and influence the reasoning processes that Tom and his classmates use to determine whether Tom's hostility toward Dr. Andrews is justified. An overview of the mental structures and processes involved in these framing and analytic aspects of social cognition is presented next.

### Tom: The Aggressive Individual

In the above example, the description of Tom illustrates a prototypical aggressive personality. His aggressiveness stems from a desire or motive to overcome opposition forcefully, to fight, to revenge an injury, to attack another with intent to injure or kill, and to oppose forcefully or punish another (Murray, 1938). Contemporary work on aggression combines this motive with trait-based behavior to describe the *aggressive individual*. An aggressive individual (a) chooses to use some form of aggression to deal with evocative, especially frustrating, situations; (b) dislikes if not hates the target of aggression; (c) desires to inflict harm on this target; (d) has diminished self-regulatory capacities, which suggests underdeveloped internal prohibitions or standards against aggressing (although sufficient self-regulation may be present to make the aggression indirect and/or passive); and (e) sees limited response options, which denotes that aggression is seen as the most efficacious response to frustration and anger (cf. Anderson & Bushman, 2002; Bandura, 1973, 1999; Baron & Richardson, 1994; Berkowitz, 1993; Bettencourt, Talley, Benjamin, & Valentine, 2006; Gay, 1993; Huesmann, 1988; Laursen & Collins, 1994; Todorov & Bargh, 2002).

Expression of the motive to aggress may take many forms (Buss, 1961; Folger & Baron, 1996). We see a myriad of aggressive behaviors in Tom's case, including direct aggression (insubordination), indirect aggression (filing gratuitous grievances), and passive-aggression (ignoring e-mail). Each of these behaviors shares the common denominator that it is intended to harm another individual(s)—namely, Dr. Andrews. Tom also bullies other students, which involves both direct and instrumental aggression (see Bushman & Anderson, 2001).

Nearly all individuals want to believe that their behavior is rational and appropriate as opposed to irrational and inappropriate (Bandura, 1999; Cramer, 2006; James, 1998). Attributions of rationality come easily when the behavior is consistent with social norms and cultural ideologies, or what Bandura (1999) referred to as the *moral standards* that define and buttress socially adaptive behavior in our society. When a behavior is inconsistent with a moral standard (e.g., when Tom attempts to harm Dr. Andrews via filing gratuitous grievances, launching verbal assaults in the classroom, and passive-aggressively ignoring her e-mail messages), then self-ascriptions of rationality are less easily attained. Although admissions of aggressiveness are possible, self-deceptions aimed at salvaging some semblance of reasonableness are more likely (Cramer, 2006; Westen, 1998). This particular self-deceptive process often involves the defense mechanism of rationalization (see James & Mazerolle, 2002; James et al., 2005).

## Rationalization of Aggression

A model describing rationalization of aggression was recently presented in James et al. (2005) and is reproduced in Figure 2.1. The model begins with

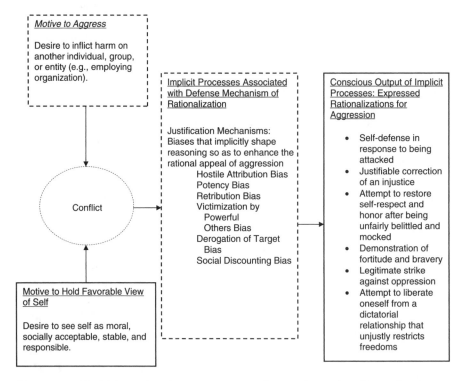

*Figure 2.1.* Model for rationalizing aggression. Dotted line: primarily implicit (unconscious). Solid line: primarily explicit (conscious). Adapted from "A Conditional Reasoning Measure for Aggression," by L. R. James, M. D. McIntyre, C. A. Glisson, P. D. Green, T. W. Patton, J. M. LeBreton, . . . L. J. Williams, 2005, *Organizational Research Methods, 8,* p. 71. Copyright 2005 by Sage Publications, Inc. Adapted with permission.

two conflicting motives, the first of which is the motive to harm others, or the aggression motive. A strong motive to harm others predisposes people like Tom to respond to frustrating situations with anger, accompanied by desires to inflict harm on the perceived source of the anger (i.e., the target; Baron & Richardson, 1994; Berkowitz, 1993). Included here are immediate verbal or physical attacks as well as the more long-term seeking of vengeance and retribution via indirect or passive means (e.g., instrumental aggression; see Bushman & Anderson, 2001; Buss, 1961).

One of the foundations of the defense-mechanism concept and many psychological theories that followed it is that aggressive people are often not aware of the full extent of their powerful desire to inflict harm (see Baumeister et al., 1998; Baumeister, Smart, & Boden, 1996; Cramer, 1998, 2000, 2006; A. Freud, 1936; Westen, 1998). For example, Westen (1998) indicated that the first and most central postulate that defines contemporary psychodynamic theory is that "much of mental life—including thoughts, feelings, and motives—is unconscious, which means that people can behave in ways or develop symptoms that are inexplicable to themselves" (p. 334). Westen (1998) went on to argue that motives and the defense mechanisms that develop to protect motives have central roles in unconscious mental activities.

Our approach is founded in the writings of authors such as Baumeister, Cramer, Freud, and Westen, and closely parallels McClelland, Koestner, and Weinberger's (1989) theory that motives have both implicit and explicit components. As discussed in Chapter 1, the implicit part of the motive is not subject to introspection because it conflicts with the motive to hold a favorable view of the self, that is, to possess a moderate to high sense of self-worth (or self-esteem; see Bandura, 1999; Baumeister, Campbell, Krueger, & Vohs, 2003; Cramer, 1998, 2000, 2006). The great majority of people, including aggressive ones like Tom, need to think of themselves as being moral, prosocial, stable, and capable of self-control (see Bersoff, 1999; Loewenstein, Weber, Hsee, & Welch, 2001; Sykes & Matza, 1957). This motive is largely explicit, although it too has some implicit components (e.g., unrecognized propensity to attribute frustration to external factors to protect self-esteem).

The conflict within aggressive individuals between the motive to hold a favorable view of the self and the motive to aggress sets in motion unconscious defensive processes. The intent of these processes is to allow for the release of the aggression motive while not damaging the sense of self-worth. These unconscious self-protective processes are known as *defense mechanisms*, and they consist of mental operations designed to keep painful thoughts and emotions, such as that one is disposed to be hostile and inclined to harm others, out of consciousness (see Cramer, 2006; Kihlstrom, 1999). The CR system focuses on a defense mechanism that protects people by influencing what they believe to be rational reasoning. This defense mechanism is *rationalization*, defined as the use of ostensibly plausible reasons to justify behaviors that are unknowingly caused by unconscious, unacceptable, and/or unwanted motives (Baumeister et al., 1996; Westen & Gabbard, 1999). For example, a violent act motivated by an unconscious desire to harm a rival may be consciously rationalized as self-defense.

It is noteworthy that rationalization allows many aggressive people to maintain their socially adaptive norms, values, and moral standards (Bandura, Barbaranelli, Caprara, & Pastorelli, 1996; Bandura, Caprara, Barbaranelli, Pastorelli, & Regalia, 2001). Bandura (1999) suggested that aggressive people use justification to "disengage" their moral standards so that self-regulatory mechanisms are not activated during aggression. He observed, "People do not ordinarily engage in harmful conduct until they have justified to themselves the morality of their actions" (Bandura, 1999, p. 194). A similar view was proposed by the "drift" or "neutralization" model of Sykes and Matza (1957). These investigators proposed that delinquents develop justifications for their anti-social behaviors that allow them to temporarily drift from, or neutralize, their otherwise strong sense of moral obligation to conform to the social order.

Rationalization may be thought of as one of the primary defense mechanisms used by aggressive individuals to create the self-delusion that they can behave aggressively and remain socially worthy (Baumeister et al., 1996; Westen & Gabbard, 1999). Rationalizing aggression is accordingly an act of self-deception. This act is intended to conceal from awareness the true, but unacceptable, cause of aggression, specifically, a strong motive to inflict harm. Rationalization accomplishes this self-deception while sparing the aggressive person the anxiety and guilt of self-perceptions that she or he is a hostile, malicious, or malevolent person (see James et al., 2005). Rationalization typically occurs when an aggressive person is building an ostensibly rational case to aggress (see Bandura, 1999), although spontaneous acts of aggressive behavior may require justification after the fact (see Loewenstein et al., 2001; Winter, John, Stewart, Klohnen, & Duncan, 1998).

Possible self-deceptive judgments that illustrate rationalizations for aggression are presented in the last component of Figure 2.1. These ostensibly plausible reasons for acts that harm others appear reasonable to the aggressive individual because he or she arrives at them via what appear to be rational analyses (see James et al., 2004; James & Mazerolle, 2002; Kuhn, 1991). What aggressive people do not realize is that the true but unconscious purpose of their reasoning is to enhance the logical appeal of their rationalizations for aggressive behavior. James (1998) proposed the term *justification mechanisms* to describe the unconscious or implicit proclivities that shape the reasoning that aggressive people use to build logical foundations for their rationalizations. Justification mechanisms may be thought of as implicit predispositions that direct seemingly logical ways of framing and reasoning that are in fact biased and serve rationalizations by making the rationalizations seem reasonable and sensible. More specifically, justification mechanisms are unrecognized (implicit, unconscious, automatic) biases to reason in ways that enhance the rational appeal of self-deceptive explanations for aggression—that is, rationalizations (James, 1998). In a real sense, justification mechanisms enable rationalizations, as we explain next.

### Justification Mechanisms for Aggression

Six proposed justification mechanisms for aggression are presented in the middle component of Figure 2.1. These mechanisms were identified by James (1998; see also James & Mazerolle, 2002) via searches of aggression literatures in psychology and other social sciences. Searches of the scientific literature were augmented by searches of the popular press (e.g., Anderson's [1994] account of street gangs in *The Atlantic Monthly*, Finnegan's [1997] treatment of the unwanted in *The New Yorker*, and Gay's [1993] treatise on the psychoanalytic antecedents of aggression in *The Cultivation of Hatred*). The intent of these searches was to identify a set of biases that implicitly (unconsciously, unknowingly) define, shape, and guide the framing and reasoning that enable aggressive individuals to build rationalizations for their aggression. This process produced six implicit biases that we hereafter refer to as *justification mechanisms for aggression* because they make it possible for aggressive people to build rationalizations for aggression. The six mechanisms are summarized in the following discussion. How each mechanism assists in the construction of one or more rationalizations for aggression is included in the summaries.

Aggressive individuals such as Tom often attempt to rationalize their hostile acts by casting them as forms of self-defense, intended to respond to physical or verbal attacks initiated by their targets (Anderson, 1994; Averill, 1993; Baron & Richardson, 1994; Baumeister et al., 1996; Berkowitz, 1993; Brehmer, 1976; Crick & Dodge, 1994; Felson & Tedeschi, 1993; Gay, 1993; Huesmann, 1988; James, 1998; Millon, 1990; Tedeschi & Nesler, 1993; Toch, 1993). Tom, for example, feels that he has to defend himself against Dr. Andrews's use of unfair tests to create a reason for demeaning and criticizing students. But Tom's attempt to rationalize his aggression as self-defense is a product of justification mechanisms (implicit biases) in the causal attributions he made about the behavior of Dr. Andrews.

To illustrate, like many aggressive people, Tom harbors an unconscious predilection to see or to seek out malevolent purpose or harmful intent in other people (cf. Crick & Dodge, 1994; Dodge & Coie, 1987). This is a justification mechanism (implicit bias) that may permeate the implicit cognitive system, such that perceptions of Dr. Andrews (and others) are seen through a perceptual filter that causes Tom to focus on indications of hostile or malevolent intent (cf. Anderson, 1994; Tedeschi & Nesler, 1993; Toch, 1993). With this justification mechanism in place, even a benign or friendly act by another person, such as an offer by Dr. Andrews to assist on one of Tom's assignments, may be seen by Tom as having a hidden, hostile agenda designed to inflict harm either now or in the future (e.g., by pretending to assist, Dr. Andrews can sabotage Tom's work or make him look incompetent). The implicit proclivity to see or seek out hostile intent as a reasonable cause of the behaviors of others has been designated the *hostile attribution bias* (cf. Crick & Dodge, 1994; Dodge & Coie, 1987).

Our primary concern is that biased attributions of hostile intent help shape the aggressive person's attempts to rationalize his or her own hostile behaviors by casting them as acts of self-defense. It is the ability to enable rationalizations of self-defense that make the hostile attribution bias a justification mechanism in our theoretical model. The enabling process follows a mediation model. Initially, individuals with this justification mechanism selectively attend to information in their environments suggesting that others should not be trusted, while discounting information that disconfirms these perceptions. This results in a heightened sense of threat, engendered by overestimating hostile intent, that triggers sensations of peril and alarm. A concern for self-protection follows, which enables the aggressive person to infer that harming another is justified inasmuch as one is merely protecting oneself, not initiating a hostile action. Thus, the desire to harm another is made to seem rational via a justification mechanism to overestimate malevolent intent in the behavior of the intended victim.

We will take a moment to discuss what we mean by the term *bias* in relation to the hostile attribution bias justification mechanism (and by analogy other justification mechanisms). If the intentions of others such as Dr. Andrews were truly hostile, and the danger from an attack was real and imminent, then use of aggression in the name of self-defense would be rational (in the minds of many). However, if, as is the case here, the attributions of hostile intent reflect an unrecognized (implicit) bias to overestimate the degree to which antagonism is present, perhaps even to see antagonism when it is not there, then the ensuing feelings of peril and desire for self-protection that are used to justify aggression as self-defense are an illusion. Basically, an implicit predilection to see hostile intent (the justification mechanism) sets off processes that create the self-deception that one is under attack and therefore aggression in the name of self-defense is rational (the rationalization).

Thus, we might say that aggressive individuals often miss the true state of a person's intentions because they are predisposed to see hostile intentions. That is, they are inclined to give greater emphasis to hostile intentions than to nonhostile intentions. The result is that sometimes they are correct in their attributions of hostility—a person really does mean them harm. However, more often they overestimate the degree of hostile intent. Overall, they see many more cases, and more severe cases, of hostile intent than are factual. It is the pattern of consistently seeing hostile intent when other attributions are at least equally plausible that is the key to possession of the justification mechanism of the hostile attribution bias.

A second implicit bias in reasoning that serves to justify aggression, and is therefore a justification mechanism for aggression in our thinking, is referred to as the *potency bias* (James & Mazerolle, 2002; James et al., 2005). This justification mechanism consists of a tendency to frame and think about interactions with others as contests to establish dominance versus submissiveness (Anderson, 1994; Bandura, 1999; Baron & Richardson, 1994; Crick & Dodge, 1994; Gay, 1993; Hogan & Hogan, 1989; Millon, 1990; Tedeschi & Nesler, 1993; Wright & Mischel, 1987). The actions of others pass through a perceptual prism (implicit bias, justification mechanism for aggression) primed to distinguish (a) strength, assertiveness, dominance, daring, fearlessness, and bravery from (b) weakness, impotence, submissiveness, timidity, compliance, and cowardice (James & Mazerolle, 2002). Such framing promotes biased inferences that the use of aggression to establish dominance indicates strength, bravery, control, and fearlessness. Not acting in an aggressive, domineering manner is associated with weakness, fear, cowardice, and impotence. When biased inferences such as these are furnished by the potency bias justification mechanism, they serve as a foundation for, and therefore enable, rationalizations such as aggression is an act of strength or bravery that gains respect from others. An individual's failure to act aggressively to gain dominance indicates weakness and invites others to be aggressive because it shows that he or she is willing to submit.

Tom's framing and reasoning revealed the operation of a potency bias. He described Dr. Andrews as having an "intense desire to be powerful" and as using her position of authority to dominate students by controlling their thoughts and behavior. He characterized her as engaging in tyranny and forcing students to bend to her will. The fact that classmates did not share these inferences about Dr. Andrews's motives and behavior suggests that Tom is biased toward thinking of his interactions with her in terms of a dominance contest. He sees Dr. Andrews as dominant and resents this. What he wants is to enhance his personal potency, his ability to personally dominate, control, intimidate, assert his will, and instill fear in Dr. Andrews (Winter, 1973). His use of aggression (e.g., insubordination, filing grievances) appears to him to be rational, for it paints him, he thinks, as strong, assertive, brave, powerful, bold, and seeking control. These positive but self-deceptive rationalizations (enabled by the justification mechanism of the potency bias) suggest that attempts to gain control over others by accruing personal power is not only reasonable but also laudatory (Doesn't everyone respect bravery?).

Further evidence of a potency bias at work is Tom's inference that his classmates are weak, afraid, and incapacitated by Dr. Andrews's dominance. Such reasoning projects one of the great fears of aggressive individuals, which is that of being seen as "weak" (Veroff, 1992). It follows that if their quest for dominance is frustrated, and they are at risk of being seen as weak, then aggressive people are prepared to use injurious and unjust methods to show that they are strong, powerful, bold, and in control (Baumeister et al., 1996; James & Mazerolle, 2002). In fact, their pride, honor, and self-respect are tied to their personal potency and status (Baumeister et al., 2003). Anything that threatens such potency and status is regarded as a form of personal disrespect and dishonor that is deserving of immediate retribution. When engaging in such retribution, they believe that others secretly respect them even though these others may express public disapproval (James, 1998).

Whereas the hostile attribution bias and the potency bias appear to be central justification mechanisms shaping Tom's reasoning, there are indications of a third justification mechanism that relates to his inferences about his experiences in Dr. Andrews's classroom. Aggressive individuals are often selectively attentive to, indeed may seek out, what they regard as acts of inequity, exploitation, injustice, and oppression by authority figures and/or their organization. Selective attentiveness and confirmatory searches both engender and reinforce implicit tendencies in such an individual to assume that he or she is being victimized by powerful others. This occurred several times for Tom, when he framed himself and his classmates as victims of oppression.

The justification mechanism at work here is the *victimization* (by powerful others) *bias*. This justification mechanism consists of an implicit bias to see oneself as the victim of inequity, exploitation, injustice, and oppression by those who are more powerful in one's life (e.g., parents, teachers, supervisors, employing organizations, institutions such as the Internal Revenue Service; Averill, 1993; Bandura, 1999; Finnegan, 1997; Tedeschi & Nesler, 1993; Toch, 1993). Framing of events, hypotheses about cause and effect, and confirmatory searches for evidence reflect an obsession with oppression and victimization (and the operation of the victimization bias justification mechanism). These inferences stimulate feelings of anger and injustice. The inferences produced by the victimization bias justification mechanism and the emotions of anger and injustice together set the stage for rationalizing aggression toward the powerful as legitimate strikes against oppression, rightful redressings of wrongs, and reasonable corrections of inequities, prejudices, and injustices.

Often accompanying the victimization bias is another justification mechanism that contributes to rationalizing aggression by making a target more deserving of being harmed. The *derogation of target bias* justification mechanism is an unrecognized tendency to characterize targets of aggression in negative terms (e.g., corrupt, dishonest, evil, immoral, underhanded, unethical, untrustworthy; see Averill, 1993; Bandura, 1999; Gay, 1993; Toch, 1993; Wright & Mischel, 1987). Alternatively, positive traits of the target may be ignored, undervalued, or depreciated. Tom's reasoning appeared to be shaped by this justification mechanism when he referred to Dr. Andrews as an "abusive, unethical, and untrustworthy instructor" and implied that his classmates were traitors with respect to his efforts to seek retribution for, and liberation from, Dr. Andrews.

A fifth justification mechanism pertains to implicit biases that shape aggressive individuals' reasoning about how to resolve interpersonal conflicts. The *retribution bias* consists of a predisposition to decide that retaliation will be a more effective and reasonable way to resolve a conflict than reconciliation (Anderson, 1994; Baumeister et al., 1996; Bradbury & Fincham, 1990; Crick & Dodge, 1994; Dodge, 1986; Laursen & Collins, 1994; Nisbett, 1993; Sykes & Matza, 1957). Similar to the potency bias, this justification mechanism is often stimulated by perceptions of wounded pride, challenged self-esteem, or disrespect (Baumeister et al., 1996). To restore self-respect, retribution is judged to be more reasonable than forgiveness, vindication is preferred to reconciliation, and obtaining revenge appears more sensible than attempting to retain a relationship. Aggression is thus seen as justifiable if it is intended to restore respect or to exact restitution for a perceived wrong. Or one could say that the retribution bias promotes aggression in response to the humiliation and anger of being demeaned. It does so by enabling the rationalization that one is restoring honor and respect.

To illustrate, the retribution bias shapes conscious experience by heightening aggressive individuals' sensitivity to any hint of insult or disrespect, which some believe to be exacerbated by aggressive individuals' high but unstable sense of self-worth (see Baumeister et al., 1996). Should insult or disrespect be sensed (e.g., when Dr. Andrews critiques Tom's homework), the latent predilection for retribution promotes conscious reasoning that the insult is belittling and undeserved. These biased inferences serve as a justification mechanism for aggression because they encourage retaliation toward the offending source, using a rationalization such as that one is avenging an unfair insult and thereby regaining one's rightful sense of pride and respect.

Note that the retribution bias encourages aggressive individuals to retaliate against perceived wrongs and yet does not interfere with their maintaining the self-deception that they are basically moral and socially worthy individuals. Aggressive individuals believe that they can justifiably disengage or suspend moral standards in order to exact restitution for being belittled and disrespected (Bandura, 1999; Sykes & Matza, 1957). If we were to observe aggressive individuals over time, we would likely find consistent patterns of retribution, enabled by use of the retribution bias and perhaps other justification mechanisms to disengage moral standards and neutralize social norms.

The sixth and final justification mechanism is the *social discounting bias*, which consists of a proclivity to frame social norms as repressive and restrictive of free will (James et al., 2005; Sykes & Matza, 1957). This framing promotes disdain for traditional ideals and conventional beliefs (cf. Finnegan, 1997; Gay, 1993; Huesmann, 1988; Loeber & Stouthamer-Loeber, 1998; Millon, 1990; Toch, 1993). Attempts to understand social events typically lean toward the cynical and critical. Reasoning will further evidence a lack of sensitivity, empathy, and concern for social customs, frequently calling upon socially unorthodox and antisocial theories to interpret and analyze social events and relationships. Such reasoning reflects the operation of the social discounting bias, and it serves as a justification mechanism for aggression because it is used to rationalize socially deviant behavior intended to harm others. For example, it allows aggressive individuals to rationalize harming others as a means to attain freedom of expression, to gain release from the shackles of social customs, and to procure liberation from confining social relationships (Sykes & Matza, 1957). In effect, reasoning that emphasizes societal restrictiveness promotes feelings of reactance. These feelings furnish a foundation for justifying socially deviant behaviors as ways to liberate oneself from repressive social customs and to exercise one's lawful right to freedom of expression (Frost et al., 2007).

To summarize, the illusion that harming others can be rationally justified often rests on a foundation of biased inferences about the behaviors of others. We refer to these biases as justification mechanisms because they enable rationalizations for harming others. We have presented six justification mechanisms for aggression. A brief definition of each justification mechanism is offered in Exhibit 2.2. Thumbnail sketches of how each of the justification mechanisms might enable a rationalization for aggression are included in the definitions.

The justification mechanisms in Exhibit 2.2 are the product of searches designed to collect a seminal set of the primary implicit biases that define, shape, and guide the framing and reasoning that enable aggressive individuals to build rationalizations for aggression. We do not suggest that this set of six justification mechanisms is exhaustive or complete, and we continue to be alert to new biases to add to the set.

## Nonaggressive Individuals' View of Rationalizations Based on Justification Mechanisms for Aggression

Nonaggressive individuals lack the desire to harm others and thus tend not to engage in dominance contests with authority figures such as teachers and supervisors. Nor are they prone to fight with their peers, coworkers, or

## EXHIBIT 2.2
### Justification Mechanisms for Aggression

1. Hostile attribution bias: A propensity to sense hostility and perhaps even danger in the behavior of others. The alarm and feelings of peril engendered by this heightened sensitivity to threat trigger a concern for self-protection. Apprehension about self-preservation enhances the rational appeal of self-defense, thus promoting the self-deceptive illusion that aggression is justified.
2. Potency bias: A proclivity to focus thoughts about social interactions on dominance versus submissiveness. The actions of others pass through a perceptual prism primed to distinguish (a) strength, assertiveness, dominance, daring, fearlessness, and power from (b) weakness, impotence, submissiveness, timidity, compliance, and cowardice. Fixations on dominance versus submissiveness promote rationalizations that aggression is an act of strength or bravery that gains respect from others. Failing to act aggressively shows weakness.
3. Retribution bias: A predilection to determine that retaliation is more rational than reconciliation. This bias is often stimulated by perceptions of wounded pride, challenged self-esteem, or disrespect. Aggression in response to the humiliation and anger of being demeaned is rationalized as justified restoration of honor and respect.
4. Victimization by powerful others bias: A bias to see inequity and exploitation in the actions of powerful others (e.g., parents, teachers, supervisors, the Internal Revenue Service). The ensuing perceptions of oppression and victimization stimulate feelings of anger and injustice. This sets the stage for rationalizing aggression as a legitimate strike against oppression and a justified correction of prejudice and injustice.
5. Derogation of target bias: This bias consists of an unconscious tendency to characterize those one wishes to make (or has made) targets of aggression as evil, immoral, or untrustworthy. To infer or associate such traits with a target makes the target more deserving of aggression.
6. Social discounting bias: A proclivity to frame social norms as repressive and restrictive of free will. Perceptions of societal restrictiveness promote feelings of reactance. These feelings furnish a foundation for justifying socially deviant behaviors such as aggression as ways to liberate oneself from repressive social customs and to exercise one's lawful right to freedom of expression.

*Note.* Adapted from (a) "Measurement of Personality via Conditional Reasoning," by L. R. James, 1998, *Organizational Research Methods, 1*, p. 155. Copyright 1998 by Sage Publications, Inc., and (b) "A Conditional Reasoning Measure for Aggression," by L. R. James, M. D. McIntyre, C. A. Glisson, P. D. Green, T. W. Patton, J. M. LeBreton, . . . and L. J. Williams, 2005, *Organizational Research Methods, 8*, p. 74. Copyright 2005 by Sage Publications, Inc. Adapted with permission.

neighbors or to cause harm to powerful entities such as a disliked merchant or the police by engaging in obstreperous or intentionally disruptive behavior. There is little or no incentive to possess justification mechanisms to enhance the rational appeal of aggressive behaviors. Thus, reasoning tends not to be shaped by the types of biases summarized in Exhibit 2.2. Nonaggressive individuals are not disposed to frame others through a lens of dominance/submissiveness, nor is malevolent intent the default option for attributions regarding the causes of others' behavior. Nonaggressive people are not constantly looking for slights or disrespect in the comments of others, and they are not inclined to reason in ways that give preference to retribution over reconciliation. They are also not disposed to see themselves as victims of oppression.

Basically, nonaggressive people have no compunction to engage implicit biases that enhance the rational appeal of aggression. Moreover, they are likely to view the attempts to rationalize aggression via reasoning produced by justification mechanisms as superficial, farfetched, and inappropriate (cf. Gay, 1993; Huesmann, 1988). On the other hand, reasoning based on the justification mechanisms in Exhibit 2.2 can be subtle and exploit uncertainties in fact and evidence. This means that (a) the reasoning cannot be rejected outright on logical grounds, and therefore (b) the reasoning should be considered tenable, at least for the moment. However, even in conditions of uncertainty, nonaggressive individuals will tend to be skeptical or doubtful of reasoning based on justification mechanisms (Crick & Dodge, 1994; Dodge, 1986; Dodge & Coie, 1987; Dodge & Crick, 1990; Gay, 1993; Huesmann, 1988; James, 1998).

To illustrate, nonaggressive individuals are likely to be skeptical of aggressive individuals' assertions that the behaviors of others are due to hostile intent. Unless there is clear supporting evidence or logic suggesting otherwise, nonaggressive people are also likely to question that retribution and retaliation are more reasonable responses to social discord than attempts to cooperate and reconcile. And they will tend to grow weary of aggressive individuals' consistent attempts to decipher hidden agendas, designed to victimize and exploit people like them, in the behaviors of powerful others.

Our basic suggestion is that (a) even though nonaggressive people may be unable to reject reasoning based on justification mechanisms on strictly logical or empirical grounds, (b) they regard such reasoning as improbable, dubious, socially unorthodox, unrealistic, provocative, extreme, nonconstructive, and/ or slanted. Simply stated, reasoning based on justification mechanisms for aggression typically will not be convincing or logically persuasive to nonaggressive individuals.

More logically persuasive to nonaggressive individuals are arguments for socially adaptive or prosocial behaviors such as civility, politeness, friendliness, and cooperation (James et al., 2005). (*Socially adaptive* and *prosocial* are used interchangeably and refer to dynamics that move "people closer together" [Buss & Finn, 1987, p. 435] and that act as contrasts to aggression [Wright & Mischel, 1987].) These are the normative (expected, role-prescribed) standards for appropriate conduct in most social situations because they promote harmony, cooperation, and peace. Nonaggressive individuals tend to internalize the ideologies and values that support society's normative behaviors as part of being socialized (Bandura, 1999; James et al., 2004). Their reasoning about what constitutes rational behavior in social situations is often automatically (i.e., implicitly; Schneider & Shiffrin, 1977) shaped by the socially adaptive values and ideologies that they have internalized. Consequently, nonaggressive individuals are prone to make determinations about whether a behavior is reasonable, sound, and rational on the basis of standards that reflect internalized, socially adaptive ideologies and rationales (James et al., 2004; Kuhn, 1991). The ensuing reasoning appears to them to be more plausible, balanced, probable, and sound than rationalizations for aggression.

For example, in contrast to aggressive individuals' proclivities to reason in terms of justification mechanisms, James and Mazerolle (2002) described nonaggressive individuals as being inclined

- to see greater probabilities for amicable or benign intent (as opposed to hostile intent) as the default option in seeking explanations for the actions of others;
- to perceive others through a prism that frames them on a continuum ranging from (a) likely to be a friend, companion, confidante, partner, or colleague to (b) likely to have only a neutral, unemotional, or uninvolving relationship (nonaggressive individuals are less likely than aggressive individuals to perceive others through a prism of potency [i.e., the potency bias] that evaluates others as dominant or submissive in relation to themselves);
- to reason from the perspective that people can operate in society without being exploited, demeaned, or made victims of injustices and inequities (as opposed to selectively focusing on being victimized by powerful others);
- to build dialectics that include both the positive and negative characteristics of others (as opposed to just negative characteristics);
- to selectively focus on promoting friendship, harmony, collaboration, and trust over assuaging wounded pride, defending self-esteem, or seeking retribution for perceived disrespect (nonaggressiveness is reflected in reasoning that favors forgiving, cooperating, and maintaining relationships as more rational options than retaliating, seeking vindication, or obtaining revenge); and
- to analyze social events from the perspective that society benefits from respect for traditional ideals and conventional beliefs as well as from acceptance of social customs (as opposed to reasoning grounded in rejection of conventional beliefs and social ideals).

Tom's classmates evidenced much of the above reasoning. It is also noteworthy that, unlike Tom, reasoning by his generally nonaggressive classmates had no sense of justification. This is because there is no need to justify being friendly, cooperative, trusting, or agreeable. More generally, nonaggressive people have no sense of obligation to justify acting in normative, socially acceptable ways. According to the norms of our society, being agreeable, friendly, polite, peaceful, cooperative, and trusting is the sensible and reasonable thing to do in normal circumstances. It does not require justification or rationalization in the sense that deviating from these norms (by being aggressive) does.

We do not wish to imply that nonaggressive people are immune to social information processing biases. For example, by framing others through a prism of friendship, nonaggressive individuals may miss cues that they are about to be exploited. However, this is not the type of biased reasoning that is of interest for our contrast with the reasoning of aggressive individuals. We are interested in nonaggressive individuals' *implicit hypotheses*, which is to say the internalized, or implicit, socially adaptive ideologies and rationales that shape what they believe to be rational behavior.

We do not assume that nonaggressive people are equal in social adaptability or prosocialness. Indeed, we expect individual differences in the strengths of prosocialness. However, for the purposes of the present discussion, all people referred to as nonaggressive are regarded as having satisfied a minimum threshold for social adaptability. Their reasoning about sensible behavior is shaped by the same general implicit hypotheses (internalized socially adaptive ideologies and rationales), although the strength of those hypotheses may vary.

## Conditional Reasoning

When aggressive individuals and nonaggressive individuals frame the same events differently and regard contrasting behaviors to be rational, reasoning is said to be "conditional" on the reasoners (James, 1998; James & LeBreton, 2010). By *conditional reasoning* we mean reasoning that is dependent on personality; that is, it is reasoning that is dependent on the motives, framing proclivities, and justification mechanisms of the reasoners. CR is used in a manner such as the following: Whether framing and analyses will identify aggression or nonaggression as being a sensible behavioral adjustment to an environment is conditional (i.e., dependent) on whether the person doing the reasoning is aggressive or nonaggressive. Aggressive people like Tom tend to reason in ways that justify the expression of aggression. Nonaggressive people like Tom's classmates tend to reason in ways that foster the expression of friendship, harmony, cooperation, and trust.

CR occurs because the interpretations and analyses of events used to furnish logical support to a given type of behavior are unconsciously shaped, defined, and guided by the motives, framing proclivities, and implicit assumptions of individual reasoners. Thus, for example, an individual's reasoning that culminates in viewing hostility as justifiable self-defense is conditional on his or her personality when this reasoning was shaped by the motivation to act aggressively in the first place and by the use of the hostile attribution bias to enable the self-deception that aggressing is rational.

Whereas CR is grounded in a dependency between the reasoning of an individual and his or her personality, the full scope of CR is captured only by considering individual differences in reasoning, particularly differences in reasoning about the same event. CR conveys the notion that differences in motives, framing proclivities, and implicit assumptions shape, define, and guide reasoning so as to furnish a predictable pattern of individual differences in the judgments of what is and what is not reasonable behavior in the same situation or context. Differences in what is considered to be reasonable adjustments in the same context are thus conditional on differences in the personalities of the persons doing the reasoning.

CR is an area of personality that is concerned with patterns of individual differences in reasoning about behavior that are unknowingly engendered by differences in underlying personalities. A key feature of CR is that even though aggressive individuals and nonaggressive individuals come to disparate judgments about what constitutes reasonable behavior, both sets of individuals believe that their reasoning is rational and sensible as opposed to irrational and inappropriate. A novel contribution of CR to the study of personality has been the charting and assessment of the types of reasoning biases—referred to here as justification mechanisms—that aggressive individuals use to enhance the rational appeal of hostile behavior. We shall discover in the next chapter how the understanding of justification mechanisms opened the door to a new measurement system for personality.

## THEORY OF THE INSTRUMENT FOR THE CONDITIONAL REASONING TEST FOR RELATIVE MOTIVE STRENGTH[1]

Alex Haley, the author of *Roots* (1976), famously reported receiving a great many rejections from publishers before receiving his first acceptance. For years, he submitted manuscripts on a regular basis, considered rejections to be learning experiences that helped him to hone his writing skills, and persisted in his belief that he would, though dedication and tenacity, become a published author. Alex Haley's persistence and his ultimately publishing highly regarded articles and books illustrate what is commonly referred to as *achievement motivation*. People high in achievement motivation have intense desires to make something of themselves, to accomplish something important in their lives, and to "do better" simply for the pleasure of succeeding at something important and demanding (McClelland, 1985). They are willing to

---

[1]This section and the section that follows concerning identifying justification mechanisms draw liberally from prior discussions in James (1998) and James and Mazerolle (2002), to which new material has been added.

commit intense effort to achievement-relevant goals and tasks, often for long periods of time. They associate enthusiasm, intensity, and commitment with the pursuit of achievement and a sense of accomplishment, self-respect, and pride with attainment of both incentives along the way and the ultimate objective.

Many individuals are attracted to the idea of becoming a famous author. However, some of these people focus on the risk of spending years preparing a manuscript and then having it rejected. Unlike Alex Haley, who continued to concentrate on the rewards of publishing, these individuals fixate on the disappointment, humiliation, embarrassment, and shame that would follow if they attempted to publish and failed. People who habitually focus on failure and its consequences are prone to experience fear of failure.

*Fear of failure* is an anticipatory feeling of uneasiness, apprehension, dread, and anxiety about attempting a difficult task, failing, and appearing incompetent (Atkinson, 1957, 1978). Fear of failing, or the desire to reduce anxiety over failing, dampens the enthusiasm for achievement and stimulates affected individuals to avoid achievement-oriented tasks completely or to withdraw from such tasks if success is not immediately forthcoming. It is also the case that anxiety over possible failure may become a self-fulfilling prophecy if demanding tasks are not avoided. That is, attempting a difficult task may trigger even more negative arousal, and this heightened apprehension about failing can increase anxiety to such a level that it interferes with the performance on the difficult task.

Whether or not to attempt to publish is one example of a human dilemma in which individuals must periodically decide whether to approach or to avoid high-press-for-achievement objectives (goals, tasks). As an adolescent and young adult, these decisions may involve such things as whether to attempt to obtain a high grade point average in school or whether to devote long hours to developing proficiency as a musician, an athlete, an artist, or an actor. Later in life, these decisions could entail whether to seek a job in a high-pressure occupation, whether to dedicate the majority of one's waking hours to being a success, whether to seek promotion to a more responsible but less secure position, whether to make a career change, whether to start a business, or whether to engage in an innovative task such as attempting to publish an article or novel, write music, or pursue a career in art.

Most individuals experience some aspects of both attraction (e.g., attractiveness of becoming wealthy by owning one's business) and apprehension (e.g., misgivings about investing savings in a business venture that can fail) when faced with decisions of whether to approach or to avoid a high-press-for-achievement activity. Whether to approach or to avoid becomes a form of approach–avoidance conflict (Atkinson, 1978). How these conflicts tend to be resolved provides the foundation for behaviors, as discussed in the following sections.

## Behaviors Associated With Achievement Motivation

We see a recurring pattern in which some people consistently resolve their approach–avoidance conflicts in favor of approaching achievement-oriented objectives. An *achievement-oriented goal* is one that (a) relative to one's skill and ability, is personally challenging or demanding; (b) requires intense and persistent effort to attain; and (c) is perceived by the individual as an important and worthwhile accomplishment. Examples of achievement-oriented goals for college students include selecting a personally demanding major in college, striving for promotion in the jobs that follow college, seeking and accepting progressively greater responsibilities, or engaging in innovative activities such as research or writing. Over a career, we are likely to see attempts to accomplish progressively more difficult objectives. These attempts often reflect continuing enhancement of competencies through experience, training, practice, and, of course, engaging in progressively more difficult tasks.

A recurring pattern of seeking successively more challenging goals and tasks is also likely to include a willingness to devote intense effort to whatever demanding objective has been selected at the time. Intensity is reflected by such things as competitiveness, long hours of honing skills required for success, and what may be a level of involvement in goal accomplishment that engenders neglect of other aspects of one's life. Accompanying intensity is tenacity, exemplified by a willingness to persevere for long periods of time to accomplish demanding objectives. A writer's determination, despite repeated rejections, to see his or her work published, a student's perseverance in completing graduate programs such as medical school, or an athlete's willingness to endure years of hard work and practice to gain professional competence are all illustrative of achievement-oriented behaviors.

In sum, we have described a consistent tendency to resolve approach–avoidance conflicts in favor of approaching high-press-for-achievement tasks. Accompanying this recurring pattern of selecting challenging objectives is the willingness to devote intense and persistent effort to accomplishing the objectives. These consistent behavioral tendencies illustrate what many refer to as the behavioral disposition of *achievement motivation* (cf. Epstein, 1979; James, 1998; Kenrick & Funder, 1988; Wright & Mischel, 1987).

## Behaviors Associated With Fear of Failure

As a response, fear of failure refers to a consistent tendency to respond to achievement-oriented tasks with apprehension and anxiety about failing and being deemed incompetent. The direct consequence of apprehension, anxiety, or fear of failing is "to oppose and dampen the tendency to undertake achievement-oriented activities" (Atkinson, 1978, p. 15). A salient aspect of such dampening is to resolve approach–avoidance conflicts in favor of avoiding achievement-oriented tasks. A reasonably intelligent person high in fear of failure is likely to have a history that includes choice of a college with only modestly rigorous standards, choice of a major that is largely devoid of intense competition and "weed out courses," and choice of a career that is high in security and stability.

However, to characterize those who possess fear of failure as merely avoidant would be to miss many of this construct's important subtleties. James and Mazerolle (2002) described how these subtleties may occur in organizational settings, with a possible result being potentially serious impacts on organizational functioning. We shall summarize James and Mazerolle's illustrations of behavioral indicators of fear of failure at work. Following Atkinson (cf. 1978), these indicators are referred to as *inhibitory behaviors*. The term *inhibitory* denotes that these behaviors are designed ultimately to reduce anxiety over failing—that is, to reduce fear of failure—by dampening—that is, inhibiting—the undertaking of achievement-oriented activities.

A moderately subtle form of inhibitory behavior is a *compensatory* action, which involves substituting an easier goal or task for a more demanding, achievement-oriented goal or task. For example, a soon-to-be college graduate in computer science may be apprehensive about the competition and uncertainty of success that accompanies accepting a job offer from a high-profile software company. Indeed, fear of failing dampens his or her enthusiasm for the job to such an extent that he/she spends sleepless nights worrying about failing. Loss of sleep and other indicators of fear-engendered stress (e.g., irritability) create a situation in which job security and stability are more important to this individual than the challenge and opportunity offered by the software company. The computer scientist thus rejects the job offer, preferring instead to seek employment in a safe, secure work environment.

Subtlety of inhibitory behaviors increases when high-press-for-achievement demands are unavoidable, such as when achievement demands occur only periodically in an otherwise unchallenging job. Fear of failure behaviors may now involve *overly conservative* actions. Examples of such actions include discounting the adoption of new ideas (because new ideas could fail), avoiding any form of risk (because risk implies the possibility of failure), and when given the opportunity, selecting the least demanding tasks rather than the more exacting but potentially rewarding tasks. The latter case is a form of compensatory behavior often justified by imbuing the less difficult tasks with positive, socially desirable qualities (e.g., low risk).

Other subtle forms of inhibitory behaviors involve *counterproductive*, *self-defeating*, or *self-handicapping* behaviors (e.g., Berglas & Jones, 1978). For example, students high in fear of failure may engage in a *defensive lack of effort*. As the term implies, a defensive lack of effort consists of a purposeful lack of an attempt to achieve. Illustrations of this inhibitory behavior include not attending class, not completing homework assignments, and not studying for tests. A review of self-defeating behaviors by Baumeister and Scher (1988) suggested that this form of inhibitory behavior serves implicitly to shift attributions for low test scores away from deficits in intellectual skills (very threatening) toward lack of interest or exertion of effort (less threatening).

Additional counterproductive behaviors involve *precautionary processes*, such as the strategy of only attempting tasks for which an excuse of nonaccountability is available (e.g., lack of sufficient resources to complete the task), should failure occur. Procrastination is a form of precautionary process, often justified by arguments that it is more reasonable to "remain flexible" and to "withhold judgment" than to act precipitously and commit to what may be a futile action. A key form of precautionary process in business settings is *unnecessary diffusion of responsibility*. This occurs when, in an attempt to avoid complete responsibility for important decisions or to delay decision making, an executive disperses the responsibility to others, such as committees and teams. Unnecessary diffusion of responsibility is often presented as a form of empowerment, delegation, or participation. In truth, however, it is a defensive strategy used by an executive to avoid or to delay making a decision that he or she should make.

A final set of illustrative inhibitory behaviors that are also counterproductive involves *dispositionally induced lowered performance* on demanding tasks. Lack of persistence is the major problem here. People who fear failing tend to discourage (inhibit) perseverance on tasks where success is not immediate, often because they tacitly assume that the task is too difficult, given their abilities. This lack of persistence may be rationalized by reasoning that one should know when to exercise self-discipline and avoid escalating commitment to a lost cause. Unlike people who persist, people who avoid or quit early afford themselves less opportunity to develop or enhance their skills via continued practice, experience, study, and learning.

In sum, fear of failure involves both direct and indirect behaviors designed to reduce apprehension (anxiety, fear) about failing by engaging in acts that dampen, inhibit, or replace approach tendencies. Simple avoidance of achievement-oriented goals is the most direct behavioral indicator of fear of failure. However, avoidance may not be socially desirable or even possible, in which case subtle, inhibitory behaviors such as overly conservative decisions, diffusion of responsibility, and counterproductive strategies may occur. These latter manifestations of fear of failure can be devastating to both individuals and organizations.

### A Caveat of Multiple Causation

The preceding discussion should not be construed to suggest that achievement motivation and fear of failure are the only individually based causes of behavior. Depending on the context, other constructs, such as critical intellectual skills or innate physical/psychomotor abilities, also influence performance. Nevertheless, taking multiple causation as a given, we must consider that the potential to accomplish high-press-for-achievement objectives is realized only when effort (intensity, persistence) is applied to the task. It is difficult, if not impossible, to perform successfully on most demanding tasks unless one approaches the task and then devotes intense and persistent effort to its accomplishment. Moreover, factors such as excessive fear, anxiety, and apprehension adversely affect performance even when other skills and abilities are above average. Thus, while neither exclusive nor exhaustive, motivation contributes significantly and substantially to performance, however it is operationalized.

## MOTIVATION TO APPROACH VERSUS AVOID: MOTIVES (NEEDS)

To say that a person is achievement motivated means that he or she consistently, over time and in evocative situations, directs intense and persistent effort toward accomplishing demanding tasks. Note that we are describing this person's behavior. Now suppose we ask: Why does this person approach (select) demanding tasks and then devote intense and persistent effort toward accomplishing them? In other words, why does this person behave in ways that we describe as achievement motivated?

### The Motive to Achieve

An answer to this question appears to be that people who apply intense and persistent effort to achieving demanding objectives have a strong motive (need, desire) "to do things better" (McClelland, 1985). A need to do things better involves a desire to experience the challenge, enthusiasm, and involvement that ensue from pitting oneself against a difficult and important task and demonstrating that one is capable of mastering it. Extrinsic factors, such as competition and recognition from peers are not important. However, the natural incentives for the motive to achieve are "intrinsic" to the act of attempting to achieve. That is to say, the incentives for achievement focus on the "thrill of the chase," especially when achievement behaviors such as approach, intensity, and persistence are associated with positive emotions, such as the experience of challenge, excitement, enthusiasm, and involvement. Additional incentives for the need to achieve involve the sense of pride and the feelings of accomplishment and mastery that accompany accomplishment of a demanding task (Atkinson, 1957, 1978; McClelland, 1985; McClelland et al., 1989; Raynor, 1978).

Thus, we may say that some people are attracted to high-press-for-achievement goals and tasks and are willing to devote intense and persistent effort to accomplishing these goals and tasks because they have a desire to show themselves that they are capable of mastering challenging tasks. The motive to achieve derives its potency or forcefulness from the natural incentives of positive emotions or feelings, wherein the pursuit of demanding tasks is associated with enthusiasm, excitement, and involvement. Pride in having demonstrated mastery is also to be considered, as are winning approval and recognition for having competed successfully, given that many achievement-oriented tasks involve competition with others.

### The Motive to Avoid Failure

What, then, causes other people to experience considerable anxiety or fear over failing and to engage in avoidance or other forms of inhibitory behaviors? Consider that one of the reasons that an achievement-oriented objective is considered an "achievement" is because it is "difficult." People fail out of college or are not accepted into graduate schools. It is not uncommon to be passed over for promotion at least once in one's life. A majority of new business ventures fail. One may practice unrelentingly for an athletic event and yet still fail to win or even place among the top finishers. Basically, striving to achieve carries with it a degree of uncertainty, a risk that the venture may be unsuccessful. This sense of uncertainty is strongest when the probability of success is approximately 5 in 10, for it is here that one is least able to predict the outcome and thus is most likely to experience apprehension about the result (Atkinson, 1978).

Uncertainty and risk suggest that even though an achievement-oriented opportunity may trigger the motive to achieve and anticipations of the thrill of the chase, it is also likely to stimulate an opposing or antagonistic motive that performs a self-protective function. This motive is a form of safety mechanism designed to protect individuals from engaging in activities that will cause them psychological damage. The protective mechanism consists of a natural proclivity to consider the downside of achievement striving, which is failure and the resulting humiliation, embarrassment, and sense of incompetence that, for many, follow failing.

This motive is referred to as the *motive* or *need to avoid failure*. Everyone who cognizes normally has some concern with avoidance of failure. Nevertheless, people vary in the strength of the need to avoid failure. Those who have an intense aversion to uncertainty and are strongly concerned with protecting themselves from failure are predisposed to experience considerable fear of failure (e.g., apprehension, anxiety, dread, worry) when faced with high-press-for-achievement goals or tasks (cf. Atkinson,

1957, 1978; Nicholls, 1984; Rothbaum, Weisz, & Snyder, 1982; Schlenker & Leary, 1982).

### Resultant Achievement-Oriented Tendency

People have a desire to avoid failing in order to protect themselves from humiliation, shame, and embarrassment. When presented with an achievement-oriented opportunity, the motive to avoid failure acts to counterbalance the motive to achieve by stimulating concerns about the ramifications of attempting to succeed and falling short. The opposing forces of the motive to achieve and the motive to avoid failure create what we referred to earlier as approach–avoidance conflicts.

Attempts to resolve approach–avoidance conflicts when faced with achievement-oriented goals or tasks involve what Atkinson (1978) referred to as the *resultant achievement-oriented tendency,* or simply the *resultant tendency* (p. 16). The resultant tendency varies on a continuum from a high probability of approach to a high probability of avoidance for a given task. These probabilities are determined in part by which of the two motives is stronger and by the degree of this dominance.

For some people, the resultant tendency is represented by an *approach* or *excitatory* tendency because the motive to achieve is stronger than the motive to avoid failure. When the motive to achieve is strong and the motive to avoid failure is only modest or weak, then the excitatory tendency or probability of approach is quite high. Indeed, when a strong motive to achieve dominates a modest or weak motive to avoid failure, people tend not only to resolve approach–avoidance conflicts by engaging in achievement activities but also to devote intense and persistent effort to succeeding at these activities. As a pattern of approach and effort expenditure recurs over time and in various situations, individuals who exhibit this pattern are identified as high in achievement motivation.

For other people, the motive to avoid failure is stronger than the motive to achieve. These people are prone to avoid or at least to dampen their enthusiasm for achievement-oriented activities in an attempt to relieve anxiety and apprehension. These individuals are thus said to possess an *avoidant* or *inhibitory* resultant tendency (Atkinson, 1978, p. 16). When a strong motive to avoid failure dominates a modest or weak need to achieve, the inhibitory tendency is quite high. People with this motive pattern consistently tend to resolve approach–avoidance conflicts by avoiding achievement-related activities or by engaging in one or more of the inhibitory behaviors described earlier (e.g., defensive lack of effort, unnecessary diffusion of responsibility). Over time and in various situations, people who consistently experience fear of failure and exhibit inhibitory tendencies are described as high in fear of failure.

Research has demonstrated that many people can be classified as having either a clearly dominant motive or at least a tendency to favor one of the two motives (James, 1998). The resultant tendency is thus a function of a scale anchored by a dominant motive to achieve on one end and a dominant motive to avoid failure on the other end. Between these anchors reside gradations in the relative strengths of the motives. For example, just below a dominant motive to achieve is a preference for the motive to achieve over the motive to avoid failure. The motive to achieve does not always prevail over the motive to avoid failure in this case. Nonetheless, on the average, individuals in this range have a relatively high probability of approaching demanding tasks. This probability is, however, lower than that for individuals for whom the motive to achieve is clearly dominant.

Residing at the middle of the scale are people classified as *indeterminate* because neither need dominates (James, 1998). Indeterminacy could result from various patterns, including high (motive to achieve)–high (motive to avoid failure), moderate–moderate, or low–low. The psychological dynamics are different among these patterns. For example, a high–high pattern, and to a less pronounced degree a moderate–moderate pattern, suggest intense approach–avoidance conflicts. In contrast, a low–low pattern suggests indifference to achievement-oriented events. The behavioral outcome is similar, however, for all of the patterns. Indeterminacy is likely to engender vacillation, equivocation, and hesitancy. Moreover, the final choice to approach or to avoid is likely to be based on factors other than resultant tendency.

## Implicit Components of the Motives

Evidence suggests that individuals are unaware of portions of their motives to achieve and to avoid failure and that these implicit components are instrumental in behavior (Brunstein & Maier, 2005; McClelland et al., 1989). Presumably, the implicit portions of the motives are those most in need of the defenses and rationalizations that we address below in the discussion of justification mechanisms. It is not difficult to surmise what these implicit components involve. For example, self-esteem is largely a product of social comparison (Baumeister et al., 2003), and people's sense of self-worth is affected by how achievement-oriented others perceive them to be. This suggests that many people may be a bit self-enhancing in their self-ascriptions of achievement motivation. The latent portion of the motive, however, may be closer to the truth.

Conversely, avoidance of demanding tasks is not self-enhancing. As developed below, this is one of the reasons why avoidance is masked by rationalizations such as lack of resources or unacceptable risk. Of course, some people may obsess in their apprehensiveness, which could be a product of a very traumatic failure. They consciously overestimate their fear of failure.

And people with extremely high achievement motivation are not likely to be fully aware of what they are willing to sacrifice in the name of perfection and success (e.g., their families). Thus, consciously, they underestimate the true forcefulness of their achievement motive, which is also shrouded in justifications (e.g., commitment to a goal).

This brings us to the issues of justification mechanisms for the motive to achieve and the motive to avoid failure. We are specifically interested in justification mechanisms for the different configurations of the implicit motives that represent the primary variations in relative motive strength. Differences in reasoning between people with different motive configurations are explored next. We have adopted a form of shorthand to facilitate this discussion: People for whom the motive to achieve dominates the motive to avoid failure are referred to as AMs; people driven by a fear of failure, for whom the motive to avoid failure dominates the motive to achieve, are referred to as FFs.

## JUSTIFICATION MECHANISMS

We have described a system in which people with opposing needs often behave differently in the same environment, in part because they have different ideas about what constitutes reasonable adjustments to that environment. Let us now delve a bit deeper into why reasoning is conditional on whether the person doing the reasoning is an AM or FF. To justify engaging in their respective desired behaviors, both AMs and FFs depend on implicit biases in reasoning that are designed to enhance the rational appeal of those behaviors. We introduced the term *justification mechanism* to refer to implicit biases whose purpose is to define, shape, and otherwise influence reasoning so as to enhance the rational appeal of behaving in a manner consistent with a motive or, in the present case, the relative strength of opposing motives. We now apply this concept to describe the justification mechanisms for AMs and FFs.

A brief note of clarification is in order here. The implicit biases that make up the justification mechanisms for AMs and FFs have the same general purpose as the implicit biases that make up the justification mechanisms for aggressive individuals. All of these mechanisms provide a foundation for creating an artificial sense of rationality for motive-driven behaviors. However, as noted at the beginning of this chapter, the justification mechanisms for aggression have a more defensive connotation than the justification mechanisms for either achievement motivation or fear of failure. This is because the justification mechanisms for aggression are used to create self-deceptively rational excuses for what are often antisocial behaviors, including illegal ones. The justification mechanisms for achievement motivation and fear of failure typically do not have to defend against antisocial and perhaps illegal actions. However, they are used to build rationalizations for what are often socially undesirable behaviors, such as unbridled ambition or persistent procrastination, and thus, like aggression, involve defensive processes, just less extreme ones.

Justification mechanisms for AMs and FFs are unknowingly mapped into conscious thought by (a) implicitly influencing the cognitive schemas (interpretative categories) that AMs and FFs, respectively, use to frame events (justification mechanisms define and shape many of the framing proclivities used by AMs and FFs) and (b) shaping and defining many of the implicit hypotheses that AMs and FFs use to determine whether to approach or to avoid demanding tasks. The products of justification mechanisms are unrecognized slants and biases in (a) how AMs and FFs respectively interpret achievement and success and (b) what AMs and FFs believe to be rational decision making about whether to approach or to avoid a demanding task.

Justification mechanisms for AMs are defined as implicit biases whose purpose is to define, shape, and otherwise influence reasoning so as to enhance the rational appeal of approach behaviors. Justification mechanisms for FFs are defined as implicit biases whose purpose is to define, shape, and otherwise influence reasoning so as to enhance the rational appeal of avoidance (or inhibitory) behaviors.

We now describe justification mechanisms for AMs and then for FFs. This presentation is based on an article by James (1998) and a book on personality by James and Mazerolle (2002). It is important to reiterate that the individuals who rely on these justification mechanisms are unaware of the conditional nature of their reasoning and the biases in their thinking. To them, their analyses involve natural framing and sensible assumptions that offer logical guides for inferences about the effects of behaviors (e.g., approach to or avoidance of demanding tasks) on such things as success/failure at work, health, interrelationships with others, and a general sense of emotional well-being (Wegner & Vallacher, 1977).

We will use Exhibit 2.3 to illustrate how an AM (Joan) and an FF (Diane) differ in their framing and reasoning about their experiences as college students. We will then suggest how these and other differences in framing and reasoning are shaped by disparities in the justification mechanisms for AMs and FFs. As previously with Tom and his nonaggressive classmates, our objective is to demonstrate how CR provides us with a means for understanding how and why AMs and FFs frame the same events differently and then use dissimilarities in framing to arrive at different logical inferences about why the events occurred and what additional events are likely to follow.

### Justification Mechanisms of AMs

AMs have an unrecognized tendency to attribute behavior to personal responsibility (cf. Bandura, 1986; Hall, 1971; Jones, 1973; McClelland &

# EXHIBIT 2.3
## Illustration of Framing and Reasoning by Joan (an AM) and Diane (an FF)

Joan and Diane are in their first year of college at a state university. Joan is majoring in biology and is excited by the prospect of going to graduate school in a biological field or in medicine. She works intensely to obtain high grades. For example, she regularly attends class, takes copious notes, completes all homework assignments on time, attends all labs, and studies many hours each day, often closing the library in the evenings, including Friday and Saturday evenings. Diane has yet to declare a major. In fact, she is ambivalent if not apprehensive about continuing in college after this year. Her reticence is traceable to the anxiety she experiences every time she has to take a test, hand in a paper, or engage in some other form of evaluation. This anxiety tends to increase in intensity on the next evaluation if she is humiliated with receiving low evaluations on the prior one—a not infrequent event. Never keen on attending college, she senses a continuous eroding of what little interest she had. She often misses classes, takes only rudimentary notes when she does attend, hands homework in late if at all, and may or may not cram for a test, depending on the availability of alternatives.

Not surprisingly, Joan and Diane differ in their thinking about their respective college experiences. Joan is convinced that her success in college is directly attributable to how hard she is willing to work (e.g., selecting demanding classes and then working intensely and persistently). Tests are seen as challenges where she can demonstrate how hard she has studied and how much she has learned. Diane assumes that no matter how hard she works, her efforts will be nullified by tests that focus on the most arcane and tangential aspects in the subject matter, with little concern given to real substance and crucial points. She is convinced that she will do poorly and be humiliated even if she were to have a reasonable understanding of the material. She feels helpless to influence her evaluations, and she consistently feels threatened with visions of failure.

Joan and Diane differ in a number of other respects. For example, where Joan sees studying and sacrificed evenings as acts of dedication and commitment to excellence, Diane sees stress, overload, and obsessiveness about getting good grades. Diane wonders if leaving the high-pressure environment of college might not benefit her immediate quality of life as well as enhance her likelihood of avoiding stress-related illnesses later in life. Further consideration of these hypotheses triggers another inference, which is that she has pretty much maxed out her basic problem-solving abilities and critical intellectual skills. If she cannot succeed at this juncture, then there is little hope for upper division courses that are even more difficult. The concept that her problem-solving and critical thinking skills might be enhanced by practice and intense study is never entertained. To Joan, however, these thoughts are central to her desire to master the subject matters of her courses.

Lately, Diane has begun to seek out alternatives to college. She has become increasingly interested in jobs that do not require written examinations, offer job security, and reward those who are loyal and build seniority. Joan, in contrast, grows even more committed to attending and doing well in college. She believes that her personal commitment to doing well has resulted in her mastering new and important skills and that it is reasonable to expect that she will continue to master new and important skills. The key is effort, and she is dedicated to providing that effort. In the few cases that she has failed in her initial attempts, perseverance and resolve have overcome the obstacles. She thinks of these efforts as some of her most valuable learning experiences.

*Note.* AM = a person for whom the motive to achieve dominates the motive to avoid failure; FF = a person driven by a fear of failure, for whom the motive to avoid failure dominates the motive to achieve.

Boyatzis, 1982; Weiner, 1979, 1990, 1991). They are predisposed to reason from the perspective that people should, if the opportunity arises, take initiatives and be responsible for decisions and strategies. They are also predisposed to reason from the perspective that people should be held personally accountable for the success or failure of these endeavors. This implicit hypothesis that people should be held personally accountable for success or failure on demanding tasks engenders a tendency to favor internal attributions (initiative, perseverance, conscientiousness) as explanations for performance in achievement situations. In Exhibit 2.3, Joan's consistent attributions of her success in college to her own efforts (e.g., studying diligently) illustrate this implicit hypothesis. Predilections to invoke internal attributions (explanations) indicate a lack of inclination to use external attributions (e.g., helpful coworkers contributed to success when performance is good, inadequate resources restricted performance when one fails) for explanatory purposes.

Note that an exclusively rational (i.e., unbiased) analysis might uncover reasonable support for both internal (e.g., effort, skills) and external (e.g., resources, excellent instruction) explanations for performance. Individuals like Joan, however, are predisposed to reason from the perspective (i.e., have an implicit assumption) that success or failure on demanding tasks is largely a function of personal initiative, intensity, and persistence (i.e., internal attributions). Thus, in their attempts to justify approach to demanding goals and objectives and the pursuit of achievement, AMs are inclined to give greater emphasis to internal factors than is deserved (cf. Weiner, 1979, 1990, 1991). This is what is meant by an *implicit bias* in this context.

Bias does not denote error, for internal factors constitute one plausible explanation for performance. But a purely rational model calls for a dialectic in which both personal and external factors are viable as causes of behavior. The connotation of bias is thus a predilection to favor one side of a dialectic when a rational analysis can identify two (or more) alternative, often conflicting, plausible explanations, for which there is no logical basis for favoring one explanation over any other.

AMs may well subscribe consciously to the idea of a dialectic and may even express strong beliefs in the validity of explanatory models that espouse both internal and external causes. However, when asked to analyze specific events and to rationally determine causes of success or failure, AMs consistently favor internal causes as rational explanations.

AMs tend unconsciously to favor explanations based on personal responsibility because (a) they want to believe that success on demanding tasks is not only possible but also controllable via their efforts, and (b) attributing success to personally controllable factors such as initiative and perseverance suggests that they are competent, self-reliant, and talented. It is also noteworthy that a predilection to attribute success on demanding tasks to internal, personal agents fosters an optimistic view of the likelihood of one's success, which is to say the likelihood that demanding goals and tasks will succumb to one's intense and persistent efforts. Joan, for example, is well along the way to inferring that there is little in her chosen discipline of biology that she cannot master, given sufficient time and effort. This is an example of an implicit bias, although not necessarily an error (cf. Funder, 1987), whose purpose is to enhance the logical appeal of approach behaviors. It illustrates the presence of a justification mechanism—namely, a *personal responsibility bias*—in framing and analyses (James, 1998).

Reasoning that has been unconsciously shaped, defined, and guided by the personal responsibility bias is said to be conditional because framing and analyses are dependent on the reasoner's having a strong motive to achieve. An individual's reasoning is said to be conditional on his or her personality when this reasoning is shaped by a motive to achieve in the first place and relies on one or more justification mechanisms to enhance the logical plausibility of engaging in, and persisting in, achievement-oriented behaviors.

The full scope of CR is captured by contrasting the reasoning of AMs with the reasoning of FFs, as we illustrate in Exhibit 2.3. Arguments that champion approach over avoidance, or vice versa, as the most reasonable adjustment to a demanding task highlight the conditionality of reasoning on individual differences in the personalities of the persons doing the reasoning. This issue is addressed shortly.

An implicit affinity to personal responsibility is just one illustration of how justification mechanisms shape, define, and otherwise influence the framing and analyses of AMs. Other justification mechanisms for AMs are presented in Exhibit 2.4. Included in this set is the *positive connotation of achievement striving bias*. This justification mechanism often affects AMs' framing of working long hours, with minimal rest and attention to other facets of their lives. A sustained and single-minded concentration on the attainment of a demanding goal is framed or interpreted as a demonstration of "dedication, intensity, commitment, involvement, or tenacity." Joan exemplifies this framing when she attributes studying on Friday and Saturday evenings to dedication and commitment. Tacit in this framing is an unrecognized predilection on the part of AMs to ignore or to discount the many forms of stress (e.g., overload, conflict between work and nonwork roles) that they are likely to encounter in their quests to achieve (McClelland, 1985; Spence & Helmreich, 1983).

One of the reasons that AMs do not frame working on demanding tasks as stressful is that they tend to regard these tasks as "challenges" or "opportunities" (Spence & Helmreich, 1983). This framing is reflective of an implicit bias to assume that demanding activities are opportunities to take on important objectives, to demonstrate noteworthy skills, to learn and improve one's skills, and to make contributions in areas that count. This is the *opportunity*

## EXHIBIT 2.4
## Justification Mechanisms for Achievement Motivation

1. Personal responsibility bias: Tendency to favor personal factors such as initiative, intensity, and persistence as the most important causes of performance on demanding tasks.
2. Opportunity bias: Tendency to frame demanding tasks on which success is uncertain as "challenges" that offer "opportunities" to demonstrate present skills, to learn new skills, and to make a contribution.
3. Positive connotation of achievement striving bias: Tendency to associate effort (intensity, persistence) on demanding tasks to "dedication," "concentration," "commitment," and "involvement."
4. Malleability of skills bias: Tendency to assume that the skills necessary to master demanding tasks can, if necessary, be learned or developed via training, practice, and experience.
5. Efficacy of persistence bias: Tendency to assume that continued effort and commitment will overcome obstacles or any initial failures that might occur on a demanding task.
6. Identification with achievers bias: Tendency to empathize with the sense of enthusiasm, intensity, and striving that characterizes those who succeed in demanding situations. Selectively focus on positive incentives that accrue from succeeding.

*Note.* From "Measurement of Personality via Conditional Reasoning," by L. R. James, 1998, *Organizational Research Methods, 1,* p. 134. Copyright 1998 by Sage Publications, Inc. Adapted with permission.

*bias* justification mechanism. Our illustrative AM, Joan, demonstrates reasoning based on this justification mechanism in several ways, one of which is to view taking tests as opportunities to demonstrate what she has learned.

Note how this framing contrasts with that of FFs, as represented by Diane in Exhibit 2.3. The essence of being an FF such as Diane is to associate threat and anxiety with the same demanding tasks that AMs perceive as challenges and opportunities. AMs are able to take this perspective because they *expect to succeed*. Indeed, unlike FFs, who fixate on the downside of achievement striving, AMs attend selectively to the upside. This orientation is manifested by a selective focus on the positive incentives that accrue to successful achievers, both material (e.g., promotion, selection to graduate school) and emotional (e.g., involvement, a sense of efficacy).

Another important justification mechanism for AMs is the *efficacy of persistence bias*. A hallmark of being an AM is to reason from the perspective that continued effort and perseverance will ultimately result in the successful accomplishment of achievement-oriented objectives (McClelland, 1985; McClelland et al., 1989; Revelle & Michaels, 1976; Weiner, 1979). This bias was clearly manifested in our description of Alex Haley's 7-year odyssey to publish his ideas. The efficacy of persistence bias is especially likely to influence reasoning when AMs must overcome obstacles and transitory failures. Examples include the following: (a) a scientist who frames a failed experiment as a learning experience and moves on to continue experimentation; (b) an entrepreneur who begins anew after a business failure, with even greater determination to build a successful enterprise; (c) an athlete who persists and intensifies practice sessions after having failed to meet his or her standards in competition; (d) aspiring authors, musicians, and artists who continue in their toils despite having their works rejected repeatedly; and (e) Joan's perseverance after her initial failure and her belief that the knowledge she gained during these quests furnished her with some of her most valuable learning experiences.

An alternative explanation could have been invoked in each of these illustrations. A number of these alternative explanations could have resulted in abandoning the objectives (e.g., attributions to uncontrollable outside forces). However, an unrecognized willingness to invoke reasoning that justifies persisting on the tasks demonstrates the efficacy of persistence bias and the dominant motivational force that this justification mechanism serves (i.e., the motive to achieve). It is also noteworthy that the tendency of AMs to slant their reasoning to favor efficacy of persistence is often accompanied by a corollary and supporting tendency to think that the skills necessary to accomplish a demanding task can, if necessary, be learned or developed via training, practice, and experience (cf. Dweck & Leggett, 1988). This reasoning is often at least partially influenced by the justification mechanism termed the *malleability of skills bias*.

Again, this bias was seen in our description of the author Alex Haley. He framed repeated rejections of his manuscripts not as failures but as opportunities to improve his writing skills—skills that he framed as malleable. This bias is in Joan's reasoning when she infers that the amount and intensity of the effort she provides is directly correlated with mastering new skills. Similarly, this bias is manifested by athletes who spend countless hours practicing and preparing for competition, by dancers who regularly attend master classes to hone their skills, or by teachers eager to acquire new instructional techniques to improve their performance in the classroom.

In sum, justification mechanisms serve the motive to achieve by implicitly shaping, defining, and guiding the reasoning that AMs use to enhance the rational appeal of approaching demanding tasks. Thus, it is justification mechanisms that make it possible for AMs to approach and to persevere on personally challenging tasks without experiencing debilitating anxiety about the uncertainty of success or being intimidated by the risk to security that often accompanies failure on important tasks. Indeed, the conscious reasoning engendered by justification mechanisms encourages AMs to engage in steadfast pursuit of difficult objectives because this reasoning frames the objectives as opportunities worth commitment and sacrifice, in which willingness to expend intense and persistent effort will eventually produce success.

## Justification Mechanisms of FFs

Individual achievement commands respect in our Western culture, and demanding tasks that invite achievement are imbued with considerable valence. As we have seen, high task valence triggers approach tendencies on the part of AMs. Approach is corroborated and sanctioned as being rational by a set of justification mechanisms that make demanding goals attractive and success primarily a function of dedication and commitment. FFs are also aware of the importance of achievement and the rewards that accrue to those who succeed on difficult tasks. However, this knowledge does not engender the attraction to the tasks experienced by AMs. Rather, for FFs the recognized significance of doing well on difficult tasks stimulates fear and anxiety about the consequences of not doing well, the primary concern being whether one will be perceived as incompetent. Basically, the types of goals and tasks that serve as challenges and opportunities for AMs create psychological hazards (e.g., apprehension, debilitating anxiety, threat) for FFs. Such was the case for Diane, the illustrative FF in Exhibit 2.3, who experiences threat, fear, and apprehension frequently as a college student.

FFs seek relief from their fear of failing by avoiding the demanding activities in which they see themselves as likely to fail. As discussed, avoidance (and other, nondestructive types of inhibitory behaviors) are often viewed as *self-protective processes*, or *coping mechanisms*, for FFs. Especially important ingredients of this coping process are means to justify avoiding the tasks, goals, problems, and environments in which failure is perceived as probable. FFs want to believe that the avoidance/inhibitory behaviors they engage in to relieve their anxiety about failing are both reasonable and will produce the desired results. The framing and inferences employed by FFs to justify avoidance behaviors are often based on some aspect of the justification mechanisms summarized in Exhibit 2.5. A number of these justification mechanisms are described in greater detail in the following section.

FFs often reason that engaging in achievement striving is stressful (cf. Atkinson, 1957, 1978; McClelland, 1985; Nicholls, 1984; Rothbaum et al., 1982; Schlenker & Leary 1982). Such reasoning is often implicitly shaped by the justification mechanism termed *negative connotation of achievement striving bias*. Basically, FFs are unknowingly predisposed to frame achievement striving in negative terms. Illustrative occasions in which this justification mechanism is revealed include FFs' framing of achievement-oriented activities such as intensity and persistence as "overloading" and "sources of potential burnout." (Note Diane's reasoning that striving for good grades is indicative of obsessiveness and brings about stress and overload.) These are the same activities that AMs regard as indicators of perseverance and commitment.

## EXHIBIT 2.5
### Justification Mechanisms for Fear of Failure

1. External attribution bias: Tendency to favor external factors such as lack of resources, situational constraints, intractable material, or biased evaluations as the most important causes of performance on demanding tasks.
2. Liability bias: Tendency to frame demanding tasks as personal liabilities or "threats" because one may fail and be seen as incompetent. Perceptions of threat are euphemistically expressed in terms such as "risky," "costly," or "venturesome."
3. Negative connotation of achievement striving bias: Tendency to frame effort (intensity, persistence) on demanding tasks as "overloading" or "stressful." Perseverance on demanding tasks after encountering setbacks or obstacles is associated with "compulsiveness" and "lack of self-discipline."
4. Fixed skills bias: Tendency to assume that problem-solving skills are fixed and cannot be enhanced by experience, training, or dedication to learning. Thus, if one is deficient in a skill, then one should not attempt demanding tasks or should withdraw if one encounters initial failures.
5. Leveling bias: Tendency to discount a culturally valent but, for the reasoner, a psychologically hazardous event (e.g., approaching demanding situations) by associating that event with a dysfunctional and aversive outcome (e.g., cardiovascular disease).
6. Identification with failures bias: Tendency to empathize with the fear and anxiety of those who fail in demanding situations. Selectively focus on negative outcomes that accrue from failing.
7. Indirect compensation bias: An attempt to increase the logical appeal of replacing a threatening situation with a compensatory (i.e., less threatening) situation by imbuing the less threatening situation with positive, socially desirable qualities.
8. Self-Handicapping bias: An attempt to deflect explanations for failure away from incompetence in favor of self-induced impairments such as not really trying or not being prepared (e.g., defensive lack of effort).

*Note.* From "Measurement of Personality via Conditional Reasoning" by L. R. James, 1998, *Organizational Research Methods, 1,* p. 137. Copyright 1998 by Sage Publications, Inc. Adapted with permission.

Dedication for AMs becomes mental or physical overload for FFs, from which spring feelings of anxiousness, strain, and tension.

FFs such as Diane tend to see the intensity and persistence of AMs as signs of compulsiveness and obsessiveness. As a result, FFs tend to reason that people who take a more relaxed approach to work are less likely to experience exhaustion, illness, burnout, and chronic anxiety about how one's life, especially career, is progressing (Crocker, 1981; Crocker & Major, 1989; Raynor, 1978; Schlenker & Leary, 1982; Taylor & Brown, 1988; Taylor & Lobel, 1989; Wood, 1989). Such reasoning is also a product of an implicit tendency to justify avoidance of demanding tasks by invoking the negative connotation of achievement bias.

Other justification mechanisms shape FFs' reasoning. For example, FFs possess a strong predilection to conclude that the failure on which they have focused their attention is due to external agents that are beyond their control (e.g., lack of resources, societal inequities, poor leadership). Such reasoning often reveals an underlying justification mechanism termed the *external attribution bias* (see the first justification mechanism in Exhibit 2.5 and Crocker & Major, 1989; Hinshaw, 1992; Schlenker & Leary, 1982; Taylor, 1991).

As a specific illustration of reasoning based on this justification mechanism, consider FF students who conclude that low to moderate scores on an important, difficult exam were products of uncontrollable external agents such as lack of resources (e.g., inadequate study time), situational constraints (e.g., loud roommates), impenetrable material, biased professors, or in Diane's case, poorly designed tests that focus on the arcane and tangential issues. Thus, whereas AMs tend to reason from the perspective that less than stellar performance can be improved upon by control of internal factors (e.g., increased study time, greater effort), FFs tend to focus reasoning on external factors over which they have no control and that will likely nullify whatever effort they expend to master material. Like Diane, they often feel helpless to influence events that have an impact on their well-being. It is also the case that FFs are less than enthusiastic about AMs' tendency to hold people personally accountable for performance on demanding tasks. To FFs, it hardly seems reasonable to be held personally responsible for failures that were caused by factors over which one had little or no control (e.g., loud classroom).

AMs' tendency to champion the efficacy of intense and persistent effort comes under logical attack by FFs from yet another perspective. Research has shown that people who concentrate their attention on failure and its aversive consequences also tend to conclude that basic cognitive problem-solving abilities and critical intellectual skills are fixed and cannot be enhanced by experience, training, or dedication to learning. Diane, for example, is convinced that the demands of college exceed her basic problem-solving abilities and critical intellectual skills. She has never considered that these abilities and skills could be enhanced by practice and study. This reasoning is frequently shaped by a justification mechanism designated the *fixed skills bias* (cf. Crocker & Major, 1989; Dweck & Leggett, 1988; Nicholls, 1984; Taylor, 1991; Taylor & Brown, 1988; Taylor & Lobel, 1989; Weiner, 1979, 1990, 1991; Wood, 1989). We extend this bias to noncognitive areas of performance such as athletics and the arts. Reasoning engendered by a fixed skills bias contrasts sharply with the reasoning of AMs, who tend to analyze behavior from the perspective that the skills necessary to accomplish a demanding task can, if not present at the onset of a difficult assignment, be developed via training, experience, practice, and learning (i.e., effort). FFs, by contrast, are skeptical of pursuing goals for which they perceive themselves as having deficient critical skills (i.e., they experience an inhibitory or restraining tendency).

The preceding discussion paints a picture in which FFs logically associate demanding, achievement-oriented activities with such things as stress, uncontrollable agents, risk, intractable difficulties, and a sense of helplessness. These logical connections furnish FFs with what are often rationalizations for avoiding demanding tasks, such as Diane using reasoning based on FF justification mechanisms to build rationalizations for leaving college. In place of high-press-for-achievement situations, FFs seek secure and safe environments, where the futures of their jobs and careers are predictable and certain. Such jobs and careers are often less glamorous or prestigious, stimulating the implicit operation of a justification mechanism termed the *indirect compensation bias*. Indirect compensation consists of an attempt to justify replacing threatening goals and tasks (i.e., high-press-for-achievement objectives) with less threatening (i.e., compensatory) goals and tasks by imbuing the latter objectives with positive qualities (e.g., reasoning that emphasizes the valence of job security, enhanced work-family balance, or improved quality of life). Diane is illustrative in the sense that she has become increasingly interested in finding a job outside of college that does not require written examinations but does offer job security and rewards for those who are loyal and stay put.

In sum, the justification mechanisms possessed by FFs encourage them to reason from the standpoint that venting inhibitory tendencies is feasible and sensible as opposed to unrealistic, defensive, or irrational. Framing and inferences based on these justification mechanisms help make it possible for FFs to avoid demanding tasks without seeing themselves as unmotivated, indecisive, untalented, risk avoidant, or lacking in initiative. In particular, justification mechanisms and the reasoning they shape both define and sustain FFs in arriving at conclusions that they are cautious and patient individuals who, in the interest of maintaining a realistic, stable, and predictable lifestyle, are making decisions and engaging in behaviors that promote balance, security, lack of stress, and tranquility.

## Are Justification Mechanisms for AMs and FFs Enablers of Rationalizations?

With respect to aggression, we defined *rationalization* as "the use of ostensibly plausible reasons to justify behaviors that are unknowingly caused by unconscious, unacceptable, and/or unwanted motives" (Baumeister et al., 1996; Westen & Gabbard, 1999). Avoiding achievement-oriented tasks because they are stressful, risky, subject to shortages in resources, and conducive to escalating commitment could be characterized as rationalizations designed to shield FFs from knowledge of their true motive structure. Moreover, justification mechanisms for FFs serve the same roles they serve for aggressive individuals, which is to enable rationalizations for motive-driven behavior. However, unlike aggression, avoidance of demanding tasks is not generally antisocial (or illegal), and justification mechanisms for avoidance typically do not involve moral disengagements (like aggression—see Bandura, 1999). The same is true for the justification mechanisms for AMs. AMs have biases toward inferring that personal initiative and effort are the likely causes of behavior, and that working 70-hr weeks is indicative of commitment and sacrifice (while simultaneously discounting stress and its ramifications). Although overzealous to the point of being a bit obsessive, let us not forget that such biases have produced more than one Nobel Prize and a host of Olympic medals.

Thus, the justification mechanism implies an implicit bias that serves as an enabler of rationalizations in the sense that one attempts to enhance the rational appeal of motive-driven behavior. There is no connotation of antisocial behavior or moral disengagement as there was with aggression. Nonetheless, the justification mechanisms for AMs and FFs (and the rationalizations they enable) serve a defensive function because overascribing or underascribing one's achievement motivation and/or fear of failure often involves protecting one's sense of self-esteem. Here again, however, the consequences of engaging in approach or avoidance behaviors is not as extreme as those for harming others. In fact, rationalizations for AMs may produce great feats. Justification mechanisms and the ensuing rationalizations for FFs often reduce anxiety and help individuals to cope (Atkinson, 1957, 1978; Kuhl, 1978; Nicholls, 1984; Rothbaum et al., 1982; Schlenker & Leary, 1982; Sorrentino & Short, 1986). Thus, the general model of rationalization applies to AMs and FFs, but in a less intense and more socially acceptable form than for aggression.

## DEVELOPING ONE'S OWN SET OF JUSTIFICATION MECHANISMS

Suppose that one is interested in identifying a set of justification mechanisms associated with a motive such as affiliation, autonomy, nurturance, or power. What guidelines might one follow to seek out implicit biases—that is, framing proclivities and implicit hypotheses—that serve to enhance the rational appeal of behaviors induced by the motive? To begin to answer this question, we first consider individual differences in the behaviors we believe to be induced by the motive. How, for example, are individuals with a strong desire for power likely to behave, and how does this behavior differ from that of individuals with modest and low power motives? We might also ask what parts of the motive are likely to be explicit and what components are likely to be implicit. Fortunately, the literature assists us in this query (e.g., McClelland, 1985; Winter et al., 1998).

Given a reasonable understanding of the motive and its behavioral manifestations, we next seek to understand how people attempt to enhance the rational appeal of their power-induced behaviors. We search for answers to questions such as the following: What adjectives do people high in need for power use to frame acts of power and dominance? How do they characterize behaviors meant to act as substitutes for, or replace, the use of power? How do they frame people who are dependent and/or submissive? What theories of causality do people with strong power motives employ to justify their (or others') use of power and dominance? In particular, when do they see the use of power as mandated or especially useful? What attributions do these people make about the intent or character of power users? What are their attributions of followers? What are the probabilities of success (as they define it) associated with the use of power? With substitutes or replacement for power? What evidence is put forth to support their rationales and theories regarding power?

These questions are illustrative. Analogous questions would be asked of people with low power motives as well as those with modest power motives. We would also ask parallel questions of people with strong dependence needs. What will likely follow across all searches are strong individual differences in framing, causal theories, attributions, expectations, and what is regarded as supporting evidence. This is CR. At this point, likely candidates for implicit biases in framing and inference begin to emerge.

Naturally, exhaustive reviews of the literatures in areas such as social cognition, defense mechanisms, power, and dependence should assist in the quest for implicit biases. We would also make considerable use of the nonscientific literature (e.g., autobiographies, biographies, theoretical treatises) for power, which is voluminous and contributes insights (as we found for aggression). Interviews and discussions with prototypes of key individual differences are useful throughout the process.

Our task for the remainder of this chapter is to review the types of implicit biases that have contributed to justification mechanisms in our prior research. We have also included implicit biases that we think might be useful even though we have not yet had occasion to use them. Hopefully, this will provide others with a road map of what to look for and what to ask about when seeking justification mechanisms for a motive, or perhaps a set of contrasting motives. To set the stage for this discussion, it will be useful to distinguish more fully between justification mechanisms as they relate to *reasoning content* (e.g., a type of attribution bias such as the hostile attribution bias for aggressive individuals) and to *reasoning strategy* (e.g., confirmatory biases and selective attention).

Justification mechanisms are informed by implicit biases that, unknown to the reasoner, shape, define, and guide perceptions, understandings, hypotheses, causal explanations, and expectancies that a person employs to give meaning to events and to reason about how best to behave in an environment. The biases are designed to enhance the rational appeal of motive-based behavior. Thus, for example, highly motivated individuals are implicitly biased to reason that achievement is largely a product of initiative, intensity, and persistence as opposed to being dictated by outside, uncontrollable forces. Though often partially accurate, such reasoning also frequently involves a justification mechanism referred to as the *personal responsibility bias*, which is an unrecognized proclivity to arrive at the conclusion that one has more control over personal success/failure than is actually true.

Note that justification mechanisms have content; they involve identifiable biases that produce reasoning that attempts to enhance the logical appeal of specific behaviors. Justification mechanisms may also influence the strategies that individuals use to reason. For example, a bias toward personal responsibility is likely to stimulate a directed search process wherein the reasoner seeks occasions on which initiative, intensity, and persistence did in fact lead to success. Such a directed search represents a strategy in how one reasons known as a *confirmatory bias* because the reasoner selectively seeks out only that information (evidence, data, historical events) that supports or confirms his or her underlying justification mechanism.

Reasoning strategies are temporary mental actions that serve justification mechanisms but themselves lack indigenous content. A particular process such as a directed search for confirming evidence may serve any number of justification mechanisms. Thus, we do not think of reasoning strategies as justification mechanisms but rather as implicit biases in reasoning that are shaped and directed by justification mechanisms. Here we focus on the substantive content of justification mechanisms. Numerous reviews of biases in reasoning strategies are available in the literature (cf. Hafer & Begue, 2005; Hahn & Oaksford, 2007; Kunda, 1990; Nisbett & Wilson, 1977; Pyszczynski & Greenberg, 1987; Wilson & Brekke, 1994).

Unfortunately, no taxonomy exists for the types of implicit biases that might inform either present or future justification mechanisms. This is largely because current research is actively attempting to chart an ever-expanding cognitive terrain. The best that can be offered now is an overview of what appear to be promising domains of the types of implicit biases that could give rise to the substantive content of other justification mechanisms.

The overview presented below is drawn primarily from the implicit personality and cognition literatures. In the past 30 or so years, substantial advances have been made in identifying cognitively and/or motivationally inspired biases, many of which operate unconsciously, that affect the analyses, judgments, explanations, models, and inferences that constitute reasoning in everyday social contexts. A nonexhaustive but representative sampling of research domains that have recently contributed to the understanding of reasoning biases includes attribution models and theories, defense mechanisms, framing, heuristics in decision making, implicit (personality) theories, biases in person perception, cognitive mechanisms for self-protection and self-enhancement, object relations, measurement of implicit attitudes, social inference, and systematic biases in performance evaluation (see Cramer, 2000, 2006; Fazio & Olson, 2003; Fiske & Taylor, 1984, 1991; Funder, 1987; Greenwald & Banaji, 1995; Hogarth, 1987; Kahneman & Tversky, 1973, 1984; Kihlstrom, 1999; Kruglanski, 1989; Kruglanski & Ajzen, 1983; Kruglanski & Klar, 1987; Kunda, 1990; Miller, 1987; Nisbett & Wilson, 1977; Pyszczynski & Greenberg, 1987; Ross, 1977; Schneider, 1991; Tversky & Kahneman, 1973, 1974, 1981, 1983; Wegner & Vallacher, 1977; Weiner, 1979, 1991; Westen, 1991, 1998).

## Types of Implicit Biases That Give Rise to Justification Mechanisms

We now discuss nine categories of implicit biases that have been instrumental in building justification mechanisms. Some of these biases have long histories in research and theorizing about human cognition (e.g., halo). Others have shorter but illustrious histories (e.g., attribution biases). Still others are essentially new, having been identified in recent research, including that on CR (e.g., leveling). We suspect that new domains will be added to this list as research continues to accumulate on implicit biases in a number of areas of psychology.

*Differential framing* refers to the qualitative disparities in the meanings imputed to (i.e., the adjectives used to describe) the same attributes or event(s) by different individuals (James, 1998). For example, FFs tend to frame perseverance on a demanding task following initial failure as "compulsiveness," whereas AMs tend to frame this same perseverance as "dedication."

To frame an event is to place that event in an interpretative category, or *cognitive schema* (e.g., people high in fear of failure place demanding tasks in the interpretative category of "stressful"). Cognitive schemas are internal prisms through which external stimuli pass, and in passing are translated into interpretive adjectives that indicate personal meaning. Individuals draw repeatedly on the same cognitive schemas to give meaning to events. It is the recurring use of the same schemas to give meaning to events that determines a *framing proclivity*, which is a disposition to use only certain schemas and adjectives to interpret the same or similar events.

Differential framing often involves unrecognized tendencies to frame behaviors and/or behavioral objectives in ways that encourage or discourage specific actions. For example, AMs implicitly believe that demanding tasks provide "challenges" that offer "opportunities" to demonstrate present skills, to learn new skills, or to make a contribution (see opportunity inclination in Exhibit 2.4). AMs also tend to impute positive connotations to effort, seeing intensity and persistence as forms of "dedication," "concentration," and "involvement." These perceptions are driven by a tendency to slant the meaning of effort toward perceptions that enhance the rational appeal of approaching demanding tasks. In contrast, FFs are predisposed to slant framing toward dampening the logical appeal of approach to challenging tasks. For example, FFs unknowingly tend to frame demanding tasks as "threats" that create "risk" and to impute to these tasks negative connotations such as "overloading" or "stressful." Such framing reveals an unconscious tendency to seek out negative connotations in achievement striving.

Unrecognized biases that enhance or dampen the attractiveness of motive-inspired behaviors via framing were also prevalent for aggression. Consider, for example, the potency bias that shapes the framing of aggressive individuals. A potency bias involves a tendency to frame and analyze other people using the contrast of strength versus weakness. People with a strong potency bias tend to frame others on a continuum ranging from (a) strong, assertive, powerful, daring, fearless, or brave to (b) weak, impotent, submissive, timid, sheepish, compliant, conforming, or cowardly. This bias is used to justify aggression via arguments such as that (a) aggression (e.g., confrontations with teachers, fights with coworkers) results in being "respected" by others and that (b) weakness/submissiveness invites aggression because it shows that one is willing to submit. Nonaggressive, socially adaptive individuals tend not to perceive others through a prism of potency. In place of the potency bias, they tend to perceive others through a prism that frames them on a continuum ranging from (a) likely to be a friend, companion, confidante, partner, or colleague to (b) likely to have only a neutral, unemotional, or uninvolved relationship (James, 1998).

Additional examples of personality-based differences in framing—that is, differential framing—abound in personality. For example, extraverts are predisposed to frame meeting new people as opportunities for making new friends, whereas introverts tend to frame meeting new people as occasions associated with discomfort and potential embarrassment. Emotionally stable people perceive delaying decisions until information is obtained as being careful and cautious. Emotionally unstable, impatient people frame these same delays as indicators of indecisiveness and timidity. Agreeable, trusting individuals are inclined to frame interactions with authority figures such as the police from the perspective of one who is being defended and protected. Disagreeable, aggressive people are prone to frame these same interactions from the perspective of one who is being tyrannized and oppressed.

Framing proclivities and differential framing set the stage for the analyses and hypothesizing that make up reasoning about real-life events. How events are framed often shapes and bounds the thinking and inferences about these events. Thus, differential framing is viewed as the first stage of the CR process.

*Attribution biases* are predilections to ascribe behavior to causal factors that implicitly justify expressions of motives. After differential framing, attribution biases are perhaps the single most prevalent source of the implicit biases that underlie justification mechanisms. Earlier we described the hostile attribution bias, which is a tendency on the part of aggressive individuals to infer that the targets of their aggression acted malevolently and with harmful intent toward them, thus triggering the need for self-defensive reactions.

We also discussed how AMs favor initiative, intensity, and persistence as the most important causes of (i.e., attributions for) performance on demanding tasks. This bias toward ascribing performance to personal responsibility is a manifestation of a more general proclivity known as the *internal attribution bias*, which is opposed by the *external attribution bias*. People whose relative motive strength favors fear of failure (i.e., FFs) are prone to invoke external factors such as lack of resources, situational constraints, intractable material, or unfair evaluations as the most important determinants of high or low performance on demanding tasks. Such favoritism sets the stage for rationalizing avoidance because the inevitable failure will not be one's fault.

Other forms of attribution biases pertain to such matters as whether causes of a behavior are judged to be (a) more stable or unstable than is factual or (b) more controllable or uncontrollable than is factual (cf. Weiner, 1990). An illustration of an overattribution to controllability is an extravert who presumes that he or she has greater mastery over social situations than is authentic, whereas an example of an underattribution to controllability is an introvert who reasons that her or his life is dominated by capricious social forces. A bias favoring stability involves an intelligent person who, in the pursuit of deeper explanations, fails to appreciate the effects of random shocks on behavior. A bias favoring instability appears in the imperceptive person who fails to recognize an underlying pattern in events that appear to him or her to be unrelated.

*Halo* (also known as *implicit* or *illusory correlation*) is a tendency to associate behavior in one area with behavior in a different area. For example, an individual who demonstrates conscientiousness is expected to be stable, agreeable, wise, and sociable. Or an individual who is demonstrably undependable is expected, based on this evidence alone, to be anxious, unintelligent, disagreeable, and withdrawn. A related source of halo occurs when a rater forms a general impression of an experiment's (or a study's) participant (e.g., I like this person), and this general impression influences all or most of the judge's ratings of the target across multiple traits (e.g., this person is friendly, smart, helpful, supportive, a good leader, trustworthy, and dependable; Cooper, 1981).

Halo has been studied extensively by industrial psychologists interested in performance evaluation (for reviews, see Feldman, 1981; Ilgen, Barnes-Farrell, & McKellin, 1993; Landy & Farr, 1980; Murphy & Anhalt, 1992). Although many questions remain, the literature has consistently demonstrated a tendency for a rater's ratings on one category of behavior (e.g., creativity) to be correlated higher than would be indicated by the facts with a different category of behavior (e.g., conscientiousness). Moreover, much of the systematic variance in ratings of ostensibly different behaviors tends to be accounted for by a single underlying factor. These results suggest that raters are prone to form general impressions of others and to assume implicitly that behavior in one domain may be used to forecast, with reasonable accuracy, behaviors in other domains.

Halo gives rise to justification mechanisms when individuals with different motives forge different expectations based on the same stimulus behavior. For example, aggressive individuals are prone to associate lack of an aggressive manner with weakness or cowardice and to expect nonaggressive individuals to act in humble and deferential manners. These associations and expectations are products of halo, and they contribute to the formation of the potency bias justification mechanism. In contrast, nonaggressive, socially adaptive people are likely to associate the same lack of aggressiveness with civility, courteousness, and good-naturedness. Expectations for future behavior flow from these associations.

*Identification* is a tendency to empathize with the plights, experiences, perceptions, emotions, and behavioral dispositions of specific types of persons. Identification often reflects one's own predilections and experiences. For example, FFs tend to empathize with the fear and anxiety of those who fail in achievement situations because they themselves experience fear and anxiety in achievement situations. People with high achievement motivation (AMs) tend to identify with the sense of enthusiasm, intensity, and striving that characterize those who succeed in demanding situations. Here again, identification mirrors tendencies of AMs to be excited, intense, and enthusiastic in achievement situations. Other illustrations of identification include occasions in which agreeable people feel a sense of bonding with those who are kind, amiable, generous, and trusting. Disagreeable people tend to identify with people whom they believe to be assertive, nonvulnerable, realistic, and strong.

*Indirect compensation* is a tacit or typically unrecognized attempt to increase the logical appeal of replacing a threatening situation with a compensatory (i.e., less threatening) situation by imbuing the compensatory situation with positive, socially desirable qualities. For example, FFs tend to place greater value on job security than on opportunities for advancement, learning, and rewards. Introverts rank peace and quiet over affectionate and warm interpersonal relationships. Unimaginative people prefer the simple, practical, and bottom-line explanation to a more thoughtful and abstract explanation.

*Discounting* is a predilection to invoke assumptions, explanations, or evidence that disputes, rejects, or invalidates critiques of one's justifications for favored behaviors. For example, AMs are predisposed to discount FFs' use of indirect compensation to impute socially desirable qualities (e.g., job security) to non-achievement-oriented tasks. AMs devalue such tasks by characterizing them as routine, boring, uninteresting, or dull. Conversely, FFs discount AMs interest in achievement-oriented tasks by characterizing them as risky, uncertain, or stressful.

*Leveling* is a special form of discounting in which a culturally relevant but, for the reasoner, psychologically hazardous event is devalued by associating that event with a dysfunctional and aversive outcome. For example, FFs tend to associate approach to achievement-oriented situations with increased risk of heart disease. Here the unrecognized desire to devalue achievement striving engenders a potentially false causal inference, perhaps fueled by correlational data, for example, that business executives have an above-average frequency of heart distresses. Another example of leveling appears when shy individuals associate an attempt to initiate a social interaction with being rebuffed and embarrassed.

*Positive leniency* and *negative leniency* are unrecognized tendencies to overestimate or underestimate one's proficiencies in a behavioral domain. Examples of positive leniency are (a) overconfidence by AMs that they have a greater likelihood of success on a difficult task than they actually do, (b) benevolent self-perceptions by persons with high intellectualism that they possess keen insight, and (c) overestimates by aggressive individuals of their ability to intimidate others. Negative leniency is illustrated by (a) FFs' partially unwarranted lack of confidence in their likelihood of success on demanding tasks, (b) introverts' lack of confidence in their social skills, and (c) anxious individuals' perceptions of their inability to cope with evocative situations.

*Rationalization* is the use of ostensibly plausible reasons to justify behaviors that are unknowingly caused by unconscious, unacceptable, and/or unwanted motives. Justification mechanisms are part of the rationalization process. They consist of implicit biases that enable rationalizations, such as when the hostile attribution bias (justification mechanism) is used to enhance the rational appeal of the use of self-defense (rationalization) to harm someone. People's rationalizations for their behaviors are especially important sources of the implicit biases that represent justification mechanisms. On any specific occasion, the argument for self-defense based on the hostile intent of the target of aggression may be hard to disconfirm (if indeed it is false). However, a pattern of altercations over time, each preceded by attributions of threat and intended hostility and followed by pleas of self-defense, suggest the possibility, at least, of a justification mechanism at work.

This is also the time to note that the line between justification mechanism and rationalization may become blurred. The ostensibly plausible reason for behavior (rationalization) may also involve the implicit bias that enhances its rational appeal (justification mechanism). In this case, the two concepts are fused. The important point here is to recognize the implicit bias in the reasoning. Whether one refers to that bias as a rationalization or a justification (mechanism) is not important. However, our experience has been that rationalizations tend to be accompanied by, and distinguishable from, the types of biased supporting arguments that we refer to as justification mechanisms.

To conclude, this overview of sources for justification mechanisms is meant to be illustrative. The specific justification mechanisms constructed for motive-induced behavior must be predicated on the types of implicit biases that pervade the framing and analyses that people use to defend manifestation of the motive. Potential domains of implicit biases and the justification mechanisms they engender are still being identified, and will be for some time, as knowledge grows in the area of implicit personality. Those with an interest in pursuing the identification of justification mechanisms are advised to review the recent implicit social cognition and implicit personality literatures.

## Implicit Biases: Wanted or Unwanted

We have attempted to identify prominent domains of implicit biases that explain how and why different individuals make divergent behavioral adjustments in the same environment. Simply stated, people who behave differently think differently. Salient components of these differences in thinking are (a) differential framing and (b) reasoning that on the surface appears sensible to the reasoner (at least) but in reality is implicitly influenced by biasing mechanisms (i.e., justification mechanisms) whose purpose is to enhance the logical plausibility, and thereby justifiability, of rationalizations for that reasoner's motive-based dispositions.

Interestingly, in constructing rationales for their behaviors, individuals often try to overcome their self-perceptions of their biases through employing what they believe to be principles of reasoning (cf. Einhorn & Hogarth, 1978; Feldman & Lindell, 1989). The conviction that they have been successful in their pursuit of objectivity may be at least partially true. What individuals fail to realize, however, is that the arguments that they have carefully constructed via reasoned judgments are subject to biased processing of which they are unaware and over which they have no control. Their reasoning may thus be characterized as *conditional*, a term connoting that the probability of a person's judging a behavior to be reasonable is dependent on the strength of that person's motive to engage in the behavior. A related connotation of *conditional* is that what one considers a reasonable behavior in a given context is often dependent on one's underlying personality.

It is noteworthy that justification processes are especially likely to occur when CR opportunities are evocative, such as when the events trigger motives to protect/enhance one's self-concept, to be secure, to be accepted, and to achieve a reasonable degree of success (and to avoid demonstrating incompetence). For example, as discussed previously, unrecognized biases in reasoning have a self-protective function in the sense that they are components of defense mechanisms that protect FFs from engaging in high-press-for-achievement activities that might cause them psychological damage. Thus, unless biases in reasoning are being used to rationalize illegal and/or pathological behavior, it is perhaps best to think of them as a natural part of human functioning. Basically, people want to believe their behavior is justified—which is to say, rational or sensible, as opposed to irrational or inappropriate. It is often, although not always, functional and healthy psychologically to engage in nonconscious processes that assist in realizing this belief.

# 3

# THE DEVELOPMENT OF CONDITIONAL REASONING PROBLEMS

In Chapter 2, we presented the theoretical foundation of measuring the implicit personality and its justification mechanisms through the use of conditional reasoning (CR) problems. This chapter is devoted to describing the content of the CR measurement system, which consists of procedures for measuring justification mechanisms. These procedures are based on the following four principles:

1. It is possible to design logical assertions that support or challenge the implicit bias or biases (e.g., unrecognized preconceptions, assumptions, theories) that constitute a justification mechanism and shape reasoning.
2. The presence or absence of a justification mechanism in a person's implicit cognitive system predisposes him or her to react positively or negatively to these logical assertions.
   - People who possess a justification mechanism will accept logic that projects the implicit bias on which the mechanism is founded and reject logic that challenges this implicit bias.
   - People who do not possess a justification mechanism will reject logic that is based on the implicit bias and agree with logic that challenges the implicit bias.

3. People will believe that the soundness of the reasoning contained in the logical assertions determined their judgments—they will be unaware that their judgments were conditioned by whether the assertions projected or challenged their implicit biases.

4. The presence (and strength) or absence of a justification mechanism in the implicit personality is revealed by the judgments a person makes of logical assertions that project biases and logical assertions that offer challenges to those biases.

We use measurements of justification mechanisms based on these principles to make inferences about the strengths of motives (e.g., the motive to aggress) or the relative strengths of contrasting motives (e.g., relative motive strength of achievement motivation in relation to fear of failure). The CR measurement system is introduced by illustrating how to develop a single CR problem to measure fear of failure.

## STEPS INVOLVED IN BUILDING A CONDITIONAL REASONING PROBLEM FOR FEAR OF FAILURE

People whose motive to avoid failure exceeds their motive to achieve have been referred to as *FFs*. In the previous chapter, FFs were described as being disposed to logically associate achievement-oriented activities with such things as stress, uncontrollable agents, risk, intractable difficulties, and a sense of helplessness. These logical associations serve as justification mechanisms because they enable FFs to build rationalizations for avoiding demanding tasks (e.g., the tasks should be avoided because they will lead to burnout, are insufficiently funded, or dangerous). Avoidance is thus reasonable and realistic to FFs, as opposed to unrealistic, defensive, or inappropriate. Moreover, reasoning based on justification mechanisms makes it possible for FFs to avoid demanding tasks without seeing themselves as unmotivated, indecisive, untalented, risk avoidant, or lacking in initiative. In fact, as noted previously, justification mechanisms guide FFs toward forming conclusions that they are cautious and patient individuals who, in the interest of maintaining a realistic, stable, and predictable lifestyle, are making decisions and engaging in behaviors that promote balance, security, lack of stress, and tranquility.

By way of brief review, the mental processes that we believe underlie FFs' development of rationalizations for avoiding demanding tasks are illustrated in Figure 3.1. This figure highlights the relations among the different concepts involved in the rationalization process, namely, evocative stimuli,

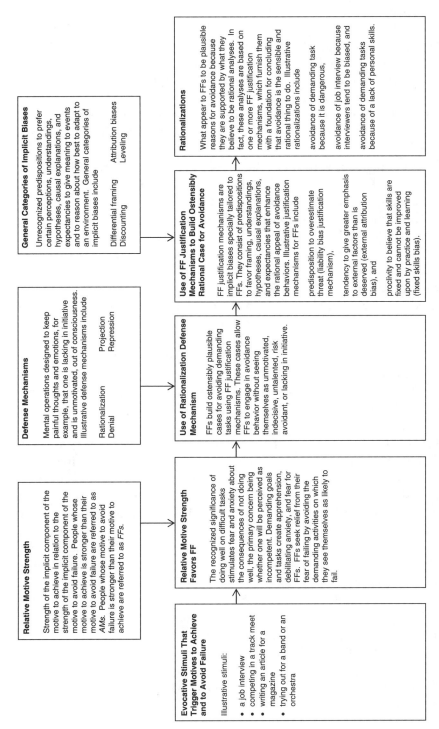

*Figure 3.1.* Relationships among motives, defense mechanisms, implicit biases, and justification mechanisms.

motives, defense mechanisms, implicit biases, and justification mechanisms. These relations are displayed in the linear progression of mental events represented by the five boxes in the bottom row of the figure. This progression of events is intended to illustrate the primary experiences of FFs as they build toward a rationalization for avoiding a demanding task. The three boxes in the top row of the figure represent the latent variables or general constructs (factors, general categories) that inform (i.e., give substance to) the specific mental events in the lower boxes (or the specific events that stem from the general constructs).

The progression begins with an evocative stimulus that triggers the motives to achieve and to avoid failure. As described in greater detail below, illustrative stimuli include a job interview or attempting to write an article for a magazine. A stimulus such as writing an article triggers fear and anxiety in FFs, as indicated in the second box in the progression. Being an FF is a specific expression of the general construct we have referred to as *relative motive strength* (top of figure). One way for FFs to gain relief from their fear is to avoid the source of fear. Avoidance can be attained without seeing oneself as unmotivated, indecisive, untalented, risk avoidant, or lacking in initiative by building an ostensibly plausible case that avoidance is a rational course of action (third box in progression). To embark on this course is to employ the rationalization defense mechanism, which is one of a number of possible defense mechanisms.

Rationalizations are (ostensibly) logical conclusions and, like any other logical conclusion, are dependent on a supporting case made up of premises, arguments, and evidence. Unlike the case for an objective logical conclusion, however, the supporting case for a rationalization involves reasoning that, unknown to the FF involved, is slanted and biased toward justifying avoidance. This is where justification mechanisms enter the picture (fourth box in progression). Justification mechanisms for FFs stem from the general domain and construct of implicit biases (top of figure). Only specific biases of use to FFs are selected, and these biases are tailored to the needs of FFs. The resulting justification mechanisms consist of predispositions to favor framing, understandings, hypotheses, causal explanations, and evidence that enhance the rational appeal of avoidance.

For example, an aspiring author who is an FF may conclude that it is not worthwhile to attempt to publish an article because most articles are ultimately rejected. This is a rationalization for avoiding a demanding task, and it belongs in the fifth box in the progression. To support this rationalization, the FF argues that most aspiring authors are rejected because they lack the skills to write in the first place, and such a skill set is largely fixed at birth and not subject to improvement, irrespective of practice and training (fourth box again). Such support is based on the fixed skills justification mechanism. We proceed now to give substance to this theoretical treatment by describing how we build a CR problem for fear of failure.

## Identify a Stimulus for the Motive to Avoid Failure

With this knowledge as a foundation, our first step in building a CR problem is to ask what types of events, theories, data, arguments, and the like can be expected to trigger FFs' strong motive to avoid failure. Triggers for this motive likely involve such things as evaluative situations (e.g., academic tests, job interviews), contests (e.g., athletics, promotions), high-stress occupations (e.g., astronauts, physicians), situations that require taking responsibility (e.g., leadership), situations that ask for creativity (e.g., author, artist, inventor), moderate to high-risk situations (e.g., commodities broker, mountain climber, entrepreneur), and education and training programs that have strong demands (e.g., military commando, neurosurgeon). We focus on the job interview for this illustration.

## Design an Inductive Reasoning Problem

The next step in problem development consists of asking: What about job interviews could serve as the basis for an inductive reasoning problem? (Our rationale for focusing on inductive reasoning is discussed later in this chapter.) Inductive reasoning asks people to reason "from given premises to a reasonable but logically uncertain conclusion" (Sternberg, 1982, p. 235). In more specific terms, inductive reasoning involves tasks such as the following:

1. Inference—discriminating among degrees of truth and falsity of conclusions (e.g., causal inferences) drawn from given premises (e.g., arguments, data, models, assumptions).
2. Recognition of assumptions—recognizing unstated assumptions in a given statement or logical assertion. A variation on this theme is to identify unstated assumptions that strengthen or weaken a logical assertion.
3. Evaluation of evidence—weighing evidence to decide if generalizations or (general) conclusions based on the given (specific) data or assumptions (premises) are warranted. This often involves determining which testimony is trustworthy, which evidence is untainted, and which samples are representative in regard to evaluating the reasonableness of a logical conclusion.

4. Relevance of arguments—distinguishing between arguments that are strong and relevant versus those that are weak and tangential or irrelevant to a particular issue.
5. Covariation or causation—determining whether covariation among events pertinent to a logical assertion is due to causal influences or is the product of spurious correlation.
6. Unmeasured variables—determining whether causal explanations (models, theories) offered to support a conclusion have omitted one or more key variables.
7. Expectations of outcomes—forecasting consequences, including dysfunctional ones, that might occur naturally or as the result of planned changes or proposed interventions.
8. Analogies—examining the similarities shared by two stimuli (people, situations, events) and inferring the likelihood that those stimuli share other attributes.
9. Generalization of relationships—using information about relationships among variables in a particular sample to draw inferences about those relationships in other samples (or in the larger population).

These reasoning tasks are illustrative of general categories of inductive reasoning. They are not meant to be exhaustive, mutually exclusive, or independent, and it is often the case that more than one task is involved in solving a problem. The inductive reasoning task we chose for (job) interviews is based primarily on "recognition of assumptions" (the second reasoning task in the preceding list), although generalization of relationships (the last inductive reasoning task) is also involved. The substance for this task was based on the general problem: What can people do to prepare for interviews and thereby improve the probability they will do well in interviews? The logical assertion, often referred to as a "conclusion," we used to answer this question is: "Gaining experience is one way to improve performance in the hope of doing well in interviews." Our reasons for choosing this conclusion will unfold in the following discussion.

Three variations on the "recognition of assumptions task" are presented in Exhibit 3.1. Problem 1 in Exhibit 3.1 follows a classic critical reasoning format, which begins with an argument that attempts to convince the respondent that a conclusion follows from one or more premises. The stem to the item includes (1) the conclusion to the argument, "A key to doing well in interviews is thus to gain experience at being interviewed," and (2) premises, which in this case consist of arguments to support the conclusion. A set of interconnected premises are offered to support the conclusion, the key one being "With experience at being interviewed, however, an applicant learns what to

EXHIBIT 3.1

**Problem 1**

Going to a job interview is like acting. When the applicant is new to being interviewed, he or she is likely to have stage fright and to make nervous mistakes. With experience at being interviewed, however, an applicant learns what to expect, such as what types of questions interviewers like to ask and how to answer questions in ways that impress interviewers. A key to doing well in interviews is thus to gain experience at being interviewed.

The argument that gaining experience is a key to doing well in interviews depends most strongly on which one of the following assumptions?

    A. Interviews are often conducted in airports and hotels.
    B. The applicant's early interviewers are similar to her or his later interviewers.
    C. Interviewers tend to have a personal theory as to what the perfect applicant should be like.
    D. Interviewers generally prefer short answers to their questions.

**Problem 2**
[Stem is the same.]

Which one of the following most weakens the argument that gaining experience is a key to doing well in interviews?

    A. Interviews are often conducted in airports and hotels.
    B. The applicant's early interviewers all asked the same narrow range of questions.
    C. The applicant has prepared impressive answers to the questions posed by prior interviewers.
    D. Interviewers generally prefer short answers to their questions.

**Problem 3**
[Stem is the same.]

Which one of the following most strengthens the argument that gaining experience is a key to doing well in interviews?

    A. Interviews are often conducted in airports and hotels.
    B. The applicant's early interviewers all asked the same narrow range of questions.
    C. The applicant has prepared impressive answers to the questions posed by prior interviewers.
    D. Interviewers generally prefer short answers to their questions.

expect, such as what types of questions interviewers like to ask and how to answer questions in ways that impress interviewers."

This problem is inductive because (1) whereas the premises provide support for the conclusion, (2) parts of the argument linking premises to conclusion are missing. Stated alternatively, the argument linking the premises to the conclusion is dependent on one or more unstated assumptions. This renders the conclusion logically uncertain in Sternberg's (1982) terms. The task for respondents is to search the four alternatives given for the problem to find an unstated assumption (i.e., an assumption not stated in the stem) that buttresses the argument that the stated premises lead to the conclusion.

Drawing from Sternberg's (1982) discussion of the cognitive operations involved in inductive reasoning, respondents begin the reasoning process by encoding the information given in the problem. *Encoding* refers to how respondents internally represent, or frame, the information given in the problem for the operations that are to follow. These operations involve attempts to infer what assumptions underlie the argument linking the premises to the conclusion. (Respondents may scan the alternatives to obtain direction and hints for inferences.) These operations likely contain, but are not limited to, attempts to identify gaps in the argument linking the premises to the conclusion.

A respondent may initially identify logically untenable responses. For example, the conclusion that gaining experience is a key to doing well in interviews is not assisted if it is true that each interviewer tends to have a personal theory as to what the perfect applicant should be like. This alternative suggests that interviewers' idiosyncratic stereotypes also serve as a cause of interviewee success (in addition to experience of the interviewee). Thus, alternative C cannot serve as an unstated assumption that ties experience to interview performance. The same can be said for alternatives A and D. Even if true, neither alternative is of use for the problem at hand.

The reasoning above points to alternative B as the most logically plausible solution. This alternative identifies an unstated assumption upon which the argument in the stem depends. To be specific, the argument that experience at interviewing is a key to doing well in interviews rests on the unstated assumption that the interviewers used to gain experience are representative of the interviewers that the applicant will meet in later interviews. This inference also represents a form of inductive generalization of relationships: Similarity of interviewers over time suggests that the early sample of interviewers was representative of the population of interviewers and the experience gained is thus useful for later interviews.

Problem 2 in Exhibit 3.1 is a critical reasoning task that employs a variation on the unstated assumption paradigm. The stem is the same as Problem 1, and the respondent must once again find an unstated assumption on which the argument depends. Here, however, the objective is to find the unstated assumption that best serves to weaken the argument relating the premises to the conclusion (i.e., find the alternative that represents a flaw in the argument). Problem 2 again builds on the unstated assumption that the interviewers used to gain experience are representative of the interviewers that the applicant will meet in later interviews. It follows that if the experience-rendering interviews are not representative, then the applicant will not be adequately prepared and the argument for experience is weakened. One of the ways for the experience-rendering interviews to lack representativeness is for all of the interviewers to ask the same narrow range of questions. Alternative B is thus a logically correct answer to the problem: "The applicant's early interviewers all asked the same narrow range of questions." The remaining three alternatives are untenable in the context of the problem. Alternatives A and D are untenable for the same reasons as discussed above for Problem 1. Alternative C is untenable because it strengthens, not weakens, the argument.

Problem 3 illustrates a third form of the recognition of assumptions task. The stem is the same as above, and the respondent must again find an unstated assumption on which the argument relating interview success to experience at interviewing rests. Now, however, the objective is to find the unstated assumption that serves best to strengthen the argument relating the premises to the conclusion (i.e., the alternative that fortifies the argument). Problem 3 again builds on the unstated assumption that the interviewers used to gain experience are representative of the interviewers that the applicant will meet in later interviews. The alternatives are the same as Problem 2, only here we reverse the tenability of alternatives B (the weaken alternative) and C (the strengthen alternative). Alternative C is now the most tenable answer.

A caveat: It is possible to use each of the nine inductive reasoning tasks identified above to build inductive reasoning problems. We illustrate several of the remaining inductive reasoning tasks in the remainder of this chapter. We reiterate that these tasks are meant to cover a broad range of inductive reasoning problems. They are not, however, meant to be exhaustive of all possible inductive reasoning tasks.

We recommend that one always begin development of a CR problem by first developing an inductive reasoning problem around the general theme of the task (e.g., how to improve performance in interviews via experience). We make this recommendation because, of the attempts to build CR problems that we have seen (often in the personality classes we teach), the primary shortcoming is failure to structure a CR problem around a valid inductive reasoning task. Far too often we see problems such as those shown in Exhibit 3.2. Each task offers alternative solutions, any one of which could be logically tenable. The difficulty is that the information provided is not sufficient to settle on just one of the alternatives as the most reasonable answer. Each problem needs additional information to direct respondents to the one most plausible answer. An example would be to add premises that, combined with an unstated assumption, identify one of the solutions as the most plausible. We emphasize this point because it is necessary to master building inductive reasoning problems with one logically tenable answer before attempting to build CR problems that have more than one reasonable answer. With this point in mind, we now proceed to CR.

## EXHIBIT 3.2
### Poor Inductive Reasoning Tasks

**Problem 1**

Joan would like to go to a college that she enjoys. To select a college, she should consider which one of the following?

    A. Cost of tuition and books.
    B. SAT scores of the students.
    C. Approachableness of the faculty.
    D. Ratio of female to male students.

**Problem 2**

John often gets in fights with other individuals. The most reasonable explanation for his getting into fights would be:

    A. John gets angry more quickly than most other individuals.
    B. John has poor impulse control.
    C. John was abused as a child.
    D. John does not handle alcohol well.

**Problem 3**

Susan studied for years so that she could become a physician. Unfortunately, she was not admitted to medical school on her first try. Which one of the following is most likely to occur?

    A. Susan will become a nurse.
    B. Susan will apply to medical school again next year.
    C. Susan will take a year off to think about her future.
    D. Susan will be depressed for some time.

## Conversion From Inductive to Conditional Reasoning

We now expand the role of inductive reasoning in measurement to include assessment of justification mechanisms using CR. Continuing with our illustration, a key to converting an inductive recognition-of-assumptions problem into a CR problem is (a) the redesign of the inductive reasoning problem so that (b) different personality types (e.g., FFs and AMs) recognize different unstated assumptions as reasonable solutions to it. This recommended redesign makes use of a property of inductive reasoning that is generally overlooked in the measurement of inductive reasoning skills: The logical uncertainty of inductive reasoning means that a given problem can have more than one logically tenable answer. That is, specific premises can lead to more than one general conclusion. In fact, they often lead to a number of alternative conclusions, and there is no requirement that these solutions be correlated, internally consistent, or even compatible.

The redesign process makes use of this property and is based on the four principles introduced at the beginning of this chapter. The essence of these principles is that at least one unstated assumption—that is, an answer to the problem—should be based on a justification mechanism (Principle 1). Our intent here is to make the answer logically compelling to FFs by playing to their implicit predispositions to sense psychological hazards (threat, failure, humiliation) in a demanding task such as a job interview (Principle 2). Basically, FFs will tend to be logically attracted to a line of reasoning if it concludes that demanding tasks herald threat and stress, infers skills cannot be enhanced by experience, surmises that perseverance is a reflection of obsessiveness, discounts the valence of demanding tasks by associating them with aversive outcomes, or selectively focuses on failure and the negative outcomes associated with failure.

We can give substance to these points by first asking how FFs are likely to analyze the stem to the inductive reasoning problem in Exhibit 3.1. FFs are predisposed to find weaknesses in this logical assertion. As discussed in Chapter 2, a relative motive strength favoring fear of failure engenders expectancies of failure in demanding tasks. To avoid the embarrassment and humiliation associated with failure, FFs are predisposed to reason in ways that enable them to rationalize avoiding demanding tasks. Included in the justification mechanisms that guide their reasoning are

- a propensity to assume that problem-solving skills are fixed and cannot be enhanced through experience, training, or dedication to learning (fixed skills bias—see Exhibit 2.4); and
- a tendency to overestimate the impact of external, uncontrollable factors (e.g., lack of resources, competition with more talented others) when making attributions about the causes of failure (external attribution bias).

*Analysis of Logical Assertion by FFs*

These two justification mechanisms are likely to provoke considerable skepticism regarding the logical assertion that a key to doing well in interviews is to gain experience at being interviewed. FFs are likely to seek logical weaknesses in this assertion because they would not expect to do well in interviews no matter how much experience they amass at being interviewed. Illustrative ways in which they might find the assertion logically vulnerable include the following.

- Experience at being interviewed cannot overcome preexisting (i.e., fixed) deficits in abilities and skills.

- Even with experience, when average or below-average people are compared with people who are truly talented, their inadequacy will be exposed.
- Extending the effort to gain experience at being interviewed may be doing little more than setting a person up for disappointment, humiliation, and failure.

We used these reasoning proclivities to convert an inductive reasoning problem to a CR problem for FFs.

*Conversion to a Conditional Reasoning Problem*

We converted Problem 2 in Exhibit 3.1 to a CR problem, which is shown in Exhibit 3.3. Recall that Problem 2 employs a variation on the unstated assumptions reasoning task. The objective of this problem is to find a weakness in the logical assertion that gaining experience is a key to doing well in interviews. Respondents must identify an unstated assumption in the logical assertion and then find the alternative that builds on this assumption to most weaken the assertion. A logically tenable answer to Problem 2 (in Exhibit 3.1) is alternative B. This answer is based on the unstated assumption that the interviewers used to gain experience are representative of the interviewers that the applicant will meet in later interviews. If the experience-rendering interviews are not representative, then the applicant will not be prepared and the argument for experience is weakened. One of the ways for the interviews to lack representativeness is for all of the interviewers to ask the same narrow range of questions. Alternative B is thus a logically tenable answer to Problem 2 in Exhibit 3.1.

### EXHIBIT 3.3
#### An Illustrative Conditional Reasoning Problem

Going to a job interview is like acting. When the applicant is new to being interviewed, he or she is likely to have stage fright and to make nervous mistakes. With experience at being interviewed, however, an applicant learns what to expect, such as what types of questions interviewers like to ask and how to answer questions in ways that impress interviewers. A key to doing well in interviews is thus to gain experience at being interviewed.

Which one of the following most weakens the argument that gaining experience is a key to doing well in interviews?

A. Interviews are often conducted in airports and hotels.
B. The applicant's early interviewers all asked the same narrow range of questions.
C. Applicants may be interviewed just after a smart and socially adept candidate.
D. Interviewers generally prefer short answers to their questions.

We retained alternative B for the CR problem (see Exhibit 3.3). We also retained the two untenable alternatives (A and D). We replaced alternative C by invoking the property of inductive reasoning mentioned earlier—that is, that a given problem can have more than one logically tenable solution (i.e., the stem to the problem can lead to more than one conclusion that weakens the logical assertion that experience leads to doing well in interviews). Moreover, there is no need for these solutions to be correlated, internally consistent, or compatible.

Our redesign of alternative C was aimed specifically at FFs. Alternatives based on justification mechanisms are designed to appear as logically plausible and psychologically persuasive to respondents whose reasoning is shaped by the targeted justification mechanisms. In the present case, an attempt was made to capture what FFs consider "logical analyses" as they might occur in what Kuhn (1991) referred to as *informal reasoning*. Such reasoning focuses less on the strict standards of formal inductive analyses and more on what FFs consider reasonable or logical in real, everyday human activity (Galotti, 1989; Hahn & Oaksford, 2007; Haidt, 2001). (We discuss informal reasoning in greater detail later in this chapter.)

The new alternative C in Exhibit 3.3 is an example of the type of reasoning that FFs consider reasonable in real, everyday human activity: "Applicants may be interviewed just after a truly smart and socially adept candidate." This alternative is grounded in the two justification mechanisms discussed above in relation to FFs' thinking about interviews, that (a) experience at being interviewed cannot overcome preexisting (i.e., fixed) deficits in abilities and skills, and (b) even with experience, when average or below-average people are compared with people who are truly talented, their inadequacy will be exposed. For FFs, fixed deficits and an unfavorable comparison with more talented others serve as unstated assumptions that identify a weakness in the logical assertion that experience is a key to doing well in interviews. Alternative C attempts to capture these natural, everyday, informal reasoning proclivities.

Specifically, alternative C is intended to be logically compelling to FFs because they are predisposed to find logical and sensible reasons for failing. Being interviewed just after a truly talented applicant plays directly into their implicit predispositions to assume that (a) experience will not overcome fixed deficits in intelligence and social skills and that (b) their inadequacies will be exposed when they are compared to a truly intelligent and socially skilled interviewee.

CR attempts to construct answers to inductive reasoning problems that are grounded in the same justification mechanisms people use to rationalize their motive-inspired behavior (Principle 1). In the present illustration, FFs could use their reasoning to avoid demanding activities such as job interviews. People who habitually engage in such thinking are drawn to these answers.

This is because people who typically engage in creating rationalizations (for avoiding demanding tasks) find reasoning based on the same protective thinking processes to be logically compelling (Principle 2; James & LeBreton, 2010). Protocol studies (interviews with test respondents) indicate that they believe the soundness of the reasoning contained in the CR alternatives determined their judgments (Principle 3; James, 1998).

Research results suggest that alternative C is indeed compelling to FFs. People with a demonstrated history of avoidance and inhibitory behaviors are significantly more likely than respondents in general, including those with a history of achievement behaviors, to select alternative C to solve the problem. These results suggest that the presence (and strength) or absence of the justification mechanisms used to build the problem is partially revealed by how a person solves the CR problem (Principle 4).

We are mindful that reasoning on a single problem, even one with demonstrated validity in predicting avoidance and inhibitory behaviors, is not an infallible indicator of justification mechanisms for fear of failure. Other causes may have stimulated thinking in this manner (e.g., a respondent may have just had a less than satisfactory interview experience). Thus, we track whether a respondent consistently selects reasoning based on FF justification mechanisms across a set of CR problems that vary in terms of premises, contexts, and conclusions. It is the consistent selection of answers that target FF justification mechanisms that most reliably reveals the presence of a relative motive strength favoring fear of failure.

*How Do Achievement-Oriented Individuals Respond?*

Our intent is that alternative C will appeal only to people whose relative motive strength favors fear of failure (i.e., FFs). We intend all other respondents to be drawn to alternative B because it is an inductively correct answer but one that is not shaped by justification mechanisms supporting fear of failure. Instead, it is the case that alternative B is founded on the assumptions that skills are malleable and effort devoted to gaining experience will improve performance. These assumptions are consistent with justification mechanisms for individuals whose relative motive strength favors achievement motivation (i.e., AMs). Thus, there is a double inducement for AMs to select alternative B.

**Relationships Among Inductive Reasoning, Informal Reasoning, and Conditional Reasoning**

The preceding discussion of the CR problem in Exhibit 3.3 demonstrated that more than one unstated assumption was involved in logically asserting that gaining experience is a key to performing well in interviews.

Two different unstated assumptions led to two different logical weaknesses. There are additional unstated assumptions in this argument, and thus a third, a fourth, and so on, logical weaknesses. This is the essence of inductive processing: Multiple unstated assumptions tie specific premises to different general conclusions. Another way of saying this is that multiple general conclusions derive from the same set of specific premises. As noted, there is no requirement that the alternative unstated assumptions, or the conclusions that they support, be logically consistent or even related.

The types of implicit biases of primary interest in assessing CR build on the ambiguity of reasoning inductively in everyday life. Consider the case in which a person encounters a number of circumstances across time and situations in which he or she could infer that less than stellar performance is due to personal inadequacy (e.g., lack of skills), lack of personal intensity, lack of personal persistence, lack of resources, personally uncontrollable constraints (e.g., poor leadership), or poor luck. Personal inadequacy is a logically viable inference in any one of the situations where personally uncontrollable restraints are not an overwhelmingly obvious attribution. But so are the other explanations, including insufficient effort, which implicitly suggests that the person feels capable of performing the task and simply needs to devote more intensity and/or time to it. This is the ambiguity of inductive processing in real life, in which people have multiple viable inferences at their disposal.

The terms often used to characterize this condition include *everyday reasoning* (Galotti, 1989), *motivated reasoning* (Kunda, 1990), *biased hypothesis testing* (Pyszczynski & Greenberg, 1987), and *informal reasoning* (Kuhn, 1991). We use the latter term. Informal reasoning relaxes the constraints (e.g., only one correct answer) of formal inductive reasoning problems because in everyday situations the reasoner is often required to deal with (a) subjectivity due to potential personal relevance of the problem to the problem solver; (b) incomplete information and/or tacit premises and hidden agendas; (c) conjectures, contradictions, and uncertainties about cause and effect, often manifested as the absence of established rules, procedures, or formulas for solving a problem; and (d) multiple potential or proposed solutions that not only are incompatible but also are based on conflicting and incongruous premises (cf. Galotti, 1989).

Attempts to solve informal reasoning problems, especially those that engender multiple, incompatible solutions, are often based on the development of personal dialectics (Kuhn, 1991). The reasoner first endeavors to identify as large a set of potential (incompatible) solutions to the problem as possible. Arguments are then developed to support and defend each solution, which requires identification of counterarguments that conceivably could be used to challenge (find weaknesses in) each supporting argument. The objective of this process is to attempt to exhaust the possible arguments and counterarguments and then to analyze each argument and counterargument as thoroughly as possible in order to separate valid arguments/counterarguments from invalid arguments/counterarguments (and tenable solutions from untenable solutions).

Informal reasoning via dialectic often draws from the list of inductive reasoning tasks described in the early part of this chapter. Thus, the soundness of informal reasoning is a function of such things as being able to identify unstated premises that strengthen or weaken an argument/counterargument, to ascertain which facts are relevant to a problem and which facts are not, and to discern whether an explanatory model has omitted a key causal variable (Kuhn, 1991). Justification mechanisms enter this picture when people (a) unknowingly rely on just a few favored implicit biases (external attributions, fixed skills) to build dialectics over time and different situations and (b) fail to realize that this reasoning is subject to biased processes of which they are unaware and over which they have no control.

Many, if not most, of the alternatives in CR problems that are based on justification mechanisms involve informal reasoning. These alternatives are designed to appear as logically plausible and psychologically persuasive to respondents whose reasoning is guided by the implicit biases that comprise justification mechanisms. An attempt is made to make the reasoning that appears in a CR alternative logical in a formal inductive sense. However, this is often not possible, simply because reasoning driven by implicit biases is often not formally logical. In these situations, the reasoning in CR alternatives focuses less on the strict standards of formal inductive analyses and more on what people with a specific set of justification mechanisms consider reasonable or logical in real, everyday human activity (i.e, informal reasoning; Galotti, 1989; Kuhn, 1991).

Thus, for people who possess an implicit bias, CR problems offer the opportunity to engage in what, for them, appear to be rational analyses. They do not realize that the degree of logical appeal of an alternative derives from its being based on one of their implicit biases. The reasoning may be formally logical or informally reasonable. Irrespective of logical formality, one's determination of what are the most reasonable solutions over a set of CR problems reveals one's justification mechanisms and thus implicit personality.

## BUILDING CONDITIONAL REASONING PROBLEMS FOR RELATIVE MOTIVE STRENGTH

Most CR problems developed for measuring achievement motivation or fear of failure are designed to assess relative motive strength. To briefly review points developed in Chapter 2, it is proposed that justification mechanisms are used unknowingly by both AMs and FFs to shape reasoning and define the nature and parameters of what both AMs and FFs take to be rational behavior. The difference between AMs and FFs is that each of these personality types employs different justification mechanisms (see Exhibits 2.3 and 2.4 and accompanying discussion), and thus each personality type arrives at different, and often opposing, judgments about what is, and what is not, a justifiable decision about whether to approach or avoid challenging tasks.

These differences in (conditional) reasoning have been used to design CR problems to assess the dispositional component of resultant achievement motivation (Atkinson, 1957, 1978; McClelland, 1985). This component consists of the strength of the motive to achieve in relation to the strength of the motive to avoid failure. James (1998) referred to the difference in the relative strengths of these two latent motives as *relative motive strength*. The objective of the CR problems is to determine what a person judges to be the more sensible: (a) reasoning based on justification mechanisms for approach to achievement-oriented objectives or (b) reasoning based on justification mechanisms for avoidance of achievement-oriented objectives. With these determinations in hand, it is possible to infer whether the motive to achieve is dominant or subordinate to the motive to avoid failure—that is, a person's relative motive strength.

If a person consistently sees reason in arguments that advance the logical appeal of approach over avoidance, then it is inferred that this person's relative motive strength favors the need to achieve. Conversely, if a person consistently attributes greater reasonableness to arguments that favor avoidance over approach, then it is inferred that this person's relative motive strength favors the need to avoid failure. A category also exists for cases in which neither type of reasoning or motive has a mandate.

Three illustrative CR problems designed to assess relative motive strength are presented in Exhibit 3.4. Each of these problems was constructed using the steps described earlier for constructing a CR problem. Here, however, rather than design just one alternative based on FF justification mechanisms, we have added a second alternative that is based on one or more AM justification mechanisms. We focused on AMs' predispositions to be logically attracted to a line of reasoning if it concludes that demanding tasks herald challenge and opportunity, infers that skills can be enhanced by experience, surmises that perseverance is a reflection of commitment and sacrifice, amplifies the valence of demanding tasks by associating them with positive outcomes, or selectively focuses on success and the rewards associated with achievement. (Earlier we noted that FFs tend to be logically attracted to a line of reasoning if it concludes that demanding tasks herald threat and stress, infers skills cannot be enhanced by experience, surmises that perseverance is a reflection of obsessiveness, discounts the valence of demanding tasks by associating them with

## Conditional Reasoning Problems for Relative Motive Strength

1. Studies of the stress-related causes of heart attacks led to the identification of the Type A personality. Type A persons are motivated to achieve, involved in their jobs, competitive to the point of being aggressive, and impatient, wanting things completed quickly. Interestingly, these same characteristics are often used to describe the successful person in this country. This association logically suggests that

   A. Striving for success increases the likelihood of having a heart attack.
   B. Most successful people are prone to violence.
   C. Few nonambitious people have heart attacks.
   D. People often mistake enthusiasm and drive for aggressiveness and impatience.

2. An honor graduate from a well-known law school is offered a job by a prominent law firm in a large city. The firm gives new hires 3 to 5 years to perform, and then it decides whether to make them partners or let them go. Approximately half the lawyers hired by the firm make partner. Many of these people go on to achieve fame and fortune. The young lawyer declines the firm's offer and instead accepts a position with a small law firm in a small town. Almost all new lawyers make partner in this firm.

   Which of the following is the most reasonable conclusion based on this information?

   A. It will be more difficult for the young lawyer to become nationally famous in the legal profession.
   B. The young lawyer probably grew up in a small town.
   C. The young lawyer is more likely to be employed in 5 years.
   D. The young lawyer liked the pressure to perform at the well-known law school.

3. Consider the following two statements:

   Editor 1: We receive hundreds of manuscripts each year from people who have no talent to write and are wasting their time trying to be authors. We reject the manuscripts and try to discourage these people from further writing.
   Editor 2: Alex Haley, the author of *Roots*, reported that he spent 7 years having manuscripts rejected before receiving his first acceptance.

   What inference can most reasonably be made from this exchange?

   A. Editor 1 accepts more manuscripts than he or she rejects.
   B. Having a manuscript rejected is poor evidence of writing skills.
   C. Most of the people rejected by Editor 1 will never become successful authors.
   D. Most aspiring authors turn to other occupations after having their first manuscript rejected.

aversive outcomes, or selectively focuses on failure and the negative outcomes associated with failure.)

## Problem 1

Each of the three problems in Exhibit 3.4 is based on one or some combination of the inductive reasoning tasks presented at the beginning of this chapter. Problem 1 in Exhibit 3.4 asks respondents to analyze the association between Type A personality and successful people, specifically the following assertion:

> Studies of the stress-related causes of heart attacks led to the identification of the Type A personality. Type A persons are motivated to achieve, involved in their jobs, competitive to the point of being aggressive, and impatient, wanting things completed quickly. Interestingly, these same characteristics are often used to describe the successful person in this country.

The task for the reasoner is to determine whether covariation among events is due to causal influences or the product of spurious correlation (inductive reasoning task 5). Specifically, are the causes of stress and heart attacks—namely, motivation to achieve, involvement in one's job, extreme competitiveness and willingness to harm others to achieve, and impatience—also causes of success? If so, then does achievement striving make one vulnerable to cardiovascular disease (alternative A)? Or is there something about the profile of characteristics for Type As that does not necessarily apply to successful people even though there appears to be an association?

Alternatives B and C are clearly not reasonable answers to this problem. This leaves alternatives A and D as possible answers. One of these alternatives is based on an AM justification mechanism to make it logically attractive to AMs. The other answer is designed to appeal logically to FFs because it is based on an FF justification mechanism. The design process is described below for each alternative.

### The AM Alternative

AMs are predisposed to disagree with the assertion linking Type A individuals and those who attempt to succeed. Indeed, a number of AMs (e.g., highly motivated scholars, authors, physicians, executives, and lawyers) were interviewed in the process of problem development. Their analyses of the stem typically included reasoning such as the following: It is indeed probable that overload produces stress and that some people are so obsessed with achievement that they overload themselves and create potentially injurious strains. However, this is an extreme state of affairs and does not apply to ordinary conditions. Simply because a few individuals exercise poor judgment does not imply that strong desires to achieve, to be enthusiastic about one's job, to enjoy competing with peers for promotions, and to want to progress quickly up career ladders will necessarily evolve into stress and cardiovascular disease. Indeed, motivation, involvement, initiative, competitiveness, ambition, and enthusiasm are not stressors. They are forerunners to productivity, attainment of rewards, and a sense of overall (positive) well-being.

Moreover, being competitive does not indicate that one is aggressive in the sense that she or he desires to cause harm to others or to act in hostile ways. Similar reasoning applies to ambition and enthusiasm. Desiring to move up career ladders quickly does not connote impatience. Thus, AMs' rejection of the inference that successful people are similar to Type A individuals in regard to aggression and impatience further weakens the relationship between striving to succeed and cardiovascular disease.

The reasoning above is indicative of the justification mechanism termed *positive connotation of achievement striving bias*. As discussed Chapter 2, this justification mechanism is defined by implicit proclivities to associate effort on demanding tasks with dedication, commitment, concentration, and involvement. Alternative D is designed to capture the everyday, informal reasoning of people whose reasoning is shaped by these proclivities. It states, "People often mistake enthusiasm and drive for aggressiveness and impatience."

This reasoning is intended to be logically compelling to AMs because they are predisposed to find reasons to question the proposed link between achievement striving and the Type A personality. This alternative gives them a means to question that link by tapping into their predispositions to reason that (a) enthusiasm does not connote aggression and (b) drive does not connote impatience. By breaking the association between Type A personality and achievement striving, they question the association between achievement striving and cardiovascular disease.

### The FF Alternative

The association in the stem—Type A people and successful people share the key characteristics of achievement striving, involvement, aggression, and impatience—appeals to FFs because it provides a logical foundation for rationalizing the avoidance of achievement-oriented tasks. The logical appeal derives from two FF justification mechanisms. The first justification mechanism is *negative connotation of achievement striving bias*. This justification denotes a predilection to assume that achievement striving causes stress. The second justification mechanism is *leveling,* which in the present context involves associating the stress derived from the Type A characteristics of achievement striving, involvement, aggression, and impatience with an increased risk of cardiovascular disease.

Interviews with recognized FFs (based on demonstrated behavior) in the process of problem development supported the hypothesis that people high in fear of failure would agree that achievement striving increases stress and the risk for cardiovascular disease. While aware of at least some of the counterarguments, such as that many successful people do not experience cardiovascular disease, recognized FFs were particularly sympathetic to the inference that striving to succeed increases the *risk* of heart attack.

FFs were also inclined to support this assertion with corroborating assumptions, inferences, and theories. They assumed that evidence could be garnered to support the assertion that business executives, for example, have an abnormally high rate of heart attacks. They inferred that it is possible to explain how an achievement orientation spawns stress: People striving to succeed tend to be obsessive, to overload themselves, to be intolerant of normal delays, and to become angry and hostile if their strivings are frustrated. FFs also believed implicitly that the obverse corroborates the assertion: People who take a more relaxed approach to work are less likely to demonstrate symptoms of stress such as exhaustion, illness, burnout, and chronic anxiety about how their careers are progressing.

These implicit biases suggest that FFs will find the reasoning in alternative A to be logically persuasive. They are predisposed to find an association between being Type A and being successful. This makes the inference "striving for success increases the likelihood of having a heart attack" a natural and logical conclusion. They also are likely to discount alternative D (the AM alternative) because they associate aggression and impatience with successful people. This is part of the "leveling" process.

*Relative Motive Strength*

Multiple CR problems have been developed, each of which offers a choice between AM and FF solutions. Respondents are given a +1 for every AM alternative they select, a 0 for every logically incorrect alternative they select (an infrequent event), and a −1 for every FF alternative they select. These scores are then summed to furnish a composite score on the Relative Motive Strength (RMS) Scale.

The objective of measurement is to determine whether an individual *consistently* prefers AM alternatives or FF alternatives. Respondents who consistently select AM alternatives are believed to possess a motive structure in which the motive to achieve dominates the motive to avoid failure. These respondents have strongly positive scores on the RMS Scale and are considered to be AMs. Conversely, consistent selection of FF alternatives results in a strong negative score on the RMS Scale, which is indicative of a motive structure in which the motive to avoid failing dominates the motive to achieve. These respondents are considered to be FFs. Lack of a consistent pattern of favoritism suggests that neither type of motive dominates, and relative motive strength is regarded as "indeterminate."

## Problem 2

This problem asks respondents to evaluate consequences, including dysfunctional ones, that might occur naturally or as the result of planned changes or proposed interventions (inductive reasoning task 7, which is designated "expectations of outcomes"). The stem to the problem informs respondents that an honor graduate from a well-known law school has been offered a job by a prominent law firm in a large city. This firm gives new hires 3 to 5 years to perform before a decision is made whether to make the new hires partners or to let them go. Approximately half of the lawyers hired by the firm are made partners. Many of these people go on to achieve fame and fortune. However, the young lawyer declines the prestigious firm's offer and instead accepts a position with a small law firm in a small town; an additional piece of evidence (i.e., another premise) is that almost all new lawyers make partner in this firm.

The reasoning task is to find the most reasonable projection or outcome based on the information in the stem. Two of the answers are clearly illogical (alternatives B and D) for there is no evidence in the stem to support them. This leaves the following two alternatives:

A. It will be more difficult for the young lawyer to become nationally famous in the legal profession.
C. The young lawyer is more likely to be employed in 5 years.

One of these is alternative designed for AMs (the AM alternative) and the other is the alternative designed for FFs (the FF alternative).

*The AM Alternative*

AMs are predisposed to project a negative outcome for the young lawyer. As discussed in Chapter 2, a relative motive strength that favors achievement motivation promotes expectancies of success in demanding tasks. AMs thus seek logical support and rational defenses for approaching demanding tasks, which are furnished by justification mechanisms that enable them to build rationalizations for approaching and then persisting on demanding tasks. Included among these justification mechanisms are (see Exhibit 2.4)

- a propensity to frame demanding tasks on which success is uncertain as "challenges" that offer "opportunities" to demonstrate present skills, to learn new skills, and to make a contribution (opportunity bias); and
- a proclivity to favor personal factors such as initiative, intensity, and persistence as the most important factors affecting performance on demanding tasks (personal responsibility bias).

These two justification mechanisms are likely to provoke considerable skepticism, if not a degree of cynicism, regarding the young lawyer's decision to forgo the demanding job at the prestigious law firm. Specifically, the two justification mechanisms are likely to promote reasoning such as the following:

- The young lawyer was an honor graduate from a well-known law school, which suggests that she or he is not only intelligent but also highly motivated (e.g., willing to take the initiative to solve complex problems, willing to work intensely over long periods of time if necessary to reach difficult goals).
- With these skills and values, the young lawyer has a good chance of becoming professionally famous had he or she accepted the offer from the New York firm.
- Accepting an offer from a nondistinguished small firm in a small town will likely result in considerable loss of opportunity.

Alternative A offers a conclusion that is designed to appear as logically plausible and psychologically persuasive to AM respondents whose reasoning is similar to that described above. The conclusion that it will be more difficult for the young lawyer to become nationally famous in the legal profession is a natural progression of their reasoning that the young lawyer is talented; the young lawyer has a good chance of becoming famous, especially if associated with a top law firm; and accepting a job in a nonprestigious firm will result in loss of opportunity.

*The FF Alternative*

It was intended that FFs would interpret the young lawyer's decision to reject the offer from the prestigious firm as an avoidance of possible threat. This would be a clear indication of different implicit biases promoting differential framing when contrasted to AMs' predicted framing of the same set of events as a loss of opportunity. The framing of the more prestigious job as a threat is based on the FF justification mechanism termed the *liability bias*, which was defined in Chapter 2 as a proclivity "to frame demanding tasks as personal liabilities or 'threats' because one may fail and be seen as incompetent." We attempted to heighten the sense of threat for FFs by noting that only half of the new hires were given partnerships after 3 to 5 years.

We noted also in Chapter 2 that FFs often seek alternative, less threatening tasks after avoiding demanding tasks. When thinking about these alternative tasks, their reasoning is often guided by a justification mechanism termed the *indirect compensation bias*. This bias consists of attempts to increase the logical appeal of replacing one (i.e., highly threatening) situation with a compensatory (i.e., less threatening) situation by imbuing the less threatening situation with positive, socially desirable qualities. Thus, where AMs see a routine, mundane, obscure, unproductive, or uninteresting job, FFs see a job that is stable, predictable, structured secure, and certain. They also think of people who take such jobs as loyal, dependable, reliable, respectful, and supportive.

Alternative C is designed to be logically plausible and psychologically appealing to FFs. The conclusion, "The young lawyer is more likely to be employed in 5 years," plays directly to FFs' proclivities to associate threat with the job at the prestigious law firm while imbuing a compensatory job at a small firm with little pressure with positive qualities. In Alternative C, the compensatory quality that should appeal logically to FFs is "job security." Indeed, the job security offered by the small firm contrasts sharply with what FFs are likely to view as a decided lack of job security at the prestigious firm.

**Problem 3**

Problem 3 in Exhibit 3.4 presents respondents with a dialectic or a contrast of contradictory arguments between two editors. This is primarily a "relevance of arguments" type of inductive reasoning task (reasoning task 4). Respondents must distinguish between arguments that are strong and relevant versus those that are weak and tangential/irrelevant. This problem also requires an evaluation of inferences (reasoning task 1). Respondents must discriminate among degrees of truth and falsity of conclusions (alternatives) drawn from the premises (e.g., arguments, data, models, assumptions) offered in the stem to the problem.

With respect to premises, Editor 1 focuses on the treatment of failures. This editor receives "hundreds of manuscripts each year from people who have no talent to write and are wasting their time trying to be authors. We reject the manuscripts and try to discourage these people from further writing." Editor 2 focuses on successes, noting the professional struggle of Alex Haley, who spent 7 years having manuscripts rejected before receiving his first acceptance. Clearly, this editor is in favor of additional training and perseverance in order to improve writing skills and attempt to obtain mastery in the area of writing.

It is intended that AMs and FFs will have quite different reactions to this stem and to be attracted to different conclusions based on the premises. Alternatives A and D are clearly poor answers to the problem. This leaves alternatives B and C. The perceived reasonableness of B and C is conditional on whether the respondent is an AM or an FF, as explained below.

*The AM Alternative*

Problem 3 was designed to trigger three AM justification mechanisms. These mechanisms are:

- a tendency to empathize with the sense of enthusiasm, intensity, and striving that characterize those who succeed in demanding situations (identification with achievers bias);
- a proclivity to assume that the skills necessary to master demanding tasks can, if necessary, be learned or developed via training, practice, and experience (malleability of skills bias); and
- an inclination to assume that continued effort and commitment will overcome obstacles or any initial failures that might occur on a demanding task (efficacy of persistence bias).

These three justification mechanisms are prone to stimulate the following types of reasoning:

- preference for the argument presented by Editor 2 because it focuses on successful authors;
- experience at writing can overcome deficits in writing skills and lead to mastery as an author;
- it may take a long time to master writing skills—one must be committed and perseverant; and
- one can expect to have early manuscripts rejected—what is important is to keep practicing, gaining experience, and improving.

Alternative B should be logically compelling to AM respondents because their justification mechanisms predispose them to conclude that having a manuscript rejected is poor evidence of writing skills. This predisposition can be predicted by the proclivities discussed above, that is, AMs' biases toward reasoning that one can overcome deficits in writing skills and master writing by practice, experience, and perseverance. A natural part of this process would be to have manuscripts rejected. It follows logically that having a manuscript rejected is not a valid or reliable indicator of writing skills, especially skills that are in the process of development.

*The FF Alternative*

Problem 3 was planned to stimulate a contrasting set of justification mechanisms for FFs. These mechanisms are:

- A tendency to empathize with the fear and anxiety of those who fail in demanding situations. Selectively focus on negative outcomes that accrue from failing (identification with failures bias).
- A proclivity to assume that problem-solving skills are fixed and cannot be enhanced by experience, training, or dedication to learning. Thus, if one is deficient in a skill, then one should not attempt demanding tasks or should withdraw if one encounters initial failures (fixed skills bias).

These two justification mechanisms are likely to promote the following types of reasoning:

- Preference for Editor 1's argument because it focuses on unsuccessful authors.
- Experience at writing will not overcome preexisting (i.e., fixed) deficits in writing abilities and skills. Persistence will be of little help.
- Extending effort to gain experience at writing may do little more than set a person up for the disappointment and humiliation of having manuscripts rejected.

Alternative C is intended to be logically compelling to FF respondents because they are predisposed to find logical and sensible reasons for avoiding the demanding task of writing. The conclusion that most of the people rejected by Editor 1 will never become successful authors taps directly into their implicit proclivities to identify and empathize with failures and to assume that experience will not overcome fixed deficits in writing skills.

### Conditional Reasoning Test for Relative Motive Strength

Using the principles described above and the justification mechanisms identified in Chapter 2, we have developed a 15-item CR test designed to measure the relative motive strength. As noted earlier, respondents are given a +1 for every AM alternative they select and a −1 for every FF alternative they select. These scores are summed to furnish a continuous score on the RMS Scale that theoretically ranges from +15 to −15. To interpret these scores, a transformation was constructed that maps the scores into a scale anchored by the theoretical concepts of AM and FF. A number of algorithms for scaling were examined. The following algorithm provided the best balance among theoretical and statistical issues and was used to translate the continuous scores into an RMS Scale.

| Continuous score | RMS Scale score | Interpretation |
| --- | --- | --- |
| –3 or lower | –2 | FF |
| –2 or –1 | –1 | Aspiring FF |
| 0 | 0 | Indeterminate |
| +1 or +2 | +1 | Aspiring AM |
| +3 or higher | +2 | AM |

Basically, the RMS Scale separates respondents into five categories that are ordered in terms of tendency to approach demanding tasks. Scores in the opposing extremes are believed to distinguish most clearly between AMs and FFs. Scores in the mid-ranges (+1, 0, and –1) indicate cognitive vacillation between approach and avoidance. Nevertheless, an RMS score of +1 indicates a slight overall preference for AM alternatives and a relative motive strength that very modestly favors a disposition to approach rather than to avoid (i.e., an aspiring AM). In like manner, an RMS score of –1 indicates a slight overall preference for FF alternatives and a relative motive strength that very modestly favors a disposition to avoid rather than to approach (i.e., an aspiring FF). Results of research on the RMS scale are presented in Chapter 4.

## BUILDING CONDITIONAL REASONING PROBLEMS FOR AGGRESSION

In Chapter 2, we proposed a model of measurement for aggression. A key premise underlying this model is that aggressive people are seldom aware of the full extent to which they possess a motive to harm others (McClelland et al., 1989; Westen, 1998). Possession of such knowledge would likely engender experiences of shame, guilt, and anxiety (Cramer, 2006). People are protected from these experiences by defense mechanisms, one of which is rationalization. Rationalization both masks the true motive and engenders its expression by creating the illusion that aggressive behavior is sensible and therefore justified. For example, aggressive people may rationalize harming others as acts of self-defense or as acts that right injustices, demonstrate bravery, or strike against oppression or unfair rules (James et al., 2005).

We proposed six implicit biases that serve to enhance the logical appeal of the rationalizations or illusory defenses for aggression. These six implicit biases were referred to as justification mechanisms. Included among the justification mechanisms for aggression are the hostile attribution bias, the potency bias, the retribution bias, the victimization by powerful others bias, the derogation of target bias, and the social discounting bias. These justification mechanisms are defined in Exhibit 2.2.

The development of justification mechanisms for aggression was made possible because considerable progress has been made in recent years in understanding the aggressive personality (see Chapter 2). Psychology now has a much better idea of the defensive cognitive processes that aggressive people use to create a false sense of rationality for their aggressive acts. This knowledge of defensive processes was used to design a CR measurement test to identify aggressive individuals. In a manner similar to the measurement of relative motive strength, the CR system for aggression is based on a "cover" task in the form of an inductive reasoning problem. The use of reasoning to cover the measurement of aggression is made possible because aggressive people employ the illusion of rational analyses to create defenses for their harming of others. The measurement system builds on this process by constructing answers to inductive reasoning problems that are grounded in the same defensive, self-illusory thinking that aggressive people use to rationalize harming others. Aggressive people tend to be drawn to these answers. This is because people who habitually engage in creating falsely rational defenses find reasoning based on the same types of protective thinking to be logically compelling.

Stated directly, aggressive people find reasoning based on their justification mechanisms to be logically persuasive. Specifically, aggressive individuals tend to be logically attracted to reasoning if it infers hostility or threat in the actions of others, frames the actions of others in terms of dominance versus submissiveness, concludes that retaliation will be more effective than reconciliation, surmises that exploitation is the true driving force behind the decisions of powerful others, or determines that a social norm is repressive or restrictive. It is the attraction to these types of reasoning that unveils the largely unconscious motive to harm others. That is to say, a desire to harm others is revealed by a logical attraction to reasoning that projects the implicit biases that aggressive people are known to use to justify acting aggressively.

Examples of four CR problems written for aggression are presented in Exhibit 3.5. Each of these problems is discussed in this section. Each problem was developed using the steps for problem development presented earlier in this chapter. After presenting the four problems, we offer decision aids for problem development.

## Problem 1

The premises in the stem to this problem begin with the observation that a large number of business partnerships break up. It is then asserted that one of the reasons for the large number of breakups is that they are quick and easy to get. Evidence is then furnished to support this assertion. If the partners can agree on how to split the assets of the partnership fairly, then they can break up simply by filling out the appropriate forms. It is specifically noted that lawyers need not be engaged.

EXHIBIT 3.5
Conditional Reasoning Problems for Aggression

---

1. A large number of business partnerships break up. One reason for the large number of breakups is that dissolving a partnership is quick and easy. If the partners can agree on how to split the assets of the partnership fairly, then they can break up simply by filling out the appropriate forms. They do not need to engage lawyers.

   Which of the following is the most reasonable conclusion based on the above?
   A. The longer a partnership has existed, the less likely it is to break up.
   B. If one's partner hires a lawyer, then he or she is not planning to play fairly.
   C. Partners might resolve their differences if breaking up was harder and took longer.
   D. The younger partner is more likely to initiate the breakup.

2. The old saying "an eye for an eye" means that if someone hurts you, then you should hurt that person back. If you are hit, then you should hit back. If someone burns your house, then you should burn that person's house.

   Which of the following is the biggest problem with the "eye for an eye" plan?
   A. It tells people to "turn the other cheek."
   B. It offers no way to settle a conflict in a friendly manner.
   C. It can only be used at certain times of the year.
   D. People have to wait until they are attacked before they can strike.

3. Girl Scouts and Boy Scouts teach young people a sense of discipline. They also teach respect for authority, neatness, dependability, and loyalty.

   Which of the following is the most logical prediction of what Scouts will be like when they grow up?
   A. They will be easily controlled by leaders.
   B. They will be reluctant to attend foreign films.
   C. They will be self-conscious about their height.
   D. They will be ready to take on responsibility.

4. Wild animals often fight to see who will breed. This ensures that only the strongest animals reproduce. When strong animals reproduce, their young tend to grow into powerful animals that have the best chances of succeeding. Unlike animals, people who are *not* strong often reproduce.

   Which of the following is the most logical conclusion based on the above?
   A. People do not need to be physically strong to be successful.
   B. Animals breed most often in the fall.
   C. The study of biology is getting less popular.
   D. Humans would be more successful if only the strongest were allowed to breed.

---

Respondents are asked to determine which one of four conclusions most reasonably follows from the premises. This is primarily an "inference" type of inductive reasoning problem (reasoning task 1 in the list of nine inductive reasoning tasks presented early in this chapter). To make an inference, respondents must distinguish among degrees of truth and falsity of the four conclusions drawn from the given premises. One of these conclusions is designed for aggressive individuals (the AG alternative), another is designed for nonaggressive individuals (the NA alternative), and the remaining two alternatives offer illogical answers to the problem. Each type of alternative is discussed below, beginning with the AG alternative.

### The AG Alternative

The conclusion designed for AGs builds on the premise that lawyers are not needed if the partners can agree on how to split the assets of the partnership fairly. It follows logically that lawyers may be needed if the partners cannot agree on how to split their assets fairly. The possibility of disagreement over assets was intended to trigger AGs' predispositions

- to sense hostility and perhaps even danger in the behavior of others (hostile attribution bias); and
- to see inequity and exploitation in the actions of powerful others (e.g., a lawyer in this case)—the ensuing perceptions of oppression and victimization stimulate feelings of anger and injustice (victimization by powerful others bias).

Reasoning shaped by these two justification mechanisms is likely to involve thoughts like the following:

- A partner may have no interest in being fair, but rather intends to acquire as many of the assets as possible.
- A partner who does not intend to split property fairly is unlikely to negotiate fairly.
- A partner who is after the lion's share of assets is likely to seek the assistance of a powerful other such as a lawyer, whose primary goal will be to exploit me.

Alternative B takes this reasoning above one step further by using it to infer that if one hires a lawyer, then one is not planning to play fairly. There are many reasons why a business partner might hire a lawyer (e.g., complex investment strategies). To determine that this particular answer is a good, indeed the best, answer to the reasoning problem suggests underlying predispositions to engage in hostile attributions and to see oneself as a victim of powerful others. Stated alternatively, this answer is designed to be logically compelling and psychologically persuasive to respondents who are already predisposed to sense hostility and malevolent intent in the behavior of others. Research results suggest that this answer is indeed compelling to aggressive respondents. People with a demonstrated history of aggressive behavior are significantly more likely than nonaggressive respondents to select alternative B to solve the problem (James & LeBreton, 2010; James & McIntyre, 2000; James et al., 2005).

We are mindful that reasoning on a single problem, even one with demonstrated validity in predicting aggressiveness, is not an infallible indicator of a proclivity to make hostile attributions. Other causes may have stimulated thinking in this manner (e.g., a respondent has recently had difficulty with a lawyer). Thus, we determine whether a respondent consistently selects reasoning based on a hostile attribution bias and a victimization bias across a set of CR problems that vary in terms of premises, contexts, and conclusions. It is the consistent selection of answers that target specific justification mechanisms that most reliably reveals the presence of a proclivity to make hostile attributions and to see oneself as a victim of powerful forces.

### The NA Alternative

In Chapter 2, we suggested that reasoning based on justification mechanisms for aggression are often not logically persuasive to nonaggressive individuals (NAs). Nonaggressive individuals lack the desire to harm others and thus tend not to engage in dominance contests with authority figures nor do they project malevolent intent into the actions of others. In addition, NAs are not prone to fight with their peers, coworkers, or neighbors, or to cause harm to powerful entities by engaging in obstreperous or intentionally disruptive behavior. There is, therefore, little or no incentive to possess justification mechanisms to enhance the rational appeal of aggressive behaviors. Thus, the reasoning of NAs is not usually shaped by the types of implicit biases summarized in Exhibit 2.2.

We also noted that NAs tend to find reasoning that is based on justification mechanisms for aggression to be improbable, dubious, socially unorthodox, unrealistic, provocative, extreme, nonconstructive, and/or slanted. Of greater plausibility to NAs are arguments that promote socially adaptive or prosocial behaviors such as civility, politeness, friendliness, and cooperation (James et al., 2005). These are the normative standards for appropriate conduct in most social situations because they promote harmony, cooperation, and peace. Nonaggressive individuals' reasoning about what constitutes rational behavior in social situations is often shaped by these normative standards (James et al., 2004; Kuhn, 1991). Such reasoning appears to NAs to be more plausible, balanced, probable, and sound than reasoning based on justification mechanisms for aggression.

With this knowledge as a foundation, consider that NA respondents must draw an inference that logically extends some aspect of the premises to Problem 1. We designed the problem with the intention that NAs would be drawn to the assertion that the large number of breakups among partners is a function of how quickly and easily breakups can be obtained. According to this premise, it would be logical to assume that slowing the breakup process might reduce the number of breakups. Alternative C builds on this logical extension of a premise to infer that "partners might resolve their differences if breaking up was harder and took longer." This answer builds on the socially adaptive theory that teams and partnerships can be saved if incentives are present to encourage people to devote time and effort to working together and resolving conflicts. Research demonstrates that NAs are significantly more likely than aggressive respondents to be drawn to this alternative (James et al., 2005).

*Illogical Answers*

CR problems are meant to appear to respondents as traditional inductive reasoning problems. The objective is to have respondents focus totally on finding logical answers to reasoning problems. This allows the intended CR to operate unfettered by the self-protective mechanisms that plague self-report personality surveys (e.g., socially desirable responding). To maintain the appearance of traditional inductive reasoning problems, it is necessary to include illogical responses, often referred to as *distractors*, in the problems. Two illogical alternatives are thus included in each problem. However, we do not wish to confound CR with critical problem-solving skills. Nor do we wish to have to have to consider issues such as how illogical responses are to be interpreted and scored.

Consequently, CR problems employ distractors that are clearly illogical, at least to individuals with cognitive skills consistent with a seventh-grade reading level (see James & McIntyre, 2000). Thus, virtually no one attempts to solve CR problems by selecting either of the two logically incorrect alternatives (alternatives A and D in the illustrative problem). Rather, experience with thousands of administrations indicates that one of the logical answers (i.e., the NA or AG alternative) is almost always selected to solve the problem (see James et al., 2005).

To develop illogical responses (distractors), we examined the distractors drawn from inductive reasoning problems in a number of published tests and study guides for critical problem-solving skills. Several hundred inductive reasoning problems were examined. We then informally clustered the distractors into categories based upon their content and/or the strategy that was used to construct them. The results of this analysis are presented in Exhibit 3.6. This table is basically an outline of possible errors people may make when reasoning inductively. We refer to this table frequently when writing distractors for CR problems. We then build the distractors, trying to be careful to make the error in the reasoning very apparent.

**EXHIBIT 3.6**
**Illustrative Types of Distractors in Logical Reasoning**

1. Statement goes beyond scope of argument.
   a. Too broad; goes beyond bounds of argument
   b. Overstates case—too strong; for example, exaggerates unstated assumption.
   c. Use of inexact qualifiers—most, almost always, never.
2. Statement reverses causal order.
3. Statement repeats the premise rather than going beyond premise to make an inference.
4. Statement is out of logical order; illogical progression.
5. Representativeness of sample (data) is questionable.
   a. Sample is too small to be generalizable.
   b. Base rate is too low.
   c. Regression toward the mean.
6. Statement is the opposite of implied assumption.
7. There's a problem of omitted variables; alternative causes.
8. Statement is totally nonrelevant to argument.
9. Statement has only partial relevance; tangential to argument.
10. There's no necessary connection—confuses correlation with cause.
11. Statement is a good argument in other contexts but has no real relation to the point.
12. Statement fails to be both "necessary and sufficient":
    a. A is given as necessary and sufficient for B, but is only sufficient.
    b. A is given as necessary and sufficient for B, but is only necessary.
13. Statement affirms the consequent:
    a. If A, then B; B occurs, therefore A has occurred.
    b. If A, then B; If B does not occur, then A has not occurred.

To summarize, CR problems are, first and foremost, inductive reasoning problems. Consequently, by definition, they must have logically valid and logically invalid response options. Traditional inductive reasoning problems designed to measure cognitive ability have one logical response and three or four illogical responses. These items and their distractors vary in degree of "difficulty," implying that for the difficult items, many respondents will choose an illogical (i.e., incorrect) response. In contrast, the CR application of inductive reasoning problems involves two logical responses and two illogical responses. The CR items are all easy in the sense that virtually everyone chooses at least an informally logical answer.

## Problem 2

Problem 2 in Exhibit 3.5 further illustrates the CR procedure for aggression. The reasoning task is to find a logical weakness in the well-known proverb "An eye for an eye." This is a variation of the "recognition of assumptions" inductive reasoning task. The objective is to search the four alternatives given for the problem to find (a) an unstated assumption on which the proverb rests that (b) weakens the proverb. Alternatives A and C do not satisfy this objective because they are clearly illogical. This leaves alternatives B and D:

> B. It offers no way to settle a conflict in a friendly manner.
> D. People have to wait until they are attacked before they can strike.

Which of these alternatives is judged to be the most reasonable basis for weakening the proverb is conditional on whether the respondent is an AG or an NA, as explained next.

### The AG Alternative

We focused this problem on the proverb "An eye for an eye" to stimulate AGs' predisposition to favor retaliation over reconciliation, retribution over forgiveness, vindication over understanding, and obtaining revenge over preserving a relationship. The justification mechanism underlying these implicit biases is the retribution bias and was defined in Exhibit 2.2 as a predilection to determine that retaliation is more rational than reconciliation. This bias is often stimulated by perceptions of wounded pride, challenged self-esteem, or disrespect. Aggression in response to the humiliation and anger of being demeaned is rationalized as justified restoration of honor and respect.

Our intent is that, when AGs seek to weaken the "eye for an eye" proverb through one of its unstated assumptions, they will engage in reasoning shaped by the retribution bias. This should engender reasoning such as the following:

> A. The principle underlying the proverb is that harming another is justifiable if it is intended to exact restitution for a perceived wrong.
> B. To invoke the principle, one must first be wronged.
> C. Being wronged may involve personal injury. This is a weakness.
> D. To avoid injury when one expects to be wronged, it would seem reasonable to engage in a preemptive strike.

Alternative D builds on this reasoning to frame the inference that a weakness in the "eye for an eye" proverb is that people have to wait until they are attacked before they can strike. This answer is designed to be logically compelling and psychologically persuasive to respondents who are already predisposed to favor retribution and ways to make aggression more effective and less dangerous for themselves. In addition, although this response weakens the logic of the "eye for an eye" proverb, it does not invalidate it. That is, alternative D wounds but does not invalidate the proverb. Like the CR problem above, research results suggest that this answer is indeed compelling to

AGs because people with a history of aggressive behavior are significantly more likely than nonaggressive respondents to select alternative D to solve the problem.

### The NA Alternative

It is expected that NA respondents will reject alternative D as extreme and unnecessarily provocative. Alternative B is targeted to appeal to NAs' desire for a more socially adaptive alternative to counterbalance the antagonistic and provocative tenor of alternative D. This inference follows logically from the premises but lacks the cynicism and enmity of alternative D. It offers an option whose logical credibility is conditional on reasoning being shaped by prosocial ideologies and rationales, discussed for NAs in Chapter 2. Selection of alternative B thus provides indirect evidence that the retribution bias is not instrumental in shaping a respondent's reasoning. In addition, alternative B provides a mechanism for the logic underlying the "eye for an eye" proverb to be invalidated as opposed to simply wounded or weakened.

## Problem 3

Problem 3 uses the "expectations of outcomes" inductive reasoning task to structure the reasoning problem. Respondents are asked to evaluate consequences, including dysfunctional ones, that might occur naturally or as the result of planned changes or proposed interventions. The premises in the stem to the problem center on the assertion that the Girl Scouts and Boy Scouts teach young people a sense of discipline. Evidence is provided for the assertion in the sense that both organizations teach respect for authority, neatness, dependability, and loyalty. The reasoning problem is to determine which one of four alternatives provides the most logical forecast of what Scouts will be like when they grow up. Alternatives B and C are clearly illogical. This leaves alternatives A and D to serve as the AG and NA alternatives:

A. They will be easily controlled by leaders.
D. They will be ready to take on responsibility.

### The AG Alternative

In Chapter 2, we noted that AGs are predisposed to look at social events through a window of cynicism. Their reasoning will show a lack of sensitivity, empathy, and concern for social customs, frequently calling upon socially unorthodox and antisocial theories to interpret and analyze social events and relationships. Socially deviant behavior intended to harm others is often rationalized by inferring that it allows one to attain freedom of expression, release from the shackles of social customs, and liberation from confining social relationships. These implicit biases are indicators of an underlying justi-fication mechanism referred to as the *social discounting bias*, which was defined in Exhibit 2.2 as

> A proclivity to frame social norms as repressive and restrictive of free will. Perceptions of societal restrictiveness promote feelings of opposition, resistance, and reactance. These feelings furnish a foundation for justify-ing socially deviant behaviors such as aggression as ways to liberate one-self from repressive social customs and to exercise one's lawful right to freedom of expression.

This justification mechanism is likely to provoke considerable pessimism, if not a large degree of cynicism, for the Girl Scouts and the Boy Scouts. Specifically, the justification mechanism is likely to promote reasoning such as the following:

- Teaching people a sense of discipline (e.g., respect for authority) is really designed to constrain their freedoms and make them obedient to authority.
- One must avoid organized social programs such as the Scouts in order to maintain one's freedoms.

Alternative A offers a conclusion that is designed to appear as logically plausible and psychologically persuasive to AG respondents whose reasoning is shaped by the social discounting bias. The conclusion that Girl Scouts and Boy Scouts will be easily controlled by leaders is a natural progression of their predispositions to reason that social institutions that teach respect for author-ity and obedience will produce obedient followers in later life. Like the other problems in this section, research supports the prediction that respondents who select this alternative are more likely than those who select the other alternatives (primarily alternative D) to engage in aggressive behavior.

### The NA Alternative

Alternative D was designed to be logically persuasive to NAs. It is targeted to appeal to these individuals' desire for a socially adaptive counterbalance to the cynical tenor of the AG alternative. Indeed, to NAs, a sense of discipline, respect for authority, neatness, dependability, and loyalty are positive values that people in normal society often value in a leader (as opposed to indicators of obedience and conformity, as surmised by AGs).

### Problem 4

This problem is designed to draw out AGs' propensity to view the world through a prism of potency (see Chapter 2). The potency bias justification mechanism suggests that AGs are predisposed to focus thoughts about social interactions on issues of dominance versus submissiveness. Aggressive people are especially primed to distinguish (a) strength, assertiveness, dominance, daring, fearlessness, and power from (b) weakness, impotence, submissiveness, timidity, compliance, and cowardice. Fixations on dominance versus submissiveness promote rationalizations that aggression is an act of strength or bravery that gains respect from others. Failing to act aggressively shows weakness.

Problem 4 spotlights potency and dominance and their framing by AGs as strength, dominance, and power. The stem states that wild animals often fight to see who will breed. This ensures that only the strongest animals reproduce. When strong animals reproduce, their young tend to grow into powerful animals that have the best chances of succeeding. It is then asserted that people are not like the animals just described, for people who are *not* strong often reproduce. The reasoning task is to identify the most logical conclusion based on these premises. Two of the alternatives are clearly illogical (B and C). This leaves:

A. People do not need to be physically strong to be successful.
D. Humans would be more successful if only the strongest were allowed to breed.

Which of these two alternatives is the most reasonable is conditional on the underlying personality of the respondent.

### The AG Alternative

This is an "evaluation of evidence" problem (inductive reasoning task 3). Respondents are asked to weigh evidence to decide if generalizations or (general) conclusions based on the given (specific) data or assumptions (premises) are warranted. This often involves determining which testimony is trustworthy, which evidence is untainted, and which samples are representative in regard to evaluating the reasonableness of a logical conclusion. In the present case, respondents must determine which of two conclusions best fit the evidence provided in the premises.

If the AGs among the respondents reason as predicted by justification mechanisms, then their reasoning is likely to be guided by the potency bias. In the context of the problem, this bias is likely to promote reasoning such as the following:

- Like the animals in the question, human success is often a result of factors such as bravery, strength, fortitude, and will.
- Unlike the animals in the question, humans do not as a rule engage in breeding habits that maximize these factors.
- As a result, the human population is inundated with weakness, impotence, submissiveness, timidity, compliance, and cowardice.

Alternative D was designed to be logically compelling and psychologically persuasive to respondents who are already predisposed to frame and reason through a prism of bravery versus cowardice, strength versus weakness, and power versus impotence. Alternative D takes the illustrative reasoning one step further by using it to infer that humans would be more successful if only the strongest were allowed to breed. To determine that this particular answer is a good, indeed the best, answer to the problem suggests an underlying predisposition to place considerable emphasis on potency and dominance when reasoning informally about everyday events. (As with the problems stated, this alternative and the NA alternative significantly distinguish aggressive from nonaggressive individuals in validation analyses.)

### The NA Alternative

Nonaggressive individuals do not frame and reason through a prism of potency and dominance. They are thus prone to reject the reasoning in alternative D. Alternative A was designed to be more logically persuasive and psychologically compelling to NAs. It is targeted to appeal to NAs' reasoning that strength and potency are not usually necessary to be successful among humans. Moreover, NAs are unlikely to mask an implicit bias to think in terms of potency via the use of conscious euphemisms such as bravery. This further heightens their skepticism of alternative D and moves them logically toward alternative A.

## Design Aids for Building Conditional Reasoning Problems

Our primary blueprint for designing CR problems is provided by integrating justification mechanisms with the various types of inductive reasoning tasks identified in the first part of this chapter. However, as we constructed CR problems over the years, we developed a set of heuristic design aids to help integrate justification mechanisms with the nine reasoning tasks. The design aids are most fully developed for the aggression CR problems, which does not suggest that they have been systematically or exhaustively explored. Rather, the design aids simply evolved as we searched for ideas for CR problems and approaches for writing them. Three design aids are presented below and in Exhibits 3.6 and 3.7 and Table 3.1. The aids consist of guides to differential framing for aggression, informal reasoning based on justification mechanisms, and ideas for CR problem structures. Each design aid is discussed briefly next.

### Differential Framing in Aggression

*Differential framing* was defined in Chapter 2 as qualitative disparities in the meanings imputed to (i.e., the adjectives used to describe) the same attributes

## EXHIBIT 3.7
## Informal Reasoning Based on Justification Mechanisms

People who possess specific justification mechanisms (implicit biases) tend to be unaware that, in reasoning informally on problems that are personally relevant, they are prone to:

    a. find untenable assumptions primarily in theories that disagree with their justification mechanisms.

    b. fail to see logical problems in assumptions and theories that agree with their justification mechanisms.

    a. forecast success for social programs that support their justification mechanisms.

    b. forecast failure for social programs they oppose their justification mechanisms

    a. credit objectivity to experts whose testimony is consistent with their justification mechanisms.

    b. credit bias to experts whose testimony contradicts their justification mechanisms.

    a. attend selectively to statistics that corroborate their justification mechanisms.

    b. disregard or discount statistics that impugn their justification mechanisms.

    a. judge that a single occurrence of an event is validating if it supports a justification mechanism.

    b. judge that it is a chance occurrence of it supports an alternative hypothesis.

    a. consider a sample to be representative and unbiased if it disputes an assumption that disagrees with a justification mechanism.

    b. consider a sample to be nonrepresentative and biased if it supports that same unpalatable assumption.

    a. propose alternative, unmeasured causes for theories that they wish to disconfirm because such theories are at odds with justification mechanism.

    b. judge that salient causes are already included in theories that they wish to see confirmed because such theories are consistent with justification mechanism.

    a. fail to see unexpected consequences for theories consistent with justification mechanism.

    b. project unexpected consequences, typically dysfunctional, for theories inconsistent with justification mechanism.

    a. overstate causal salience and relevance of causes that confirm justification mechanism.

    b. understate causal salience and relevance of causes that disconfirm justification mechanism.

    a. attribute causality to correlational relationships that reflect a justification mechanism.

    b. attribute spuriousness to correlational relationships that disagree with a justification mechanism.

Basically, people unconsciously map the implicit biases that define their justification mechanisms into their informal reasoning. Among the products of this mapping are unrecognized, systematic biases in judgments of what is and what is not valid evidence or a reasonable assumption, advocacy, model, projection, or program. The actual mapping process is unobservable, but its results are not. Mapping is indicated by

- the experts that one considers trustworthy,
- the assumptions that are judged to have been corroborated,
- the statistics that are used to support positions,
- the samples that are considered to be representative, and
- the expectations projected for the success or failure of programs and ventures.

## TABLE 3.1
### Illustrations of Differential Framing by Nonaggressive Individuals and Aggressive Individuals

| Nonaggressive | Stimulus | Aggressive |
|---|---|---|
| Advice, constructive criticism | Feedback from authority figure | Personal attack, insult |
| Potential friend, confederate | Meeting a new person | Potential opponent, adversary |
| Diplomatic, considerate, cooperative | Attempt to heal conflict | Submissive, weak, disrespected |
| Belligerent, uncivilized | Intimidation attempt | Will be feared, respected |
| Effect on others | An aversive event (e.g., economic slowdown) | Effect on me |
| Negotiate, seek harmony | Interdepartmental disagreement over resources | Fight, win |
| Resolve | Quarrel | Win |
| Benefactor, source of opportunity | Employing organization | Exploiter, enemy |
| Protectors | Police | Oppressors |
| Rules and regulations | Laws | Infringements of rights |
| Impartial | Internal Revenue Service | Vengeful |

*Note.* Differential framing-qualitative disparities in the meanings imputed to the same attributes or event(s) by different individuals. Framing of nonaggressive individuals is contrasted above with the framing of aggressive individuals.

or event(s) by different individuals. For example, as shown in Table 3.1, nonaggressive people tend to frame feedback from authority figures in terms such as "advice" or "constructive criticism." In contrast, aggressive individuals are predisposed to frame this same feedback in terms of a "personal attack" or an (intentional) "insult." The latter framing is likely a product of AGs' reliance on justification mechanisms such as the hostile attribution bias and the victimization by powerful others bias to make inferences about meaning in their perceived world. As discussed in Chapter 2, differential framing is especially important because it sets the stage for how a person is likely to reason about such things as how to react to environmental stimuli.

We will not review the associations between justification mechanisms and framing. We note only that Table 3.1 is a design aid that we review quickly for ideas and directions when beginning to build a CR problem. Its role is that of a catalyst or trigger for ideas and directions for problem development.

### Informal Reasoning Based on Justification Mechanisms

The information in Exhibit 3.7 plays a similar catalytic/stimulus role. Here, we have proposed various ways that the six AG justification mechanisms may influence (bias) reasoning about specific events. Depending on subject matter, one of these types of bias can be integrated with one of the reasoning tasks listed at the beginning of the chapter to build a CR problem. Indeed, several of the implicit biases are tied specifically to one of these tasks. Please note that the information in Exhibit 3.7 is used as a heuristic to stimulate ideas for generating CR problems. We are not proposing a typology of biases in informal reasoning. Rather, we use the contrasts in Exhibit 3.7 to identify events and topics about which we can construct CR problems.

### Ideas for Conditional Reasoning Problem Structures

The ideas in Exhibit 3.8 are intended to augment the inductive reasoning tasks. Some of the ideas are directly analogous to one of the reasoning strategies. Others are not analogous but can be used in combination with a justification mechanism(s) and a reasoning strategy to build a CR problem. Basically, the ideas for problem structures in Exhibit 3.8 evolved over the years. These structures are based on those that we have found to be productive in generating CR problems.

## The Conditional Reasoning Test for Aggression (CRT-A)

The Conditional Reasoning Test for Aggression (CRT-A) consists of 22 CR problems such as illustrated in Exhibit 3.5, plus three traditional inductive reasoning problems (to further enhance the face validity associated with completing a reasoning test; James & McIntyre, 2000). The average Flesch-Kincaid Grade Level score for the 22 CR problems, an indicator of reading level provided by Microsoft Word, is approximately 7.0 (i.e., seventh grade). The 22 CR problems in the CRT-A evolved over a series of developmental studies, including a number of empirical validity and psychometric studies to be presented in Chapter 4. To be considered for retention, a CR problem had to significantly predict behavioral indicators of aggression and antisocial behavior, preferably in more than one sample. Retained CR problems also had to have low correlations with potential confounds, namely, intelligence, gender, and race. A significant part-whole correlation (i.e., correlation of problem with the total score described in Chapter 4) was required. Each problem was reviewed by a logician for face validity as an informal, inductive reasoning task. Problems were rewritten or deleted on the basis of this review.

An attempt was made to have each of the six justification mechanisms for aggression in Exhibit 2.2 represented repeatedly in the CR problems. This goal was attained for five of the six justification mechanisms. Each of these five justification mechanisms is represented in three or more of the CR problems that survived to become members of the 22-problem pool. The exception, the derogation of target bias, is represented by only one problem in this pool. This

## EXHIBIT 3.8
## Ideas for Conditional Reasoning Problems

Present an argument in favor of one side of dialectic (e.g., present AG side).
  Offer conclusion that is based on argument being valid (e.g., AG alternative).
  Offer alternative conclusion that is based on argument being invalid (e.g., NA alternative).

Present an intervention; offer a projection about effects/success of intervention.
  Conclusion based on projection being plausible.
  (Alternative) conclusion based on projection being implausible.

Present a causal model: A→B→C.
  Conclusion assumes model is self-contained.
  Conclusion assumes model has omitted a key cause.

Present an advocacy. Ask for most relevant evidence.
  Conclusion contains evidence that supports advocacy.
  Conclusion contains evidence that questions advocacy.

Advocate a causal relationship: A→B. Ask to weaken.
  Wounding response; hurts but does not disconfirm advocacy.
  Falsification response: strongly rejects advocacy.

Present the concurrence of two events (B followed A). Ask how explain relationship.
  Conclusion involves a causal relationship.
  Conclusion involves a chance occurrence.

Present incongruous events (People against killing send soldiers to war).
  Conclusion that rationalizes incongruity.
  Conclusion that highlights incongruity.

Present a problem; what caused it to occur?
  Conclusion that offers an internal attribution (at fault).
  Conclusion that offers an external attribution (not at fault).

Present a dialectic: Person A vs. Person B.
  Ask what evidence best resolves.
  Ask what can we infer about debaters?
  Ask what inference best follows from debates.

Present a general theory (self-esteem, causes of aggression). Ask for inference.
  Conclusion based on AG implicit theory.
  Conclusion based on NA implicit theory.

Present an analogy (or lack of such; e.g., animals breed based on strength; humans do not). Ask for logical inference.
  Conclusion based on AG implicit theory.
  Conclusion based on NA implicit theory.

Present a set of historical events (e.g., Boston Tea Party shows country was founded on disobedience). Ask for *analogous* set of events.
  Inference based on AG implicit theory.
  Inference based on NA implicit theory.

Present a mystery. Ask for most relevant evidence for solving it.
  Conclusion based on evidence A.
  Conclusion based on evidence B.

is largely a result of (a) the difficulty of writing problems to capture this bias and (b) the fact that the problems that were written did not survive the empirical tests described above.

Several methods were examined for scoring the 22 CR problems. These alternatives provided highly correlated scores and essentially equal correlations with external variables (James et al., 2005). Current scoring of the 22 CR problems thus follows a straightforward method. Respondents are given a +1 for every aggression (AG) alternative they select and a 0 for every nonaggressive (NA) or distractor response they select. These scores are summed to furnish a scale with a theoretical range of 0 to 22.

Respondents obtain high scores on the CRT-A by selecting a comparatively large number of answers based on justification mechanisms (i.e., the AG alternatives). A high score thus indicates that justification mechanisms for aggression are instrumental in shaping a person's reasoning, from which it follows that this respondent is implicitly prepared to justify engaging in aggressive behavior. The measurement scale is referred to as the Justification of Aggression Scale, or JAGS (James et al., 2005). Although the theoretical maximum score on the JAGS is 22, the highest score we have obtained has been a 14—and that is across thousands of test administrations. This discrepancy between the theoretical and operational maximums is driven by the generally low base rate for selecting the aggressive response options, which subsequently engenders a skewed distribution on the JAGS, with most individuals scoring on the low end of the continuum. Nevertheless, as we will see in the next chapter, high scores on the JAGS are predictive of future aggressive behavior. We will also show that an empirically defined standard for "high" on the JAGS is a score of 8. Most people have scores of 0 to 4. Approximately 10% of respondents have scores of 8 or higher. These are the respondents who are thought to have the strongest proclivities to engage in aggressive or antisocial acts (i.e., the strongest motives to harm others or institutions).

A low score (0–2) on the JAGS indicates that justification mechanisms for aggression are *not* instrumental in shaping a respondent's reasoning. The lack of a defensive system to justify acting aggressively suggests that respondents are unlikely to engage in acts intended to harm others. They are believed to have essentially no desire to harm others. Scores ranging between the weak and strong poles (3–7) on the scale indicate that justification mechanisms appear to be only sporadically instrumental in shaping and guiding reasoning, and implicit defenses for justifying aggression are not well developed. A weak proclivity to engage in aggressive acts is empirically indicated.

### Instructions for CRT-A

As discussed in relation to illogical alternatives, CR problems are meant to appear to respondents as traditional inductive reasoning problems. The objective is to have respondents focus totally on finding logical answers to reasoning problems. This allows the intended CR to operate unfettered by the self-protective mechanisms that many believe plague self-report personality surveys (e.g., socially desirable responding). To maintain the appearance of traditional inductive reasoning problems, and thereby protect the indirect measurement of the implicit personality, respondents are informed that they will be asked to take a reasoning test (which in fact is true). The title of the test booklet includes the term *reasoning test*, and the test instructions ("Identify the one answer that is the most logical") are intended to give respondents the impression that they are taking a reasoning test.

### Supervision

We ask that CRT-A administrations be supervised. We ask this for two reasons: to further the impression that respondents are taking a reasoning test on which unsupervised respondents might cheat and to prevent actual cheating. Several instances of cheating have occurred in which a respondent copied the answer sheet of another respondent.

### Time Limit

There is a 25-min time limit for completing the CRT-A. This time limit is designed to further the impression of a critical reasoning test, and it does not introduce an ability component to the testing process, beyond the requirement that respondents be able to read English at the seventh-grade level. (The relationship between CRT-A scores and critical intellectual skills, or lack thereof, is discussed in Chapter 4.) Thousands of CRT-A administrations have indicated that the 25-min limit provides ample time to complete the test, with most respondents completing the test within 15 to 18 min.

## Verbal/Visual Conditional Reasoning Test

For less adept readers, a test based on a verbal–visual version of a subset of the CR problems was designed to have a threshold reading level of approximately the fifth to sixth grade (Green & James, 1999). Referred to as the VCRT, this test consists of bare-bones versions of CR problems. The problems are presented both verbally and in written form using a VCR and television. The written component consists of simplified prose, which is overlaid on a photograph consistent with the basic theme of the CR problem. The current VCRT contains 14 CR problems, 12 of which are shared with the CRT-A. Work continues on converting CRT-A problems to the VCRT format. Scoring of the VCRT problems is based on the same procedures as described above for the JAGS.

# 4

## EMPIRICAL EXAMINATIONS OF CONDITIONAL REASONING TESTS

This chapter is devoted to the presentation of the results of empirical tests of the Conditional Reasoning Test for Aggression (CRT-A) and the Conditional Reasoning Test for Relative Motive Strength (CRT-RMS). The presentation focuses on aggression and the CRT-A because this is where the majority of empirical work has been accomplished. Empirical results for achievement motivation–fear of failure and the CRT-RMS are treated more briefly in the second section of this chapter. With respect to aggression, evidence is introduced regarding Ozer's (1999) second and third principles for sound psychological test development in the personality domain. Ozer's second principle is that the item characteristics, scale characteristics, and factor structure of the instrument should be consistent with the theory of the instrument (presented in Chapters 2 and 3, this volume); the third principle is that the instrument should possess demonstrably high validities for the most theoretically relevant inferences.

# EMPIRICAL RESULTS FOR AGGRESSION

Ozer's Principle 2 requests that the item characteristics, scale characteristics, and the factor structure of the conditional reasoning (CR) problems be consistent with the psychological theory used to build the problems. Principle 3 focuses on estimates of validity, where validity is viewed through the broad lens of construct validity. At issue is the validity of inferences regarding (a) the reliability of the instrument (e.g., internal consistency, stability); (b) empirical validities, with emphasis placed on the ability of the instrument to predict behavioral measures of aggression; and (c) the instrument's relations with measures of other theoretical constructs of interest (e.g., self-report personality variables; potential confounds such as intelligence, gender, and race). Additional validity concerns pertain to the potential for faking and the establishment of critical values for interpreting various degrees of aggressiveness, or the lack thereof. The following topics are discussed in this section:

- item characteristics, namely, $p$ values and item-total biserial correlations for the 22 CR problems in the CRT-A that constitute the Justification of Aggression Scale (JAGS);
- distributions of scores on the CRT-A (CRT-A and JAGS are interchangeable; here, we use CRT-A);
- the factor structure of the 22 CR problems that constitute the CRT-A;
- estimates of reliability for the CRT-A;
- estimates of the criterion-related validities with which scores on the CRT-A predict behavioral indicators of aggression in 14 primary studies;
- estimates of the empirical validity of scores on the CRT-A based on a meta-analysis of 22 studies;
- correlations between scores on the CRT-A and intelligence, gender, and race;
- correlations between scores on the CRT-A and scores from self-report measures of aggression;
- comparative criterion-related validities for the CRT-A and self-report measures of aggression in the context of dissociative studies;
- the empirically set standards or critical values for interpreting scores on the CRT-A; and
- results of a set of studies designed to examine the vulnerability of the CRT-A to faking.

## Item Characteristics and Distributions of Scores on the CRT-A

Data from 5,238 individuals were available for analyses involving item characteristics, distributions of scores, and the factor analysis of CR problems. These data were accumulated during approximately 10 years of developmental research on the CRT-A. As reported in Table 4.1, the largest share of the data comes from primarily undergraduate college students across a variety of research universities. However, more than 1,000 individual records were contributed by studies on adult working populations across a variety of occupations, including temporary employees, patrol officers, and customer service associates.

The $p$ values for individual CR problems are presented in Table 4.2. The $p$ values indicate the proportion of respondents who selected the aggressive answer (the AG alternative) to each problem. The $p$ value is also referred to as the *base rate*. The average $p$ value across the 22 CR problems in the CRT-A was .18, which indicates that only a small proportion of respondents tended to select each of the aggressive answers. In general terms, this is good news for society because it suggests that most people are *not* disposed to justify aggression. However, this is not such good news for people conducting research on the CRT-A because it means that they must deal with thorny statistical issues engendered by low base rates and skewed distributions.

TABLE 4.1
Samples Combined and Used for Item Characteristic Analyses
on Conditional Reasoning Test for Aggression

| Sample[a] | n |
| --- | --- |
| Students[b] | 370 |
| Students | 100 |
| Students | 307 |
| Students | 318 |
| Customer contact | 585 |
| Temp. employees | 216 |
| Students | 366 |
| Students | 43 |
| Students | 70 |
| Students | 581 |
| Students | 407 |
| Students | 364 |
| Students | 187 |
| Students | 283 |
| Students | 258 |
| Students | 182 |
| Students | 137 |
| Power plant operators | 115 |
| Patrol officers | 161 |
| Students | 188 |

*Note.* $N$ = 5,238. [a]Total. [b]Students were generally college undergraduates.

TABLE 4.2
*p*-Values and Item-Total Score Biserial Correlations for Conditional
Reasoning Problems in the Conditional Reasoning Test for Aggression

| Problem | *p*-Value | Item-total biserial |
|---------|-----------|---------------------|
| 1. | .31 | .35 |
| 2. | .21 | .38 |
| 3. | .05 | .41 |
| 4. | .05 | .41 |
| 5. | .07 | .38 |
| 6. | .35 | .41 |
| 7. | .06 | .51 |
| 8. | .19 | .42 |
| 9. | .37 | .49 |
| 10. | .21 | .45 |
| 11. | .26 | .49 |
| 12. | .15 | .39 |
| 13. | .13 | .39 |
| 14. | .19 | .41 |
| 15. | .04 | .46 |
| 16. | .29 | .45 |
| 17. | .22 | .45 |
| 18. | .22 | .42 |
| 19. | .08 | .24 |
| 20. | .28 | .37 |
| 21. | .14 | .46 |
| 22. | .04 | .46 |
| Mean | .18 | .42 |
| SD | .10 | .06 |

*Note.* $N = 5,238$.

One of these thorny statistical issues occurs with the correlations between individual CR problems and the total aggression score. These correlations are also presented in Table 4.2. To compute these correlations, each CR problem is scored dichotomously. Respondents receive a +1 for an aggressive answer (i.e., solving the problems using an AG alternative), or a 0 for selecting a nonaggressive (NA) alternative or, in rare cases, an illogical answer. These scores are then summed over CR problems to generate a total aggression score for each individual. This is each individual's score on the CRT-A (JAGS).

The correlation between the dichotomous scores on any given CR problem and the total aggression score is referred to as the *item-total correlation*. Calculating this correlation in a standard correlation program provides an estimate of the point-biserial correlation. Unfortunately, with an average *p* value of only .18, the item-total correlations are likely to be seriously underestimated by the point-biserial correlation (Lord & Novick, 1968).

Given that low base rates are characteristic of studies of aggression, the issue is to identify the better estimator of linear association between the dichotomous CR problems and the continuous CRT-A score. Lord and Novick (1968) spoke informatively on this issue more than 40 years ago:

> The point biserial gives the actual product moment correlation between test score, or external criterion, and item [in the present case, continuous test score and dichotomous CR problem]. We may view the biserial simply as another measure of association, one different from the product moment correlation. The biserial is widely used because it is hoped that the biserial will demonstrate a type of invariance from one group of examinees to another not provided by the point biserial.
>
> Consider several groups of examinees that differ in level of ability but not in heterogeneity or in other respects. If the necessary assumptions hold, the criterion biserial of a given item will be the same for all groups. But . . . the point biserial *must be low* in any group where the item is very easy or very difficult [i.e., base rate is very high or very low]. (p. 341; italics added)
>
> . . .
>
> The conclusion reached from practical experience is that biserial correlations tend to be more stable from group to group than point biserials. (p. 343)

Based on the above, it is possible to infer that (a) the biserial is more likely than the point biserial to offer stable estimates of linear relationships, and (b) correlations based on the point biserial will necessarily be "low," which is to say underestimated, when $p$ values for CR problems, or external criteria, are extreme, such as is the case with aggression. Guilford and Fruchter (1973) underscored the point regarding underestimation by the point biserial when $p$ values depart from .50 (see especially their Appendix G, which gives the factor by which the point-biserial correlation underestimates the biserial correlation). Given this information, it would appear that the biserial is the better estimator of linear association when studying aggression relationships that involve a dichotomous variable with $p$ values that depart from .50.

The average biserial correlation between the individual CR problems and the total aggression score on the CRT-A was .42. The pattern of item-total correlations in Table 4.2 is consistent with those expected for reasoning problems that have been sampled from the same general domain of content (see Nunnally & Bernstein, 1994). As shown later, these correlations produced estimates of internal consistency reliability in the mid-.70 range.

The distribution of total scores on the CRT-A is presented in Table 4.3. Noticeable features of this distribution are (a) positive skews and (b) leptokurtosis, with a peak occurring at a score between 3 and 4. Statistical tests of skew and kurtosis are reported at the bottom of Table 4.3. The test values (based on Z values) all exceeded their respective standard errors by margins indicating significance ($p < .05$). These results indicate that the justification mechanisms for aggression were instrumental in shaping the reasoning of

TABLE 4.3
Distribution of Scores on the Conditional Reasoning Test for Aggression
(Justification of Aggression Scale)

| Score | % | Cumulative % |
|---|---|---|
| 0 | 3 | 3 |
| 1 | 10 | 13 |
| 2 | 15 | 28 |
| 3 | 19 | 47 |
| 4 | 18 | 65 |
| 5 | 14 | 79 |
| 6 | 9 | 88 |
| 7 | 6 | 94 |
| 8 | 3 | 97 |
| 9 | 1 | 98 |
| 10 or higher | 2 | 100 |

Note. $M = 3.89$; $SD = 2.19$; $N = 5,238$; test of skewness: .650, standard error: .034; test of kurtosis: .471, standard error: .068.

approximately 6% to 12% of the respondents. (Later in this chapter we discuss setting a critical score for aggression at a value of 8 on the CRT-A, which is approximately 2 standard deviations above the mean of 3.89.) This percentage is consistent with general findings that aggressive personalities are not widespread in the general population (see Millon, 1990).

## Factor Analysis of 22 Conditional Reasoning Problems in the CRT-A

A factor analysis of the 22 CR problems in the CRT-A sought to determine whether the CRT-A measures a single dimension or multiple dimensions. (Dimensions are often referred to as *factors* or *latent variables*.) We hoped that the underlying dimensionality would reflect the justification mechanisms used to construct the CR problems. An early factor analysis conducted by James et al. (2005) indicated that this was the case. However, we were aware that several of the justification mechanisms tended to occur jointly, and thus a more parsimonious and perhaps informative dimensionality might be found. We therefore waited until we had a much larger sample than the 1,603 individuals included in the analyses conducted by James et al. (2005). By 2008, we had amassed a sample of 4,772 individuals, which seemed sufficient to provide stable results.[1] A principal axis factor analysis was conducted on the polychoric correlations between the 22 CR problems. Polychoric correlations were used for three reasons. First, factor analysis is very sensitive to scale, and it is important to distin-

---

[1] In this endeavor, we asked Dr. James S. Roberts, a very knowledgeable psychometrician on the psychology faculty at the Georgia Institute of Technology, to guide us in the use of advanced approaches to factor analysis. The results of the factor analysis were presented in a conference paper authored by Dr. Roberts and several other investigators (Ko, Thompson, Shim, Roberts, & McIntyre, 2008).

guish between the large proportion of people who selected an NA alternative on each problem and the few who selected an illogical alternative (or chose not to respond—a very rare event). Thus, for the purposes of the factor analysis only, each item was scored on a 3-point scale, where 1 = AG alternative, 0 = illogical or no response, and −1 = NA alternative. Second, polychoric correlations take this discrete categorical scoring on a 3-point scale into account (see Jöreskog & Sörbom, 2005). Third, we know from Table 4.2 that all the CR problems are highly skewed. The polychoric correlation attempts to avoid underestimation of relationships evolving from skewed data (Olsson, Drasgow, & Dorans, 1982). Use of the polychoric correlation is based on arguments analogous to those for using the biserial correlation to estimate the item-total correlations in Table 4.2.

The eigenvalues from an iterated principal axis factoring solution (using squared multiple correlations as initial communality estimates) were compared with the average eigenvalues generated from a bootstrapped parallel analysis of random item responses. The bootstrapped random responses retained the marginal distribution characteristics of all CR problems but eliminated the interitem correlations. The random responses analyzed with principal axis produced eigenvalues that were recorded and retained. This process was repeated 100 times, and average eigenvalues were computed for the 100 trials. These averages were then compared to the eigenvalues from the factor analysis for the real data from 4,772 individuals.

The results suggested that three factors (dimensions) should be extracted. These three factors were then rotated obliquely using promax rotation. An oblique rotation, which allows the factors to be correlated, made theoretical sense because neither the CR problems nor the justification mechanisms were expected to be mathematically independent. The rotated factor structure is reported in Table 4.4. In this table, each CR problem was assigned to the factor with which it maximally correlated, on the basis of the largest absolute structure coefficients (correlations with the factor). These assignments are indicated by shaded cells in the table.

Eleven of the CR problems had their highest loading on, or correlation with, Factor 1. Many of these problems were designed to measure, in whole or in part, implicit biases associated with two primary justification mechanisms, namely, the victimization by powerful others bias and the hostile attribution bias. These two justification mechanisms have as a common denominator the externalizing of bias. That is, when seeking to build a false sense of rationality for their aggressive acts, people scoring highly on this factor would tend to think of themselves as having been exploited, treated inequitably, threatened, oppressed, victimized, endangered, harassed, and treated hostilely. The locus for justification for aggression thus centers on external threats and victimization. This factor was therefore designated as External Justifications. We might add that several CR problems generated from the social discounting justification

TABLE 4.4
Factor Analysis of 22 Problems in the Conditional
Reasoning Test for Aggression

| CR Problem | Factor[a] | | |
| --- | --- | --- | --- |
| | 1 | 2 | 3 |
| 1 | 0.004 | 0.051 | 0.233 |
| 2 | 0.121 | 0.211 | 0.087 |
| 3 | 0.375 | 0.476 | 0.078 |
| 4 | 0.424 | 0.633 | −0.047 |
| 5 | 0.298 | 0.366 | 0.162 |
| 6 | 0.038 | 0.189 | 0.281 |
| 7 | 0.449 | 0.431 | 0.480 |
| 8 | 0.319 | 0.127 | 0.233 |
| 9 | 0.128 | 0.099 | 0.403 |
| 10 | 0.114 | 0.432 | 0.195 |
| 11 | 0.282 | 0.193 | 0.292 |
| 12 | 0.294 | 0.222 | 0.059 |
| 13 | 0.481 | 0.119 | 0.097 |
| 14 | 0.294 | 0.222 | −0.014 |
| 15 | 0.560 | 0.342 | 0.252 |
| 16 | 0.254 | 0.228 | 0.166 |
| 17 | 0.358 | 0.143 | 0.249 |
| 18 | 0.113 | 0.345 | 0.177 |
| 19 | 0.435 | 0.177 | −0.053 |
| 20 | 0.238 | 0.173 | −0.085 |
| 21 | 0.530 | 0.296 | 0.130 |
| 22 | 0.588 | 0.395 | 0.107 |

*Note.* CR = conditional reasoning.
[a]Each CR problem was assigned to the factor with which it maximally correlated, on the basis of the largest absolute structure coefficients (correlations with the factor). These assignments are indicated by shaded cells.

mechanism also loaded on this factor. These problems sought to identify predispositions to build rationalizations for aggression based on antisocial inferences relating to employee bonuses, police investigations of gang-related homicides, and the reasons that countries follow agreements. Each of these problems had a sense of an external force creating an inequity or miscarriage of justice.

Six CR problems had their highest loading on Factor 2. These problems generally shared the common attribute that they were designed to measure, at least partially, the retribution bias and potency bias justification mechanisms. Use of these two justification mechanisms signals that individuals look inward when seeking to build a false sense of rationality for their acts of aggression. For example, these individuals would be predisposed to associate acts of aggression with strength, bravery, dominance, daring, fearlessness, and power. They would also be prone to determine that, in relation to specific events (e.g., marital discord), retaliation is more reasonable than reconciliation, retribution is more sensible than forgiveness, and obtaining revenge is logically preferable to maintaining a relationship. These manifestations of bias generally reflect looking inward to find justifications for aggression. In other words, the locus of bias is something about the individual (e.g., his or her bravery or implicit penchant for revenge). We therefore designated Factor 2 as Internal Justifications.

Factor 3 was defined by five CR problems. These problems came primarily from the social discounting bias justification mechanism and suggested that a key source for building a false sense of rationality for aggression is anger and frustration with the lack of control over one's life. An example of a source of frustration and anger due to powerlessness and lack of influence includes the failure of organizations to appreciate loyalty and dependability in this time of downsizing, outsourcing, and technological change. Another illustration is seeing a logical association between (a) the teaching of discipline to Girl Scouts and Boy Scouts and (b) the Scouts being easily controlled by authority figures later as adults (see illustrative aggression problems in Chapter 3). The lack of control as a source of justification for aggression led to Factor 3 being designated as Powerlessness.

The three factors were significantly intercorrelated. External and Internal Justifications had a moderate correlation of .50, which indicated that many aggressive respondents were prone to use both types of justifications to build rationalizations for aggression. The number of CR problems that crossloaded on both factors further underscores this joint use of internal and external defenses. Powerlessness had much lower correlations of .21 with External Justifications and .17 with Internal Justifications. Nonetheless, these correlations were significant, suggesting the presence of a general tendency to use (or not to use) justification mechanisms for aggression.

In sum, the results of the factor analysis suggested a psychological model in which aggressive people call on different but correlated dimensions of bias to build falsely rational cases for aggression. The dimensions represented clusters of justification mechanisms, where externally oriented biases representing victimization and threat formed one cluster, internally oriented biases representing potency and retribution formed a second cluster, and biases focusing on powerlessness in society formed a third cluster.

### Estimates of Reliability

Three types of reliability were estimated. The first type involved internal consistency estimates (alpha coefficients) for each of the three factors ($n = 4,772$). The estimates were .87 for Factor 1 (External Justifications), .82 for Factor 2 (Internal Justifications), and .81 for Factor 3 (Powerlessness). The second type of reliability involved the internal consistency for scores on the CRT-A and the Verbal/Visual Conditional Reasoning Test of Aggression (VCRT), which were estimated using a derivative of the KR-20 formula (see

Equation 21, p. 389; Gulliksen, 1950). This formula, presented below, computes internal consistency reliability using item-total biserial correlation coefficients.

$$r_{xx} = \frac{K}{K-1} \left( 1 - \frac{\sum_{g=1}^{K} s_g^2}{\left( \sum_{g=1}^{K} r_{xg} s_g \right)^2} \right) \quad (1),$$

where $K$ refers to the number of items, $s_g^2$ refers to the variance of the items, and $r_{xg} s_g$ refers to the product of the item-total biserial and the standard deviation of the item. Following James et al. (2005), standardized variables were assumed; thus, variances were set to unity. This yielded the computational formula,

$$r_{xx} = \frac{K}{K-1} \left( 1 - \frac{K}{\left( \sum_{g=1}^{K} r_{xg} \right)^2} \right) \quad (2).$$

Nunnally and Bernstein (1994) suggested the lower bound reliability for tests in the early stages of development should be at least .70. We obtained an estimate of .76 based on the combination of samples reported in Table 4.1 ($N = 5,238$). The internal consistency estimate obtained for the 14-problem VCRT using the same procedure was .78 (see Chapter 3, this volume, for a description of VCRT). This estimate is based on a sample of college undergraduates ($n = 225$). These results indicate that the total scores on the CRT-A and VCRT are generally reliable estimates of the true scores that would be obtained if all possible CR problems from a heterogeneous domain of CR problems for aggression were answered.

The third and final estimate of reliability was based on a hybrid alternative forms analysis. Undergraduates in a development sample ($n = 276$) were given an early version of a CRT for aggression (25 CR problems) during the first week of a semester. Two months later they were given a VCRT, which at that time had 12 of the 25 CRT problems translated into the VCRT format. Percentage agreement was computed for each of the 12 problems. These values ranged from 64.9% to 94.6%, with a mean of 81.4% agreement. The estimated correlation between the total score on the 12-problem VCRT and a composite score based on the 12 CRT problems shared with the VCRT was .82. This correlation is suggestive of a reasonable degree of stability in responses to CR problems as well as a reasonable degree of comparability in the scores produced by a CRT format and a VCRT format.

In sum, the reliability analyses cumulatively point to the internal consistency and stability of the CR measures of aggression. In the future we would like to see higher estimates (> .80); that goal suggests the need for adding additional CR problems to the CRT-A.

## Empirical (Criterion-Related) Validities

*Validity*, according to the *Standards for Educational and Psychological Testing*, refers to "the degree to which evidence and theory support the interpretations of test scores entailed by proposed uses of tests. Validity is, therefore, the most fundamental consideration in developing and evaluating tests" (American Educational Research Association, American Psychological Association, & National Council on Measurement in Education, 1999, p. 9). A number of different types of evidence can be accumulated about a test—technically, test scores—and each of these types of evidence may be used to support a specific type of interpretation or inference concerning the test (Binning & Barrett, 1989). In this section, we focus on evidence of criterion-related validity, that is, an assessment of the extent to which scores on a measurement instrument are related to the external behaviors or outcome criteria that the instrument is intended to predict. Specifically, scores on a test designed to assess aggression should be significantly related to outcome criteria reflecting aggression.

A criterion-related validity is said to be *predictive* if the time of personality assessment occurs before the time of outcome measurement. To illustrate, measures of preparedness to justify aggression on the JAGS are obtained at the start of an athletic season by administering the CRT-A, and the outcome criterion is the number of abusive fouls accumulated over the course of the season. A criterion-related validity is said to be *concurrent* when the test and outcome criterion are measured at the same approximate time. For example, the measure of aggression on a CRT-A might be taken almost simultaneously with ratings obtained from peers regarding deviancy. Finally, a criterion-related validity may be *postdictive*, which means that scores on a CRT-A are obtained after outcome behaviors have occurred (e.g., absence rates for the 2 years prior to administration of the CRT-A).

All three forms of empirical validity are included in a report of the results for 14 studies of CR tests—see Tables 4.5 and 4.6. These tables show that both developmental and final versions of the CR tests for aggression are predictive of behavioral indicators of aggression. The validities are based on published studies (Bing, Stewart, et al., 2007; Frost et al., 2007; James & Mazerolle, 2002; James et al., 2004; James et al., 2005; Russell & James, 2008; a meta-analysis reported later incorporates unpublished studies.) One of these publications presented a compendium of results for 11 empirical validation studies (James et al., 2005). These studies were conducted by combinations of the 11 authors of James et al. (2005). We attempted to publish

(text continues on page 131)

TABLE 4.5
Criterion and Hypotheses for 14 Validation Samples

| Sample | Criterion | Hypothesis |
|---|---|---|
| 1. 140 officers who patrolled federal parks in a Southeastern state. Almost all officers were male, in their 40s and 50s, and White. | Supervisory performance ratings. $M = 3.48$ on a 5-point scale (1 = not at all effective, 5 = extremely effective), $SD = .87$. | Aggressive officers would receive lower ratings because of tendencies to be hostile to the public, engage in dominance contests with supervisors, and clash with coworkers. |
| 2. 188 undergraduates from a Southeastern University; 34% were female, and 10% were African American (the other 90% were White). | Habitual absences—lack of class attendance; 37% of students had high absences—low attendance. | Aggressive students would frame themselves as victims of inequitable treatment by powerful others (e.g., professors). Being victimized would serve as a justification for habitual absenteeism, which is often a form of passive-aggressiveness used by people in low power positions to defy or to resist oppressors (see Buss, 1961). |
| 3. 60 undergraduates from a Southeastern University; 60% were female, and almost all were White. | Lack of truthfulness about extra credit deserved from participating in a 55-min exercise, which consisted of completing the VCRT-A and the Jackson Personality Profile; 15% of students stated that they deserved 10 points (experiment lasted more than 1 hr) when they deserved 5 points (experiment lasted 1 hr or less). | Being kept waiting 10 min for experiment to start, being surprised with an announcement of having only 15 min to finish experiment, and being consistently reminded to work quickly would trigger anger and resentment (e.g., hostile attributions, victimization) among aggressive students. Aggressive students would attempt to "fight back" or "get even" by overstating extra credit they deserved. |
| 4. 97 nuclear facility operators. Mean age was 44.42 years, mean tenure in company was 15.29 years ($SD = 9.05$), 15% were female (data for race were not available), and education varied between high school graduate with no college (23%) to college graduate (31%). | Absences—lack of work attendance for the past 2.5 years. Lack of attendance consisted of nonoccupational, full-day absences. A pronounced positive skew compounded by several comparatively extreme scores in the absence data resulted in a natural log transformation (Sturman, 1999). | Aggressive operators would believe that the standards in this high-reliance work setting were overly strict, serving to render them submissive rather than just ensuring safety and reliability. One of the few legitimate means available to these individuals to seek justifiable redress for being dominated was a subdisciplinary level of habitual absenteeism (a form of passive-aggressiveness). Thus, the higher the indicated aggressiveness, the greater the absenteeism. |

| 5. 225 undergraduates from a Southeastern University; 49% were female, and almost all were White. | Conduct violations, which included formal sanctions for cheating, plagiarism, forgery, vandalism, physical violence, theft, possession of illicit drugs, public drunkenness, and misuse of computer accounts; seven students in sample (3%) had a violation. Type of violation not disclosed by university. | Aggressive students would frame themselves as victims of a domineering and uncaring academic bureaucracy that demands submission to arbitrary rules and regulations. Misconduct is an act of defiance and bravery that sends a message that the powerless have means to thwart domination and oppression. Consequently, the greater the aggression, the higher the probability of engaging in misconduct. |
| 6. 135 new restaurant employees.[a] Mean age was approximately 24, 66% were female, and company did not keep records on race. | Attrition. The minimum length of stay to be considered a "successful hire" by the company was 30 days. The following dichotomous criterion was created to conform to this standard: 0 = *newly hired worker stayed on the job for at least 30 days* (62% of sample); 1 = *newly hired worker left job before end of 30-day period* (38% of sample). | The vast majority of sample members were hosts and servers who had to deal with assertive and difficult customers. These factors were expected to trigger the motive to aggress. One key means to express the aroused aggression was to quit soon after being hired (i.e., disruptive attrition). It was thus expected that aggressive employees would be more likely to quit early. |
| 7. 105 new package handlers in an international organization that specializes in the rapid delivery of mail and packages. Mean age was 23.25, 74% were male, 52%, were African American, 24% were Hispanic, and 23% were White. | Habitual absences—lack of work attendance during the first 90 days of employment, which is used by the company to determine if employees should be retained. Rate of absenteeism was high (M = 4.9 days; SD = 5.2 days) and uncharacteristically (for the studies here) had a slight negative skew. | Work was well-known for engendering quantitative overload via its physical demands (e.g., lifting heavy packages) and rigid, rapid-paced time schedules. Aggressive individuals would attribute overload to being exploited and victimized in the interest of profit, and their absences as a way to retaliate by impeding the organization's productivity. |

*(continues)*

## TABLE 4.5
### Criterion and Hypotheses for 14 Validation Samples  *(Continued)*

| Sample | Criterion | Hypothesis |
|---|---|---|
| 8. 111 people selected to become members of a pool for temporary, entry-level jobs in local businesses in a Southern town. Mean age was 29.64, 64% were male, 82% were White (all remaining individuals were African Americans). | Supervisory ratings of "reliability" on the first assigned temporary job. Psychometric analyses provided the following 3-point scale: 0 = *performed unreliably* (34% of sample); 1 = *performed reliably* (e.g., accepted offer of temporary employment but failed to show up for assignment; did not complete assignment—61% of sample); 2 = *engaged in blatantly unreliable behavior* (e.g., threatened supervisor, falsely claimed to be injured—5% of sample). | Aggressive people are predisposed to engage in deviant, delinquent, retaliatory, dysfunctional, and obstructive behaviors, which typically earn them the label of *unreliable* (Hogan & Hogan, 1989). Aggression is an intrinsic component of unreliability because deviance, delinquency, retribution, and the like often involve intentionally hostile attempts to harm an organization by exacting revenge and retaliation in ways that disrupt work schedules, impede productivity, weaken morale, undermine authority, and encourage rebelliousness (James, 1998). |
| 9. 95 undergraduates from a Northwestern University; 55% were female, and 38% were Asian, 4% were Hispanic, 1% were African American, and 57% were White. | Theft of prizes reserved for members of the winning group (Group A; $n = 47$) by members of the losing group (Group B; $n = 95$). After completing CRT-As and psychological profiling tasks, members of Group A were given prizes (e.g., CD-ROMs) for correctly identifying a greater proportion of antisocial profiles. After members of Group A and the experimenter left the room, six members of Group B (6.3%) stole a prize (witnessed by confederate in Group B). | Profiling task for winning Group A was clearly easier than profiling task for losing Group B, which would fuel feelings of inequity and anger among members of Group B. Aggressively disposed Group B members would retaliate (e.g., get revenge) against experimenter by stealing a prize. |

| 10. | 191 undergraduate males from a Southeastern university who participated in intramural basketball. Almost all participants were White. | Number of hard fouls committed (personal foul where opponent is knocked to ground) and fights started by a player; 15 players (8%) engaged in at least one such physical altercation during five-game season. | Aggressive individuals are more likely than nonaggressive individuals to engage in physical attacks. |
| 11. | 191 undergraduates from a Southwestern university; 70% were female and most were White. Full study reported in Russell and James (2008); summary reported in James et al. (2005). | Lack of truthfulness and cheating on an IBS. Students completed an online, multiple-choice math test, ostensibly to evaluate a new assessment procedure. Unknown to students, the procedure was controlled by an IBS that frustrated their attempts to take the test by creating "program errors" (e.g., login failures, sending false messages, failing to respond to commands). The IBS also recorded retaliatory actions, including whether students (a) stated that they had read the instructions when they had not, (b) used a test key (they thought was mistakenly provided) to change answers, and/or (c) falsely reported that they had completed the test (to end their participation). | Aggressive students would be frustrated and angry about being repeatedly subjected to program errors, which would trigger a desire to retaliate against the Internet test. Aggression would be expressed by lying about the extent of their participation and/or taking advantage of the opportunity to cheat. Approximately 7% of the students engaged in two of the possible actions, and an additional 31% engaged in one of the possible actions; 62% did not react aggressively. |

(continues)

## TABLE 4.5
### Criterion and Hypotheses for 14 Validation Samples  *(Continued)*

| Sample | Criterion | Hypothesis |
|---|---|---|
| 12. 113 undergraduate and graduate males and 70 undergraduate and graduate females from a Southeastern university who participated in intramural basketball (in a different year than Study 10 above); 78% of the participants were Caucasian, 16% were African American, and the remainder (6%) represented a number of other races. Study reported in Frost et al. (2007). | Overt aggression—the behavior is of a physical or active nature and the aggressor's intention to harm the target person is blatant or unconcealed (e.g., pushing, shoving, tripping, or fighting with another player, and threats of physical violence) | Aggressive individuals are more likely than nonaggressive individuals to engage in overt aggression. |
| 13. 225 undergraduates from a Southeastern University. 49% were female, and almost all were White. Same sample as employed in Study 5, but the criterion assessment and the validation analyses for this study were conducted by a different group of investigators (Bing, Stewart, et al., 2007). Thus, the study was treated separately. This raises issues of independence, but the experimental independence of the criteria moderates any problem that might be engendered by correlated errors. | Traffic violations. Police records were searched 2 years after conditional reasoning tests were taken. Violations criterion more heavily weighted toward moving violations and the more serious parking violations (e.g., parking in loading zones). Number of traffic violations ranged from 0 to 47 with a mean of 3.87 ($SD = 5.25$); 73 % of sample had a least one violation. | Elevated numbers of traffic violations show a disregard for social norms and should be significantly related to the social discounting component of aggression. |

14. 184 adults (78% female) employed in various capacities in a hospital in the Southeast. Jobs included physical therapists, laboratory technicians, managers, administrators, and nurses. Average age was 41.41 years (*SD* = 11.59) and average job tenure was 7.47 years (*SD* = 6.63).

Active deviance. Average of 3.86 peers rated each employee on active organizational deviance (e.g., took property from work without permission) and active interpersonal deviance (e.g., acted rudely at work). Intraclass-correlation-based estimates of the consistencies of the mean ratings were .27 and .40, respectively. Active deviance is the average score on these two rating measures.

Aggressive individuals are more likely than nonaggressive individuals to engage in active workplace deviance (see discussion in text).

*Note.* Studies 1 through 11 are summarized in James et al. (2005). VCRT-A = Verbal/Visual Conditional Reasoning Test for Aggression; IBS = Internet-based simulation. Adapted from "A Conditional Reasoning Measure for Aggression," by L. R. James, M. D. McIntyre, C. A. Glisson, P. D. Green, T. W. Patton, J. M. LeBreton, . . . L. J. Williams, 2005, *Organizational Research Methods, 8,* pp. 81–84. Copyright 2005 by Sage Publications, Inc. Adapted with permission.
[a]No conditional reasoning test was used for selection in any of the industrial validation studies. Tests were generally administered during the hiring process or just after selection during orientation/initial training.

## TABLE 4.6
### Uncorrected Validities for Scores on Conditional Reasoning Tests for Aggression

| Study no. and criterion | n | Sample | Instrument | Experimental design | Uncorrected validity[a] |
|---|---|---|---|---|---|
| 1. Supervisory rating—overall performance | 140 | Patrol officers | CRT[b] | Concurrent[c] | −.49* |
| 2. Absences—lack of class attendance | 188 | Undergraduates | CRT | Predictive[d] | .37* |
| 3. Lack of truthfulness about extra credit | 60 | Undergraduates | VCRT | Experiment | .49* |
| 4. Absences—lack of work attendance | 97 | Nuclear facility operators | CRT | Postdictive[e] | .42* |
| 5. Student conduct violations | 225 | Undergraduates | VCRT | Postdictive | .55* |
| 6. Attrition | 135 | Restaurant employees | CRT | Predictive | .32* |
| 7. Absences—lack of work attendance | 105 | Package handlers | CRT-A | Predictive | .34* |
| 8. Work unreliability | 111 | Temporary employees | CRT-A | Predictive | .43* |
| 9. Theft | 95 | Undergraduates | CRT-A | Experiment | .64* |
| 10. Hard fouls and fights in intramural basketball | 191 | Undergraduates | CRT-A | Predictive | .38* |
| 11. Lying and cheating in Internet-based simulation | 191 | Undergraduates | CRT-A | Predictive | .40* |
| 12. Overt aggression in intramural basketball | 183 | Undergraduates and graduate students | CRT-A | Predictive | |
| 13. Traffic violations | 225 | Undergraduates | VCRT | Predictive | .54* |
| 14. Active deviance | 184 | Hospital employees | CRT-A | Concurrent | .22* |
| | | | | | .11 |

*Note.* CRT = Conditional Reasoning Test; CRT-A = Conditional Reasoning Test for Aggression; VCRT-A = Verbal/Visual Conditional Reasoning Test of Aggression. Adapted from "A Conditional Reasoning Measure for Aggression," by L. R. James, M. D. McIntyre, C. A. Glisson, P. D. Green, T. W. Patton, J. M. LeBreton, . . . L. J. Williams, 2005, *Organizational Research Methods, 8,* p. 88. Copyright 2005 by Sage Publications. Adapted with permission.

[a]All correlations are based on a priori scoring of CR instrument or cross-validation. *Uncorrected* means not corrected for either range restriction or attenuation due to unreliability in either the predictor or the criterion. *Concurrent* means that predictor and criterion data were collected at approximately the same time. [b]Developmental form of CRT-A. [c]*Concurrent* means that predictor and criterion data were collected at approximately the same time. [d]*Predictive* denotes that predictor data were collected before criterion data. [e]*Postdictive* refers to the use of archival criterion data to validate a contemporaneous predictor.
*p < .05

the first three or four of these studies in an early manuscript, but reviewers were concerned with the low base rates for aggression on both the CR tests and the criteria. In addition, the validities tended to run on the high side for personality (greater than an absolute value of .30—see Mischel, 1968) when correctly estimated using procedures (e.g., biserial correlations) that are not constrained to provide low values with low base rates (e.g., point-biserial correlations).

Basically, to publish we had to build a compendium of studies that replicated our moderate to strong validities across a series of studies, each of which had low base rates on aggression. This took approximately 7 years. Over this period we combined 11 individual studies, each with a publishable validity in normal circumstances, into a compendium of 11 studies. These are the first 11 studies in Tables 4.5 and 4.6. Only recently have we had single sample studies published (Frost et al., 2007; Russell & James, 2008).

Prior to discussing the samples and validities in Tables 4.5 and 4.6, we need to address a concern that has long troubled many investigators of human aggression: What constitutes an appropriate behavioral indicator of aggression? The discussion in this section is drawn from James et al. (2005) and focuses on measuring aggressive behavior in the workplace. We believe this discussion generalizes to many other social situations.

### Behavioral Manifestations of Aggression

The most dramatic manifestations of aggression are violent acts meant to be highly injurious to a target. However, acts such as physical assault and homicide have extremely low base rates and constitute only a fraction of the behaviors that are meant to harm others (cf. Baron & Richardson, 1994; Borum, 1996). For example, according to the FBI, there were approximately 14,000 murders in the United States in 2009 (U.S. Department of Justice, 2009). This number may seem quite high until we remember that roughly 300 million people reside in the United States. And, assuming that all murders were committed by different individuals, we obtain a base rate that translates into roughly 4.7 murders per 100,000 inhabitants.

Below, we review discussions of other less extreme forms of aggression that manifest at a base rate making prediction more feasible. These discussions were written for workplace contexts. However, we believe that they generally apply to nonwork environments as well. Their message is thus applicable to the six workplace studies in Table 4.6 as well as to the eight laboratory and field studies conducted in academic contexts.

Folger and Baron (1996) had the following to say about the overall domain of aggressive behaviors for industry:

> Some workplace aggression research concentrates on physical forms of assault of an active and direct nature. . . . Such assaults have the flavor

of high drama, but they *do not adequately represent the full gamut of work-place aggression*. Clearly, additional research should address other forms of aggression, such as the passive and indirect variety. (p. 70; italics added)

Folger and Baron suggested that one of the reasons that research has failed to devote attention to the passive and indirect forms of aggression is that investigators have "failed to view these behaviors as aggressive" (p. 70). Of particular concern here is that hostile intentions are easily concealed, and thus what is truly an aggressive behavior (e.g., theft, not showing up for work) is attributed to non-hostile motives, such as personal gain or laziness. However, the behavior may in fact be intended to harm (e.g., to exact retaliation or revenge for a perceived injustice by impeding productivity or undermining authority—cf. Skarlicki & Folger, 1997) and thus can certainly be fully or partially an act of aggression for many people. Neuman and Baron (1998) made this point rather forcefully with respect to a manifestation of aggression they refer to as *obstructionism*:

> With respect to obstructionism, people do fail to return phone calls, show up late for meetings, absent themselves from work, and delay action on important matters for reasons totally unrelated to aggression. However, when these acts are motivated by malicious intent (*as may often be the case*), their effects can be quite damaging to individuals and organizations (p. 399; italics added).

In addition to obstructionism (e.g., unresponsiveness, habitual absenteeism, habitual tardiness, procrastination), easily concealed, nondramatic forms of passive and/or indirect aggression include early and disruptive quitting, theft, lying, low job performance, unreliability, asocial conduct, subtle sabotage of projects or machinery, vandalism, spreading rumors, and failure to issue timely warnings of impending physical or financial danger (cf. Ambrose, Seabright, & Schminke, 2002; Baron & Richardson, 1994; Buss, 1961; Diefendorff & Mehta, 2007; Iverson & Deery, 2001; Judge, Scott, & Ilies, 2006; Neuman & Baron, 1998; O'Leary-Kelly et al., 1996; Roberts, Harms, Caspi, & Moffitt, 2007). Skarlicki and Folger (1997) included many of these behaviors in what they designated *organizational retaliatory behaviors*, or ORBs, which are negative workplace behaviors "used to punish the organization and its representatives in response to perceived unfairness" (p. 435; see also Greenberg, 1990, 1996, 2002). Not only are aggressive individuals more likely to perceive unfairness (Douglas & Martinko, 2001), but they also are more likely to experience the emotions of anger, outrage, and resentment, which engender the desires to impose "harmful consequences" or to "respond destructively" toward an organization (Skarlicki & Folger, 1997, p. 435).

Other research supports our position that aggression is one of the explanatory constructs underlying our criteria. One such line is *deviant workplace behavior*, which Bennett and Robinson (2000) defined as "voluntary behavior that violates significant organizational norms and, in so doing, *threatens the well-being* of the organization or its members, or both" (p. 349, italics added). Included among the developmental deviance measures were theft, absences, falsification of receipts (lying), and low and unreliable job performance. Our criteria can also be linked to aggression via studies of (a) counterproductive performance, which is defined as "voluntary behavior that *harms the well-being* of the organization" and includes behaviors such as absences, theft, and low productivity (Rotundo & Sackett, 2002, p. 69; italics added); (b) dysfunctional resistance tactics, which consist of passive-aggressive behaviors such as pretending not to hear a request (Tepper, Duffy, & Shaw, 2001, p. 975); and (c) displaced aggression, which consists of attempts to harm organizations by engaging in passive-aggressive behaviors such as absenteeism, tardiness, and withdrawal (especially early withdrawal; Pearson, 1998).

In sum, aggression is an integral component of organizational retribution, counterproductive performance, dysfunctional resistance tactics, obstructive behaviors, workplace deviance, and displaced aggression. This is because many, if not most, deviant, retaliatory, counterproductive, dysfunctionally resistant, obstructive, and displaced behaviors involve intentionally hostile attempts to harm an organization or its constituents by exacting retribution, revenge, and retaliation in ways that disrupt work schedules, impede productivity, weaken morale, undermine authority, encourage rebelliousness, and "get even" with a boss or coworkers. These processes seldom involve outright violence or other acts that are easily detectable—and punishable—as aggression. Rather, they focus on indirect, passive-aggressive behaviors such as failing to come to work or coming to work late, stealing from those seen as guilty of injustices (to exact restitution), lying to authority figures (to regain face and obtain retribution for being disrespected), and performing in poor, unreliable, or improper manners.

The preceding discussion indicates that it is reasonable to regard the criteria for the workplace studies in Table 4.6 as relevant indicators of aggression. There is no claim that aggression is the only latent construct underlying these behaviors or that these behaviors exhaust the domain of aggression. Nonetheless, these behaviors have often been used as behavioral indicators of workplace aggression and should suffice as "important external variables" (Ozer, 1999) on which to conduct the initial validation studies for the CR measures of aggression. We also note that these criteria are vital to research on human performance in organizations and that the facility to predict them is an important contribution of the CR approach. Finally, to the extent that these behaviors are shaped by factors other than aggression, the probability of finding comparatively strong validity coefficients is reduced.

We believe that the general message, along with the caveats of the preceding discussion, applies to nonwork contexts. Behaviors intended to harm others encompass a huge domain of actions. We attempted to capture some of the more dramatic forms of physical aggression with Studies 10 and 12.

However, none of our criteria encompass the extreme forms of aggression found in criminal samples or clinical samples. Nonetheless, we believe that our results are relevant to the vast majority of behavioral incidences of aggression that occur in everyday life. Moreover, the results reported here may be indicative of what can be expected in future research on criminal and clinical samples.

*Results of 14 Empirical Validation Studies*

With reference to Tables 4.5 and 4.6, we predicted that people who were implicitly prepared to justify aggression, as determined by high scores on one of the CR tests for aggression, would have a significantly greater probability of engaging in aggressive acts (past, present, and future) than people with low or moderate scores on a CR test. Results supported this prediction. Individuals whose scores indicated that justification mechanisms for aggression were instrumental in shaping their reasoning had significantly greater probabilities of engaging in behavioral manifestations of aggression than individuals whose scores indicated that these same justification mechanisms were not instrumental in guiding reasoning.

Table 4.5 presents an overview of samples, criteria, and hypotheses involved in the 14 validation studies. A number of the studies were conducted on undergraduates in large state universities, generally from psychology or business courses. Other studies were based on samples from working populations, including federal patrol officers, nuclear facility operators, restaurant employees, package handlers, pools of temporary employees, and hospital employees. Data were provided by laboratory studies, field experiments, and correlational field studies. Criteria involve a gamut of the behavioral manifestations of aggression discussed earlier.

For example, Study 3 was a field experiment involving 60 students from an introductory psychology course. The students consented to complete the VCRT, which consisted of 12 CR problems at the time of the study, and the Jackson Personality Research Form (PRF; Jackson, 1984). When the students reported to a classroom at 1:00 p.m. to participate in the experiment, they were kept waiting 10 min for latecomers to arrive. The VCRT, which took a little over 15 min, was then administered. This was followed by administration of the 300-item PRF, which could be finished in 20 to 25 min if respondents worked diligently. At 1:45 p.m. the students were told that the room was scheduled for another group at 2:00 p.m., so they would have to work quickly. A similar announcement was made at 1:55 p.m. A few minutes before 2:00, the students were asked to stop and fill in a slip for extra-credit points. The experimenter had presigned the slips, and students were asked to drop their completed slips in a box on the way out.

To fill in the slip, the students had to indicate how many extra-credit points they deserved. Departmental rules, well-advertised and well-known to students, granted 5 points for having participated in an experiment lasting 1 hr or less (the case here) or 10 points for an experiment lasting more than 1 hr. The hypothesis was that students with the higher scores on the VCRT would be more likely than students with lower scores to misrepresent the extra credit they deserved. The rationale for this hypothesis is as follows.

Students were in general unhappy with the extra-credit system because it was overloaded. This was in part a problem of students waiting until the end of the semester to chase what few extra-credit points were still available (this study was purposely conducted late in the semester). Being kept waiting for 10 min, being surprised with an announcement of having only 15 min remaining to finish, and being consistently reminded to work quickly were designed to further trigger anger and resentment (e.g., hostile attributions, victimization, social discounting) on the part of aggressively motivated individuals. This in turn was expected to stimulate propensities of aggressive students to "fight back" or "get even," perhaps even to seek retribution for having been tyrannized, by misrepresenting extra credit.

Nine of the 60 students (15%) misrepresented (i.e., were untruthful about) their points. As shown in Table 4.6, support was obtained for the hypothesis that the higher the score on the VCRT, the greater the likelihood of being untruthful. The biserial correlation between lack of truthfulness about extra credit and the CR score was .49. This validity was based on a priori scoring of the measurement instrument for CR. None of the PRF scores correlated significantly with untruthfulness, a point we address later in this chapter.

Two brief notes are in order. First, this study exemplifies the need to employ statistics that are not constrained to low values due to low base rates (i.e., $p = .15$). As discussed earlier, the biserial correlation was reported because of the low base rate for lack of truthfulness. The maximum value of the point-biserial correlation is seriously restricted when, as here, the point of dichotomy departs from .50. The biserial correlation, on the other hand, is less affected by the point of dichotomy and is more likely to generalize to a new sample (Lord & Novick, 1968). An argument can also be made that the measured dichotomy for truthfulness is actually a manifestation of a continuous latent variable that varies from highly truthful to never truthful. Second, dichotomous criteria are often associated with heteroscedasticity, which does not affect parameter estimation but is prone to produce too generous a test of significance. A logistic regression was conducted to ensure statistical accuracy of the significance test. This analysis supported the significance of the relationship between VCRT scores and (lack of) truthfulness.

A second example involves a field correlational study, also using students. In a study of intramural basketball (Study 12, Frost et al., 2007), 183 undergraduate and graduate students (113 males, 70 females) completed the CRT-A and the Angry Hostility Scale of the NEO-PI-R (a self-report or "explicit" measure of personality; Costa & McCrae, 1992) at the beginning of the basketball season. Each player was then tracked over the intramural season to determine the extent to which she or he engaged in multiple forms of aggression, the most hostile and clearly aggressive being *overt aggression*, defined thus: The behavior is of a physical or active nature and the aggressor's intention to harm the target person is blatant or unconcealed (e.g., pushing, shoving, tripping, or fighting with another player, and threats of physical violence).

On average, 17 out of 183 students (9%) had a score of 1 or more at the end of the intramural season on each of the aggression measures (see later discussion). The total number of games played by any given player ranged from three to nine with a mean of 4.66 ($SD = 1.34$). The mean playing time indicated that the average player in the sample played more than 15 minutes in four games. The distribution on each criterion was rescaled to protect against scores at the tails of the distributions (i.e., outliers) having undue influences on correlations. Correlational estimators appropriate to these transformations were employed (Jöreskog & Sörbom, 2005; Olsson, Drasgow, & Dorans, 1982). Gender and playing time were controlled when estimating correlations.

It is important to note that not all personal fouls, hard fouls, or technical fouls were considered acts of aggression. Behaviors on the court were only considered acts of aggression if they were "excessive" or outside the realm of acceptable, competitive behavior in basketball. For instance, hard fouls were tracked and defined as fouls that knocked an opponent to the ground, but not every foul where an opponent gets knocked down is executed with the intent to harm. Researcher observers were asked only to describe those "fouls that knocked an opponent to the ground" when the contact was obviously excessive or flagrant in nature.

Overt aggressive behaviors correlated significantly with both the CRT-A and the Angry Hostility Scale ($rs = .54$ and $.38$, respectively). A test for differences between dependent correlations (Neter, Wasserman, & Kutner, 1990) indicated that the CRT-A was a significantly stronger predictor of overt aggression than the self-report personality variable ($p < .01$).

Tables 4.5 and 4.6 include only one criterion per study. Current meta-analytic strategies recommend that when multiple criteria are involved, one should compute an average or composite validity for a predictor. When multiple criteria were collected, we chose instead to include the validity for the criterion that appeared most indicative of aggression, which in this study was overt aggression. This strategy did not always maximize the reported validity. For example, the reported validity in Table 4.6 for overt aggression in Study 12 is .54, yet the correlation between the CRT-A and a criterion measure of passive aggression was .61 ($p < .01$). Later in the chapter we return to a discussion comparing validities for the CR tests and self-report measures against various criteria.

The two illustrative studies above suggest that the CR tests for aggression are often, but not always, good predictors of behavioral indicators of aggression. Inspection of the absolute values of the 14 empirical validity studies in Table 4.6 reveals that validities for CR tests ranged from a low of .11 (not significant) to a high of .64 and had an unweighted mean of .41. If we were to follow current convention and correct .41 for such things as unreliability in the criterion and range restriction in the predictor (e.g., Schmidt & Hunter, 1998), then the .41 could surpass .60, depending on the assumptions used for corrections. However, the observed values in Table 4.6 reflect what can be expected practically, and operationally, in regard to the use of the CR tests in applications such as employee selection and placement, and thus we maintain a focus on observed values.

To put a mean validity of .41 in perspective, consider that both past and current reviews indicate that validities produced by predicting behavioral criteria from self-report, projective, and other, new implicit measures of personality peak out at individual correlations of approximately .40, with the vast majority of individual correlations falling below .30 (see Meyer et al., 2001). Average observed validities often can run as low as .12 to .14 (Barrick & Mount, 1991; Hurtz and Donovan, 2000). A mean correlation of .41 that comes from a distribution of correlations with many individual correlations over .40 suggests that CR is capable of producing a comparatively strong and empirically valid system of assessment in personality.

The generally strong validities can be traced to several likely factors. These include (a) an attempt to base CR on a coherent theory of measurement, as outlined in Chapters 2 and 3 of this volume; (b) a focus on a single, well-delineated construct like aggression; (c) presenting participants with reasoning-eliciting problems that are tied directly to specific justification mechanisms; and (d) capitalization on psychometric aggregation principles to cancel out largely random error across CR problems.

## Correlations Between Critical Intellectual Skills and Scores on Conditional Reasoning Tests

Correlations between scores on CR tests for aggression and critical intellectual skills were obtained on nine studies of undergraduates from different universities. The correlations presented in Table 4.7 are from James et al. (2005) and LeBreton et al. (2007). Measurement of critical intellectual skills was based on scores from tests developed by American College Testing Program, Inc. (ACT scores). Scores were obtained from student records after obtaining informed consent from the students.

Of initial note is that there is no theoretical reason to expect a correlation between CR for aggression and intelligence. If a correlation were observed, then critical intellectual skills might in some way be confounded with responses

### TABLE 4.7
#### Correlations Between Critical Intellectual Skills and Scores on Conditional Reasoning Tests for Aggression

| Study | Composition | Correlation* |
|---|---|---|
| 2 | 188 undergraduates | −.06 |
| 3 | 60 undergraduates | −.05 |
| 5 and 13 | 225 undergraduates | −.08 |
| 11 | 191 undergraduates | .02 |
| LeBreton et al. (2007) | 832 undergraduates | .06 |
| LeBreton et al. (2007) | 295 undergraduates | −.06 |
| LeBreton et al. (2007) | 268 undergraduates | −.03 |
| LeBreton et al. (2007) | 144 undergraduates | −.03 |
| LeBreton et al. (2007) | 86 undergraduates | −.16 |

*$p < .05$

to the CR problems. For example, NA alternatives might in some rational way, perceptible by intelligent respondents, be "more logical" than the AG alternatives. However, all nine correlations were nonsignificant, indicating that no such confounding took place.

## Correlations Between Gender and Scores on Conditional Reasoning Tests for Aggression

Correlations between gender and scores on CR tests are presented in Table 4.8. Results indicated that CR did not correlate significantly with gen-

### TABLE 4.8
#### Relationships Between Gender and Scores on Conditional Reasoning Tests for Aggression

| Study | Composition | Proportion female | Biserial correlation |
|---|---|---|---|
| 2 | 188 undergraduates | .34 | −.10 |
| 3 | 60 undergraduates | .60 | −.29* |
| 5 and 13 | 225 undergraduates | .49 | −.25* |
| 6 | 120 restaurant employees | .66 | −.08 |
| 7 | 105 package handlers | .26 | .05 |
| 8 | 111 temporary employees | .36 | .09 |
| 9 | 95 undergraduates | .55 | .00 |
| 12 | 183 undergraduates | .38 | −.09 |
| LeBreton et al. (2007) | 316 undergraduates | .49 | .01 |
| LeBreton et al. (2007) | 107 undergraduates | .29 | −.15 |

*Note.* Male = 0, female = 1. Adapted from "A Conditional Reasoning Measure for Aggression," by L. R. James, M. D. McIntyre, C. A. Glisson, P. D. Green, T. W. Patton, J. M. LeBreton, . . . L. J. Williams, 2005, *Organizational Research Methods, 8,* p. 92. Copyright 2005 by Sage Publications. Adapted with permission. *$p < .05$.

der in eight out of 10 studies from published papers. Correlations in two studies indicated a tendency for young, adult, educationally motivated males to have slightly higher scores than young, adult, educationally motivated females. This tendency was not consistent across all undergraduate samples and did not extend to workplace samples. In all, a generally low and non-significant correlation between gender and scores on CR tests for aggression is indicated.

These results may seem surprising to those familiar with the often modest but significant correlations between gender and self-reported measures of aggression, correlations revealing that females see themselves as less aggressive than males (see Hyde, 2005). In contrast, our results for implicit aggression appear to parallel findings by Bornstein (1998), wherein males did not differ significantly from females on an implicit measure of dependency. Differences were found, however, between males and females on an explicit measure of dependency, and these differences were related to behavioral manifestations of dependency.

Extrapolating from Bornstein, it may be that males and females do not differ on implicit aggression (i.e., both males and females have developed justification mechanisms). Differences do occur in explicit self-beliefs, where (a) females think of themselves as being less aggressive than males because of (b) socialization practices based directly or indirectly on social stereotypes that characterize women as less aggressive than men. These self-beliefs are channeled into aggressive behaviors, especially those that have a more instrumental or controlled component. This, of course, is a hypothesis and in need of investigation.

An additional analysis was made to search for possible differences in scores due to gender on the CR problems. This analysis consisted of an examination for differential item functioning (DIF) due to gender (Ko, Shim, & Roberts, 2008). The DIF analysis sought to determine if a gender difference existed on responses to each of the 22 CRT-A problems that could not be explained by group differences in the underlying three factors identified in the factor analysis. The occurrence of DIF signifies gender differences on a CR problem that is irrelevant to the construct being measured.

The sample used to test for DIF consisted of 2,119 individuals from the nine CRT-A studies on which we had gender data. A nonparametric DIF assessment method for polytomous (graded) test items was employed for the DIF analysis. One problem out of the 22 CRT-A problems showed possible DIF. The index of DIF (B= +0.187) indicated that (a) the severity of DIF was "mild" (Ko et al., 2008) and (b) that males were more aggressive than females (for this problem). The CR problem evidencing the mild DIF was:

> American cars have gotten better in the last 15 years. American car makers started to build better cars when they began to lose business to

the Japanese. Many American buyers thought that foreign cars were better made.

Which of the following is the most logical conclusion based on the above?

A. America was the world's largest producer of airplanes 15 years ago.
B. Swedish car makers lost business in America 15 years ago.
C. The Japanese knew more than Americans about building good cars 15 years ago.
D. American car makers built cars to wear out 15 years ago, so they could make a lot of money selling parts.

Alternative C is the nonaggressive response, whereas alternative D is the aggressive response.

Basically, the findings indicate that males had a weak tendency to evidence more aggression than females on this problem, and this tendency could not be explained by the underlying factor on which this problem loaded. Stated alternatively, part of the difference between males and females on this problem is irrelevant to the constructs being measured by the CRT-A. Ko, Shim, and Roberts (2008) surmised that the weak proclivity toward aggressiveness on this problem could likely be traced to differences between males and females in either knowledge of automobiles or interest in automobiles, or both. The most salient point for the present discussion was that no consistent DIF was found for gender for 21 of the 22 CRT-A problems.

### Estimated Relationships Between Race and Scores on Conditional Reasoning Tests for Aggression

Race has been and continues to be unrelated to the scores on the CR tests for aggression (James et al., 2005). Results based on seven samples from published studies are reported in Table 4.9. The nonsignificant biserial correlations in Studies 2 and 8 indicated that mean scores on CR tests did not differ significantly between African Americans and Whites. The nonsignificant F tests in the remaining five studies had similar implications. There is thus no indication that different races are more or less likely to score differently on implicit readiness to justify aggression.

### Correlations Between Self-Report Measures of Aggression and Scores on Conditional Reasoning Tests

In Chapter 1, we noted the consistent finding that self-report measures of conscious (explicit) personality have a history of low and often nonsignif-

TABLE 4.9

Relationships Between Race and Scores on Conditional
Reasoning Tests for Aggression

| Study | Composition | Proportion | Race | Relationship |
|-------|-------------|------------|------|--------------|
| 2 | 188 undergraduates | .90 | White (0) | $r = 0.10^a$ |
| | | .10 | African American (1) | |
| 7 | 105 package handlers | .23 | White | $F = 1.43$ |
| | | .52 | African American | |
| | | .24 | Hispanic | |
| | | .01 | Asian | |
| 8 | 111 temporary employees | .82 | White (0) | $r = 0.10^a$ |
| | | .18 | African American (1) | |
| 9 | 95 undergraduates | .57 | White | $F = 0.16$ |
| | | .38 | Asian | |
| | | .04 | Hispanic | |
| | | .01 | African American | |
| LeBreton et al. (2007) | 381 undergraduates | .29 | African American | $F = 0.98$ |
| | | .52 | White | |
| | | .02 | Hispanic | |
| | | .04 | Asian | |
| | | .01 | Native American | |
| | | .12 | Other | |
| LeBreton et al. (2007) | 316 undergraduates | .04 | African American | $F = 0.58$ |
| | | .91 | White | |
| | | .01 | Hispanic | |
| | | .03 | Asian | |
| LeBreton et al. (2007) | 75 undergraduates | .32 | African American | $F = 2.10$ |
| | | .52 | White | |
| | | .01 | Hispanic | |
| | | .03 | Asian | |
| | | .12 | Other | |

*Note.* Adapted from "A Conditional Reasoning Measure for Aggression," by L. R. James, M. D. McIntyre, C. A. Glisson, P. D. Green, T. W. Patton, J. M. LeBreton, . . . L. J. Williams, 2005, *Organizational Research Methods*, *8*, p. 92. Copyright 2005 by Sage Publications. Adapted with permission.
[a]Biserial correlation.
*$p < .05$

icant correlations with various measures of implicit personality, however implicit personality is assessed (see Bornstein, 2002; Greenwald & Banaji, 1995; McClelland et al., 1989). This pattern of modest relationships between explicit and implicit measures extended to the CR tests for aggression. As shown in Table 4.10, scores on CR tests shared no more, and typically less

## TABLE 4.10
### Correlations Between Scores on Conditional Reasoning Tests and Self-Report Measures of Aggression

| Study | Composition | Self-report measure | Correlation |
|-------|-------------|---------------------|-------------|
| 3 | 60 undergraduates | PRF Aggression | .14 |
| | | PRF Dominance | .05 |
| | | PRF Impulsivity | .11 |
| 5 and 13 | 225 undergraduates | NEO-PI-R Angry Hostility | .26* |
| | | NEO-PI-R Dutifulness[a] | −.18* |
| 9 | 95 undergraduates | Aggression Questionnaire[b] | .24* |
| 10 | 191 undergraduates | NEO-PI-R Angry Hostility | .01 |
| 12 | 183 undergraduates | NEO-PI-R Angry Hostility | .06 |
| 14 | 184 hospital employees | PRF Aggression | .23* |
| | | HPI Reliability | .14* |

*Note.* PRF = Personality Research Form (Jackson, 1967); NEO-PI-R = NEO Personality Inventory–Revised (Costa & McCrae, 1992); HPI = Hogan Personality Inventory (Hogan & Hogan, 1995). Adapted from "A Conditional Reasoning Measure for Aggression," by L. R. James, M. D. McIntyre, C. A. Glisson, P. D. Green, T. W. Patton, J. M. LeBreton, . . . L. J. Williams, 2005, *Organizational Research Methods, 8,* p. 93. Copyright 2005 by Sage Publications, Inc. Adapted with permission.
[a]An indicator of low aggressiveness. [b]Buss & Perry, 1992.
*$p < .05$

than, 7% of their variance with self-ascriptions of aggression from recognized self-report personality inventories. Bornstein (2002) suggested that the likely reason for the modest relationships between implicit and explicit measures is not, as psychometricians have mistakenly thought over the years, lack of convergent validity. Rather, self-reports and implicit assessments measure complementary aspects of traits, motives, and need states (i.e., explicit and implicit aspects), and there is no simple pattern in the way these explicit and implicit components relate. Indeed, the explicit and implicit facets may conflict, one may compensate for the other, they may work in harmony, or they may work independently—it depends on the constructs and the people.

This is clearly an issue for future research. Readers are referred to excellent new theories regarding interfaces between explicit and implicit measurements in Bornstein (2002; process dissociations models) and Winter, John, Stewart, Klohnen, and Duncan (1998; channeling models). The dissociative model is overviewed below, whereas channeling models are the subject of Chapter 5.

### Dissociative Model of Personality

The core of this model was proposed by McClelland et al. (1989; see also Koestner & McClelland, 1990; Koestner, Weinberger, & McClelland, 1991), who suggested that a low correlation between an implicit measure and an explicit measure of the same personality construct (motive to achieve, in their case) reflects not psychometric artifacts, as often believed, but different facets of personality. This proposed dissociation between the implicit and explicit components of a personality construct has been the subject of several recent studies (e.g., Bornstein, 1998, 2002; Brunstein & Maier, 2005; see also the review in Wilson et al., 2000). Results of these studies support McClelland et al.'s view that the implicit personality consists of automatically activated, unconscious forces that influence thinking and behaviors without the awareness of the individual. They further support McClelland et al.'s belief that the explicit personality consists of relatively independent (in comparison to the implicit personality), self-attributed characteristics, that is, forces that a person "openly acknowledges as being characteristic of his or her day-to-day functioning and experience" (Bornstein, 1998, p. 778).

The separation of implicit from explicit facets of personality is consistent with our description of the CRT-A as a measure of implicit biases that, unknown to individuals, influence their reasoning about the justifiability of aggression. Similarly, the various instruments that we have used to measure explicit aggression (e.g., the Angry Hostility Scale of the NEO-PI-R; Costa & McCrae, 1992) consist of these same individuals' self-attributions of whether feelings and behaviors signifying aggression are characteristic of them.

A critical aspect of the dissociation of implicit and explicit personality is McClelland et al.'s (1989) hypothesis that the implicit and explicit components of personality predict different behaviors. As described by Brunstein and Maier (2005) in relation to the implicit and explicit aspects of achievement motivation, "the implicit motive energizes spontaneous impulses to act . . . , whereas the explicit motive is expressed in deliberate choice behavior" (p. 205). These authors elaborated on these basic points by noting that the implicit motive is "affectively tinged," and "propels a person's . . . behavior in the face of challenges, . . . [whereas] the explicit motive . . . is built on a person's self-image . . . and operates as a self-regulator that shapes voluntary behavior in accordance with a person's motivational self-view" (p. 206).

We attempted to extend the idea of dissociation—that implicit and explicit measures predict different behaviors—to aggression. We used the hostile-instrumental aggression dichotomy (Anderson & Bushman, 2002; Bushman & Anderson, 2001; see also Baron & Richardson, 1994; Berkowitz, 1993) to represent the dissociative model's spontaneous (automatic) versus controlled dichotomy of behavior. *Hostile aggression* is traditionally defined as "impulsive, angry behavior that is motivated by a desire to hurt someone," whereas *instrumental aggression* "is premeditated, calculated behavior that is motivated by some other goal (e.g., obtain money, restore one's image, restore justice"; Bushman & Anderson, 2001, p. 274). In a "pure" application of the dissociative model, we would expect scores on the implicit biases assessed by the CRT-A to predict the emotional, angry, spontaneous, retaliatory behaviors that characterize hostile aggression. In contrast, we would expect people who believe that aggressive feelings and behaviors are characteristic of them to engage in more calculative forms of aggression and to consciously self-regulate voluntary behavior in accordance with their motivational self-view.

It is noteworthy that the subject of Bushman and Anderson's (2001) article was to propose that the hostile versus instrumental aggression dichotomy has "outlived its usefulness" (p. 273). Their reasoning was that many aggressive behaviors have both hot, impulsive components as well as cold, premeditated components. Our results provide partial support for this position.

We tested the dissociative model with data from the Frost et al. (2007) study, which is Study 12 in the tables. In the earlier discussion regarding Study 12, we noted that data had been collected on multiple behavioral aggression criteria for 183 female and male college intramural basketball players. Only one of the criteria was included in Tables 4.5 and 4.6. The full set of (three) aggression criteria include:

- Overt aggression—the behavior is of a physical or active nature and the aggressor's intention to harm the target person is blatant or unconcealed (e.g., pushing, shoving, tripping, or fighting with another player, and threats of physical violence).
- Obstructionism—the behavior is of a passive or covert nature, and the aggressor intends to impede an individual's ability to perform his or her duties or interfere with a group's ability to meet its objectives (e.g., standing in a player's way after the whistle, intentionally not giving the ball to the referee so play can resume).
- Verbal hostility—the behavior is primarily verbal or symbolic in nature, except for threats of physical violence (considered acts of overt aggression). Examples include loud swearing, verbal criticism or ridicule, physical gestures, mocking facial expressions, and belittling someone else's opinion.

These three classifications are based on Neuman and Baron's (1998) factor-analysis-based categories of aggression.

Means, standard deviations, and correlations for the implicit and explicit personality variables, the three behavioral (dependent) variables, and two potential control variables, gender and playing time, are presented in Table 4.11. The first five variables were positively skewed ($p < .05$), indicating a low base rate for aggression however this construct is measured. The mean CRT-A score of 4.16 indicated a slightly elevated tendency for college intramural basketball players to justify aggression in comparison to a more heterogeneous norm sample shown in Table 4.3. The mean of 19.02 on the Angry Hostility Scale also indicated a slightly elevated tendency to perceive oneself as aggressive (the Angry Hostility Scale on the NEO-PI-R has a mean of 16 and an $SD$ of 5.00; Costa & McCrae, 1992). The means for the three behavioral variables reflected the positive skews discussed above.

TABLE 4.11
Scale Intercorrelations and Descriptive Statistics

| Variable | M | SD | 1 | 2 | 3 | 4 | 5 | 6 | 7 |
|---|---|---|---|---|---|---|---|---|---|
| 1. JAGS | 4.16 | 2.15 | — | | | | | | |
| 2. A-H | 19.02 | 5.40 | .06 | — | | | | | |
| 3. Overt aggression | .25[a] | .57 | .54** | .38** | — | | | | |
| 4. Obstructionism | .14[a] | .37 | .61** | −.16* | .13 | — | | | |
| 5. Hostility | .30[a] | .61 | −.03 | .41** | .12 | −.04 | — | | |
| 6. Gender | .38 | .49 | −.09 | −.30** | −.19** | −.02 | −.31** | — | |
| 7. Playing time | 8.36 | 2.83 | .05 | .10 | .10 | .21** | .10 | −.26** | — |

*Note.* $n = 183$; JAGS = Justification of Aggression Scale; A-H = NEO Angry Hostility Scale. Reprinted from "Implicit and Explicit Personality: A Test of a Channeling Hypothesis for Aggressive Behavior," by B. C. Frost, C. E. Ko, and L. R. James, 2007, *Journal of Applied Psychology, 92*, p. 1310. Copyright 2007 by American Psychological Association.
[a]Based on the following rescaling system: 0 = person never expressed/engaged in behavior (over the course of the season); 1 = person expressed/engaged in the behavior once; 2 = person expressed/engaged in behavior two or more times.
*$p < .05$. ** $p < .01$.

The three dependent variables and playing time are technically polychotomous, ordinal representations of underlying continuous scales (e.g., number of hostile verbal expressions), gender is a dichotomous scale, and the two independent personality variables (e.g., CRT-A) are continuous scales with presumably interval properties (see Olsson, Drasgow, & Dorans, 1982, for discussions of scales). Appropriate estimators of the various types of correlations among all but the two personality variables (a Pearson $r$) involve biserial, polyserial, or polychoric correlations (Jöreskog & Sörbom, 1999). All correlations were estimated in PRELIS 2.72 (Jöreskog & Sörbom, 1999), the results of which are presented in Table 4.11.

Of initial interest are correlations with possible confounding or control variables, namely, gender and playing time. Modest but significant correlations were found between gender and explicit aggression, where females saw themselves as less aggressive than males (a common finding; see Hyde, 2005). Females were also less likely than males to engage in active forms of aggression (overt aggression and verbal hostilities). Playing time was correlated with gender, where the average male played more than the average female, and obstructiveness, which was more likely to occur for those who played longer.

Relationships with the control variables were of sufficient magnitude and breadth to warrant controlling for their influences when estimating the relationships of interest in the dissociative model. We created controls via a series of hierarchical regression analyses. Basically, we entered gender and playing time in the first step of a hierarchical regression for each of the three aggressive behaviors. The second step consisted of adding either the CRT-A or the A-H (Angry Hostility) Scale (separate regression analyses were conducted

## TABLE 4.12
### Bivariate Correlations Versus Standardized Regression Weights With Playing Time and Gender Controlled

| | Bivariate correlations | | Standardized regression weights with controls | |
|---|---|---|---|---|
| | CRT-A | A-H | CRT-A | A-H |
| Overt aggression | .54** | .38** | .53** | .35** |
| Obstructionism | .61** | −.16* | .61** | −.18* |
| Expressed hostility | −.03 | .41** | −.06 | .34** |

*Note.* CRT-A = Conditional Reasoning Test for Aggression; A-H = NEO Angry Hostility Scale.
*$p < .05$. ** $p < .01$.

for the CRT-A and A-H Scale for each criterion). We again used PRELIS to estimate correlations. Possible underestimation of standard errors, given the trichotomous, ordinal nature of the behavioral data, was addressed via the use of unweighted least-squares (Jöreskog & Sörbom, 1996; Kaplan, 2000). The standardized regression weights obtained for the CRT-A and the A-H Scale in each of the Step 2 analyses are reported in Table 4.12. Also included are the bivariate correlations from Table 4.11 for comparison purposes. It is evident that controlling for gender and playing time had little effect on relationships.

Scores on the CRT-A had a small and nonsignificant relationship with scores on the A-H Scale ($r = .06$; the CRT-A was regressed on the A-H Scale with controls for gender and playing time in effect; see Table 4.11). We begin, therefore, with an implicit-explicit relationship that is consistent with an interpretation that each scale measures a different if not independent component of personality (Bornstein, 2002; McClelland et al., 1989; Wilson et al., 2000).

Overtly aggressive behaviors related significantly to both the implicit and the explicit personality variables ($\beta$s = .53 and .35, respectively; see Table 4.12). A test for differences between dependent regression weights (Neter, Wasserman, & Kutner, 1990) indicated that the implicit personality variable was a significantly stronger predictor of overt aggression than the explicit personality variable ($p < .01$).

The regression weight linking implicit personality to obstructionism was .61 ($p < .01$), which was significant, as predicted. The regression weight linking explicit personality to obstructionism was a modest but significant −.18 ($p < .05$). The difference in dependent regression weights was again significant ($p < .01$). The negative relation between explicit personality and the measure of passive aggressiveness is noteworthy in that it suggests that passively aggressive players were rather seriously out of touch with their latent aggressive natures. These true natures, at least as they manifested in the context of intramural basketball, appeared to be better captured by the measurements of implicit personality, which produced the highest validity reported in the tables.

A reversal occurs in the previous pattern favoring implicit over explicit personality with respect to the results for verbal expressions of hostility. Verbal expressions of hostility were more strongly related to explicit personality ($\beta = .34$, $p < .01$) than with implicit personality ($\beta = -.06$, $ns$). Not only was this difference significant ($p < .01$), but also the latter weight suggests that, in this context, implicit personality has no direct, linear relationship with verbal aggression. (Tests of nonlinearity were also nonsignificant.)

The differing patterns of regression weights over the dependent variables suggest that the three aggressive behaviors were not highly, or perhaps not even modestly, related. Results reported in Table 4.11 indicate that all three of the correlations among the behavioral measures of aggression were nonsignificant. These results are consistent with the findings of Neuman and Baron (1998), who used factor analysis to identify the same three behavioral domains of aggression.

There are several ways to interpret the differential regression weights and correlations involving the aggressive behaviors, which technically are functions of predictive validities (i.e., personality was measured prior to aggressive behaviors). One alternative is that predictive efficacy reflects an underlying influence or differential weighting process involving the implicit and explicit components of dispositional tendencies, which is a central theme of the dissociative model. According to this perspective, the pattern of regression weights for verbal expressions of hostility indicates that verbal aggression is primarily under the influence of conscious, controlled, choice-making dispositional processes (i.e., the explicit personality). Conversely, passive-aggression, as represented by obstructionism, appears to be primarily under the influence of automatic, reactive, and spontaneous processes (i.e., the implicit personality). The results for passive-aggression are consistent with the predictions of the original dissociative model proposed by McClelland et al. (1989). Overt acts of aggression appear to be influenced by both the explicit and implicit personality, with implicit having the greater weight in this case.

Basically, some version of a dissociative model appeared to underlie results for each criterion. However, this conclusion is conditional; it assumes "nonintegrative" relationships in the sense that the explicit and implicit components of personality operate more or less independently to shape aggressive behavior. An alternative approach is an integrative model of aggression, which proposes that the explicit personality interacts with the implicit personality in the sense that the explicit personality channels how the implicit personality is expressed in aggressive acts (Winter et al. 1998). In fact, the implicit and explicit personality interacted strongly in this study. We return to this issue in Chapter 5 when we present and discuss channeling models of personality. In sum, the dissociative model initially appeared to be strongly supported by this study. Tests for interactions based on an integrative model of personality undermined this initial support.

## Multiple Regressions Based on Implicit and Explicit Personality

The study of dissociative relationships reported above suggests that comparisons of validities for implicit and explicit measures of personality must consider the nature of the criterion. The channeling-integrative studies reported in Chapter 5 suggest that the low correlations between implicit and explicit measures of personality often mask important interactions between the measures. Indeed, like those of Winter et al. (1998), our data indicate that implicit measures provide the motivational forces for behaviors, whereas explicit measures determine the channels (behaviors) through which those forces will be manifested. For example, two people may have a strong implicit need to aggress, but the behavioral channel for their aggression is based on their self-perceived levels of aggressiveness. The person who thinks of himself/herself as aggressive is prone to use overt channels. The person who thinks of herself/himself as nonaggressive is prone to use passive channels.

Given the accumulating knowledge of functional relationships between the implicit and explicit personalities, we are hesitant to present any more simple contrasts of validities between the measures. It is not a matter of which aspect of personality is most valid, for such a question misses the points of both dissociative and channeling models. On the other hand, zero-order validities are the starting point for more sophisticated analyses and thus need to be examined. These validities are reported in Table 4.13 for seven of the studies from Tables 4.5 and 4.6. These are the studies on which we had explicit measures of personality.

The correlations from each study in Table 4.13 were entered into a multiple regression analysis (the ACT was added for Study 3), the results of which are reported in terms of standardized regression weights. Significance of a regression weight indicates that a variable led to a significant increment in validity when added to the regression equation. Results suggest that the CR (implicit) measure contributed significantly in six of the seven studies. One or more self-report (explicit) measures contributed significantly in five of the seven studies. The implicit measure generally had the stronger validity. However, we have deleted our analyses of differences in validities because the presence of interactions between implicit and explicit measures, which we show in Chapter 5, renders such differences moot.

TABLE 4.13
Multiple Regression Analyses

| Study | Criterion | Multiple $R$ | Variable | Zero-order $r$ | Beta weight |
|---|---|---|---|---|---|
| 3 | Lack of truthfulness about extra credit | .55* | VCRT | .49* | .51* |
|   |  |  | ACT | −.07 | −.12 |
|   |  |  | PRF Aggression | .16 | .17 |
|   |  |  | PRF Impulsiveness | .14 | .14 |
|   |  |  | PRF Dominance | .05 | .04 |
| 5 | Student conduct violations | .61* | VCRT | .55* | .53* |
|   |  |  | NEO Angry Hostility | .26* | .21* |
|   |  |  | NEO Dutifulness | −.18* | −.13* |
| 9 | Theft | .70* | CRT-A | .64* | .57* |
|   |  |  | Aggression Quest. | .44* | .30* |
| 10 | Hard fouls and fights | .45* | CRT-A | .38* | .38* |
|   |  |  | NEO Angry Hostility | .22* | .22* |
| 12 | Overt aggression in basketball | .65* | CRT-A | .54* | .53* |
|   |  |  | NEO Angry Hostility | .38* | .33* |
| 13 | Traffic violations | .22* | VCRT | .22* | .22* |
|   |  |  | NEO Angry Hostility | −.02 | −.01 |
| 14 | Active deviance | .20* | CRT-A | .11 | .07 |
|   |  |  | PRF Aggression | .19* | .17* |

*Note.* VCRT = Verbal/Visual Conditional Reasoning Test; ACT = American College Testing; PRF = Personality Research Form; CRT-A = Conditional Reasoning Test for Aggression. Adapted from "A Conditional Reasoning Measure for Aggression," by L. R. James, M. D. McIntyre, C. A. Glisson, P. D. Green, T. W. Patton, J. M. LeBreton, . . . L. J. Williams, 2005, *Organizational Research Methods, 8,* p. 94. Copyright 2005 by Sage Publications. Adapted with permission.
*$p < .05$

## Setting a Nonarbitrary Metric on the CRT-A

A scale is said to be *arbitrary* when it is not known where a score on the scale locates an individual in relation to (a) an underlying psychological dimension or (b) a behavioral manifestation of the psychological dimension (Blanton & Jaccard, 2006). The metrics of many psychological scales in personality are arbitrary. This is not a huge problem when scores from the metrics are used to test theories, for here the primary question is covariation between statistical distributions. Arbitrariness of metric becomes a problem when psychologists wish "to draw inferences about the true absolute standing of a group or individual on the latent psychological dimension being measured" (Blanton & Jaccard, 2006, p. 27). Here, one wishes to make an inference about how aggressive or depressed or racially biased an individual is rather than just to describe her or his relative standing in a statistical distribution. This requires the development of nonarbitrary metrics.

In an *American Psychologist* article, Blanton and Jaccard (2006) demonstrated concerns that ensue when scores based on arbitrary metrics are treated as if they are based on nonarbitrary metrics. The illustrative test was the Implicit Association Test (IAT) for race bias, which can be taken online and purports to determine whether a respondent is unbiased or has an implicit (i.e., unconscious) preference for Blacks or Whites. The IAT attempts to measure implicit preferences via response latencies in reactions to pairings of race with positive and negative terms. The resulting scale is arbitrary, according to Blanton and Jaccard (2006), because it fails (a) to link a score on the scale to a true score on an underlying psychological dimension (e.g., latent variable) and (b) to show that changes in scores on the scale are related empirically to noticeable changes in meaningful, real-world events that represent the psychological construct in question.

It appears that new, implicit measures of attitudes and personality are to be given special scrutiny regarding arbitrary versus nonarbitrary metrics. We invite this scrutiny because it will help to show psychologists that CR tests are tied to pertinent psychological constructs. We have initiated studies designed to develop nonarbitrary, which is to say meaningful, metrics for the CRT-A. Earlier, we presented the results of factor analytic work designed to investigate the links between scores on the CRT-A and latent dimensions of justifications for aggression. We also presented results of research that showed that changes in the scores on the CRT-A are related empirically to noticeable changes in meaningful, real-world indicators of aggression. In the present section, we demonstrate how these empirical associations were used to establish a nonarbitrary metric for aggressiveness on the CRT-A. To be specific, we report on the analyses we used to determine that selection of eight or more aggressive responses on the CRT-A (on a scale of 0–22) represents a "strong" implicit cognitive readiness to aggress and thus a high probability of engaging in aggressive behaviors.

We employed data from six of the validity studies in Tables 4.5 and 4.6 (Studies 7, 8, 9, 10, 11, and 12). These studies include two work samples and four student samples (total $N = 876$) on which both CRT-A and reasonable indicators of behavioral aggression were available. The behavioral indicators of aggression included threatening supervisors, theft and aggression in basketball on the part of students, and, for employees, habitual absences from work during the first 90 days of employment. In each sample, determinations were made about what score on the criterion indicated aggressive behavior. For work samples, such determinations were based on consultations with managers (e.g., At what point does this behavior harm the organization?).

Members of each sample were then separated according to whether they were members of an aggression criterion group or a nonaggression criterion group. Scores on the CRT-A were then plotted separately for each of these two groups. The point at which the distribution of CRT-A scores for the aggression criterion group intersected with the distribution of CRT-

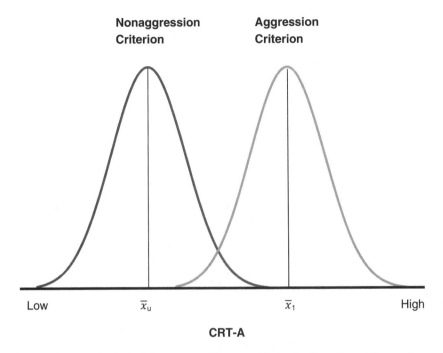

**Nonaggression
Criterion**

**Aggression
Criterion**

Low $\quad\quad\bar{x}_\mathrm{u}\quad\quad\quad\quad\quad\quad\quad\quad\bar{x}_1\quad\quad\quad$ High

**CRT-A**

*Figure 4.1.* Strategy for building a nonarbitrary metric for the Conditional Reasoning Test for Aggression. The point at which the distribution of Conditional Reasoning Test for Aggression (CRT-A) scores for the aggression criterion group intersected with the distribution of CRT-A scores for the nonaggression criterion group provided the "cutting score" or "reference point" for identifying aggressive individuals on the CRT-A scale.

A scores for the nonaggression criterion group provided the "cutting score" or "reference point" for identifying aggressive individuals on the CRT-A scale. A theoretical example of the overlapping distributions is shown in Figure 4.1.

According to Blum and Naylor (1968), this procedure furnishes the optimum cutting point on a test for distinguishing between potentially successful and unsuccessful employees. In our case, we used the procedure to map CRT-A scores onto meaningful, real-world occurrences of aggression, thus providing a foundation for establishing an empirically based, nonarbitrary metric (i.e., optimum cutting point) for distinguishing between aggressive and nonaggressive respondents on the CRT-A. We used the procedure on each of the six samples to set a nonarbitrary metric for distinguishing between aggressive and nonaggressive respondents on the CRT-A. An illustration of the results for the sample from Study 9 is presented in Figure 4.2.

The average optimum cutting point across the six samples was 8.36. We rounded to a score of 8 as the nonarbitrary cutting point for distinguishing aggressive from nonaggressive individuals on the CRT-A. Comparing this metric with the distribution of scores on the CRT-A in Table 4.3 indicates

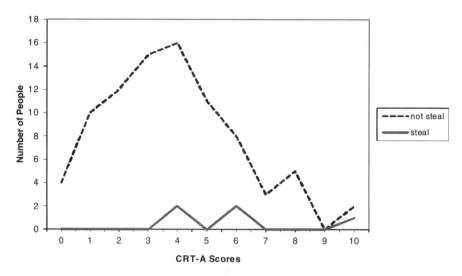

*Figure 4.2.* Nonarbitrary or optimum score based on theft criterion (Study 9). CRT-A = Conditional Reasoning Test for Aggression.

that roughly 6% of individuals would be classified as "highly aggressive." As noted earlier, this is good news for society, and it is also good news for institutions or organizations that might use the CRT-A to screen out candidates (e.g., for a job, athletic scholarship) because only a very small portion of the applicant pool would be removed. However, that small proportion also appears to be the one most responsible for acts of aggression.

## Faking Studies on Conditional Reasoning

A topic that is often raised in applied and high-stakes testing contexts is the extent to which personality assessments are susceptible to faking, intentional response distortion, and impression-management strategies. This topic has been researched extensively using self-report personality inventories (cf. Hogan, Barrett, & Hogan, 2007; Hough, Eaton, Dunnette, Kamp, & McCloy, 1990; Ones & Viswesvaran, 1998; Ones, Viswesvaran, & Reiss, 1996; Rosse, Stecher, Miller, & Levin, 1998; Snell, Sydell, & Lueke, 1999). Such research has documented that most respondents are able to "fake good" or "fake bad" on self-reports when instructed to do so. This intentional response distortion typically results in (a) a decrease in scale variance (i.e., scores tend to be clustered at the "good" or "bad" end of the response continuum), (b) an increase in scale score means (i.e., means shift toward a "good" or "bad" average), and (c) increased collinearity among scales (cf. Hough et al., 1990; Viswesvaran & Ones, 1999; Zickar & Robie, 1999).

Investigators are split on whether such changes pose a serious problem. For example, some researchers argue that intentional response distortion does not result in attenuated criterion-related validity coefficients (Barrick & Mount, 1996; Hough et al., 1990; Ones & Viswesvaran, 1998), it does not produce a pronounced effect on actual test scores (Ellingson, Sackett, & Connelly, 2007), nor does it threaten the construct validity evidence of the these measures (Ellingson, Smith, & Sackett, 2001; Hogan et al., 2007; Smith & Ellingson, 2002; Smith, Hanges, & Dickson, 2001). Other researchers have arrived at contradictory conclusions. Specifically, in high-stakes testing contexts such as employee selection, faking is prevalent, and it does impact the rank orders of potential job applicants. Thus, it affects who is ultimately hired by the organization (Rosse et al., 1998). In addition, some researchers have argued that individuals differ in the ability to fake personality assessments (McFarland & Ryan, 2000) and that faking does in fact pose a threat to the construct validity evidence of these self-report personality tests (Schmit & Ryan, 1993; Stark, Chernyshenko, Chan, Lee, & Drasgow, 2001).

In sum, there is a vigorous debate concerning faking and response distortion in high-stakes testing contexts. However, this debate has focused largely on issues pertaining to self-report personality surveys, which by definition are designed to assess elements of the explicit personality. In contrast, CR tests are designed to assess elements of the implicit personality. We have argued that if tests such as the CRT-A truly provide an indirect assessment of the implicit personality, then individuals should not be able to fake or distort their answers. This should be true for two reasons. First, the indirect nature of assessments should make it impossible for respondents to know which traits are being assessed. Thus, because respondents are not informed as to the nature of the assessment, they should not be able to adjust responses in a socially desirable manner. Second, by definition, as measures of implicit personality, the tests are assessing constructs outside of conscious awareness. Therefore, individuals should not be able to introspect on their implicit personalities (i.e., unconscious biases) and modify their responses.

Basically, there are compelling conceptual arguments for why CRTs should not be susceptible to faking or intentional response distortion, especially when the indirect nature of assessment is maintained. Nevertheless, the proof is in the empirical pudding. Recently, we conducted a series of faking studies designed to test these fundamental assumptions using the CRT-A. These studies, which were published in the *Journal of Applied Psychology* (LeBreton, Barksdale, Robin, & James, 2007), are summarized below. Our working hypothesis was that if we maintain the indirect nature of the CRT-A, problems with faking should be obviated because respondents would approach the CRT-A as a reasoning test. Thus, any attempt to "fake good" would simply result in greater efforts being expended toward making themselves look good (i.e., smarter) and, thus, greater energy would be expended trying to identify the "correct" answer to the reasoning problems.

*Faking When the Indirect Nature of the CRT-A is Violated*

In Study 1, we sought to examine the impact of disclosing the purpose of the CRT-A. That is, we sought to understand the implications of violating the indirect nature of assessment by informing participants of the purpose of the CRT-A. We adopted a between-subjects design in which participants were assigned to a control condition or two different experimental conditions. Participants in the control condition completed the CRT-A under traditional testing conditions (i.e., they were informed that they would be completing an inductive reasoning test and for each item they should try to identify the most logical or reasonable answer). Participants in the first experimental condition were briefed on the true purpose of the CRT-A (i.e., the test is designed to appear as a test of logical reasoning, but it is actually a measure of the personality characteristic known as aggression) and asked to present themselves in the most unfavorable way possible. This condition, disclose-fake, was designed to test whether respondents could identify the aggressive answers after being told the purpose of the CRT-A.

Participants in the second experimental condition, disclose-logic, were also briefed on the true purpose of the CRT-A but were asked to select the most logical or reasonable answer to each question. This condition was designed to test whether respondents might adjust their scores in a socially desirable direction after being informed as to the purpose of assessment. We expected CRT-A scores to be highest in the disclose-fake condition, indicating unwarranted aggressiveness, and lowest in the disclose-logic condition. The latter finding was expected because, once the purpose of assessment was disclosed, we anticipated that impression-management effects would motivate participants to select the nonaggressive answers as the most logical.

Data were collected from undergraduate students ($n = 316$ in the control condition; $n = 136$ in the disclose-fake condition, and $n = 99$ disclose-logic condition). A one-way ANOVA indicated substantial differences in mean scores across the conditions, $F(2,548) = 1,420.26$, $p < .001$, partial eta$^2 = .84$. A planned comparison test provided support for the hypothesis that the mean score in the disclose-fake condition ($M = 17.82$) would be significantly higher than the mean score in the control condition, $M = 3.62$; $F(1,548) = 2,707.57$, $p < .001$, partial eta$^2 = .83$. Contrary to our expectations, a second planned comparison test demonstrated that the mean score in the disclose-logic condition ($M = 4.49$) was actually a bit higher than the mean score in the control condition, $M = 3.62$; $F(1,548) = 8.02$, $p < .005$, partial eta$^2 = .01$. We were expecting that disclosing the nature of assessment would result in a mean shift in a socially desirable direction (i.e., lower aggression). However, disclosing the purpose of assessment impacted item responses, but the direction of this effect was opposite to our prediction.

Our best explanation for this counterintuitive finding is that disclosing the purpose of the CRT-A introduced a demand characteristic—the undergraduate participants thought we were expecting them to select the aggressive responses because they were told the test was designed to assess aggression. Irrespective of the reason, however, this finding, although statistically significant, explained very little variance in mean test scores across the control and disclose-logic conditions (partial eta$^2$ = .01). Much more compelling was the strong amount of variance (83%) in mean test scores accounted for by the contrast between the control and "fake bad" conditions. Individuals who were told to "fake bad" were readily able to identify the aggressive responses. These findings strongly reinforce the criticality of maintaining the indirect nature of assessment.

*Faking When the Indirect Nature of the CRT-A is Maintained*

In Study 2, LeBreton et al. (2007) sought to examine the impact of faking on the CRT-A when the indirect nature of assessment was maintained (i.e., the purpose of the CRT-A was not disclosed). We expected that respondents would not be able to "see through" the test and adjust their scores. To test this hypothesis, we adopted a within-subjects design. Participants completed a test battery containing the CRT-A, self-report measures of the Big Five personality traits, a self-report measure of aggression, and a self-report measure of achievement motivation. All participants completed this test battery twice under different sets of testing instructions, with roughly a 1-week interval between testing periods.

One set of instructions asked participants to complete the test battery under normal testing conditions. Thus, the indirect nature of the CRT-A was maintained, and respondents were asked to identify the most logical solution to each problem. They completed the self-report measures using a 5-point Likert scale ranging from *strongly agree* to *strongly disagree*. The other set of instructions served as a more subtle "fake good" manipulation by asking participants to complete the test battery as though they were applying for a job they really wanted, working as a customer service representative. Instruction type (traditional vs. job applicant) served as our within-subjects factor, and the order in which participants received these instructions was counterbalanced. It is critical to note that in both testing conditions, we maintained the indirect nature of assessment for the CRT-A. Thus, we anticipated no significant differences on the CRT-A under normal and job applicant instructions. However, we expected to see a mean shift on the self-report measures in a socially desirable direction under job applicant instructions, consistent with previous research involving self-report surveys.

Data from 100 undergraduate participants were used to test these basic hypotheses. As expected, a significant multivariate effect was observed for the within-subjects factor of instruction type (traditional vs. job applicant) when analyzing the self-report measures, $F(6,92) = 5.68$, $p < .001$, partial eta$^2$ = .27. An examination of the means revealed shifts in a socially desirable direction in the job applicant condition. Specifically, in the job applicant condition higher means for achievement motivation, extraversion, agreeableness, conscientiousness, and emotional stability were obtained. We also observed a lower mean for self-reported aggression.

Moving to the CRT-A, our expectation of no significant differences in mean scores across conditions was confirmed, $F(1,98) = 1.91$, $p > .05$, partial eta$^2$ = .02. Specifically, the mean score on the CRT-A under job applicant instructions (M = 4.37) did not differ significantly from the mean score under traditional testing conditions (M = 4.66). Collectively, these results suggested that even when motivated to fake, respondents were not able to significantly manipulate their scores on the CRT-A when indirect measurement was maintained.

*Evidence of Impression Management/Faking in a High-Stakes Employment Context*

The prior two studies examined the importance of indirect measurement on faking behavior using samples of undergraduate students. In Study 3 from LeBreton et al. (2007), we sought to replicate the findings of Study 2 in a high-stakes testing context. Again, the indirect nature of the CRT-A was maintained. We adopted a between-subjects design and compared the scores on the CRT-A obtained from the following three samples: (a) individuals applying for jobs working as package handlers or for jobs with a temporary staffing agency ($n = 216$), (b) job incumbents working in several financial services call centers ($n = 585$), and (c) a sample of undergraduate students ($n = 150$). Our working hypothesis was that by maintaining the indirect nature of the CRT-A, job applicants and job incumbents would not be able to see through the purpose of assessment and thus would not adjust their scores in a socially desirable direction. A simple one-way ANOVA confirmed this hypothesis. No significant differences were observed in mean CRT-A scores across job applicant (M = 3.32), job incumbent (M = 3.30), and student samples, M = 3.55, $F(2, 948) = 0.80$, $p > .05$, partial eta$^2$ = .002. This finding suggested that even in high-stakes employment testing, where there was a strong incentive to appear nonaggressive, job applicants and job incumbents were not able to significantly reduce their scores on the CRT-A compared with the student sample.

Collectively, Studies 1 through 3 from LeBreton et al. (2007) revealed that (a) violating the indirect nature of assessment impacted item responses and resulted in respondents being able to identify the aggressive answers on the CRT-A, (b) maintaining the indirect nature of assessment appeared to make the CRT-A fairly robust to traditional faking manipulations in a laboratory setting, and (c) this robustness to faking appeared to carry over to actual high-stakes testing situations using field samples of job applicants and job incumbents. These results suggest that as long as the indirect nature of the CRT-A is maintained, the likelihood of faking or intentional response distortion will be minimized.

## Meta-Analysis of Conditional Reasoning Tests

We presented results based on 14 published studies in Table 4.6 to demonstrate the predictive efficacy of the CRT-A and its predecessors. The criterion on which each of the 14 validities was based was determined to be the best indicator of aggression in each study. In this section, we offer an overview of results of a meta-analysis of validities for the CRT-A and its predecessors (i.e., developmental versions), which includes both published and unpublished studies and formal meta-analytic techniques. We attempted to accumulate data from all studies involving the developmental and final versions of the CRT-A by examining theses, dissertations, articles found using PsycINFO, and referenced articles. This search yielded 30 samples reported in 22 sources. We excluded samples on the basis of two substantive issues. First, we eliminated samples that used self-report criterion measures, because of concerns regarding biases, faking, and introspective accuracy (Nisbett & Wilson, 1977; see also Haidt, 2001; Morgeson et al., 2007). Second, we eliminated samples that used student conduct violations as the criterion measure, because of concerns over construct validity, which includes deletion of Study 5 in Table 4.6.

The student conduct criterion was appealing in our first use of it in Study 5 because it produced a strong validity and presumably included a number of aggression-related components, such as cheating, vandalism, physical violence, and theft. However, in contrast to the validity of .55 found in Study 5, five later attempts to employ this criterion furnished (a) an average validity of approximately zero, (b) no validity greater than .15, and (c) three small but negative validities. The samples varied from 105 students to 760 students. The variance in the total of six validities exceeds what would be expected by sampling error, suggesting a more stable and substantive underlying source for the variation. The consistent predictive efficacy of the CRT aggression measures demonstrated in Table 4.6 against other criteria suggests that this substantive problem most likely rests with the student conduct criterion. Specifically, it is likely that the student conduct violations were highly saturated with aggression behaviors in Study 5, thereby making them predictable by a CRT for aggression, but less saturated with aggression behaviors in the later studies (e.g., consisting of such things as public drunkenness and possession of illegal drugs, which are antisocial but not necessarily aggressive—they lack the "intent to harm" aspect noted for our other criteria.). This would make Study 5 a form of extreme on the saturation of aggression in the criterion measure and the later studies a form of regression toward the mean in regard to saturation of aggression in the criterion measures.

Unfortunately, there was no way to determine the source or content of the violations criteria because it was against university policy to divulge the source of a conduct violation. The ambiguous nature of student conduct violations raised concerns regarding the construct validity of this criterion, and as a result we decided to exclude samples using this criterion. Twenty-two samples remained after eliminating the analyses that used self-report or the student conduct criterion.

With respect to the meta-analytic strategy, several studies reported a range of sample sizes for validities without specifying which sample went with which validity. In these cases, the lower bound of this range was used to conservatively ensure that no correlation coefficient was given more weight than it was due. In addition, a number of samples included multiple aggression criteria. In these cases, the validity for the sample was calculated by taking the average of the reported validity coefficients. This method gives no weight to how representative or construct valid a criterion is as a measure of aggression (which was how we chose criteria to be included in Table 4.6). It is, however, consistent with reducing the role of meta-analyst to that of statistical mechanic by not allowing meta-analysts to make substantive scientific judgments.

Reported correlation coefficients were analyzed by weighting each $r$ value by the sample size and calculating an average. While this common method of conducting meta-analyses will be the basis for our interpretation, some have expressed concern that this method gives too much influence to studies conducted using large samples. As a result, we also calculated the unweighted average, giving each study a unit weight. We hasten to note that this is not necessarily a better or worse method of conducting a meta-analysis but simply provides an alternative result for the reader to consider. The results presented in the first column of Table 4.14 reflect the traditional weighted analysis. The results of the unweighted analyses are reported in Column 2 of Table 4.14. To provide realistic estimates of validity coefficients, the results presented below (both weighted and unweighted) are based on observed relationships and have not been artificially inflated by the use of corrections for range restriction or for the unreliability of predictor or criterion measures.

Across all studies, the mean weighted validity for the CRT-A was .24. The unweighted mean validity was .28. To discern why these means departed from the unweighted mean of .41 reported in Table 4.6, we conducted a series of moderator analyses. The moderator analyses included the effect of type of criterion on magnitude of average validity. Four criterion-related moderators

TABLE 4.14
Conditional Reasoning Test for Aggression Meta-Analysis

| Overall analyses and moderators | Weighted[a] r | Unweighted r | K | n |
|---|---|---|---|---|
| All CRT-A studies | .24 | .28 | 22 | 3,643 |
| Aggression criterion | .29 | .31 | 8 | 1,312 |
| CWB | .27 | .30 | 8 | 1,197 |
| Low OC | .08 | .12 | 2 | 623 |
| Low job performance | .18 | .21 | 6 | 969 |
| Aggression + low CWB | .28 | .31 | 16 | 2,509 |
| Performance + low OC | .17 | .22 | 6 | 960 |
| Developmental versions of the CRT-A | .35 | .35 | 5 | 763 |
| Verbal-Visual CRT-A | .28 | .36 | 2 | 285 |
| Current version of the CRT-A | .21 | .24 | 15 | 2,595 |
| Student sample | .30 | .32 | 9 | 1,507 |
| Work sample | .21 | .25 | 13 | 2,136 |
| Objective criterion | .24 | .31 | 13 | 2,443 |
| Subjective criterion | .18 | .21 | 12 | 2,084 |
| Predictive/experimental studies | .31 | .33 | 12 | 1,758 |
| Concurrent/postdictive studies | .18 | .22 | 10 | 1,885 |
| Best indicators[b] | .41 | .41 | 9 | 1,254 |

Note. CRT-A = Conditional Reasoning Test for Aggression; CWB = counterproductive work behavior; OC = organizational citizenship.
[a]Weighted by sample size. [b]Best indicators were defined as predictive studies that used objective criteria.

were examined. The first criterion-related moderator examined was aggression. Examples of aggression criteria included acts that harm others and/or the organization such theft, dishonesty, and verbal hostility. The average correlation between a CRT-A and aggression was .29 ($K = 8, n = 1,312$). The second type of criterion examined was counterproductive work behavior (CWB), which we defined as any negative work-related behavior. Examples of CWB criteria included organizational deviance, unreliability at work, and use of manipulative tactics in the workplace. The average correlation between a CRT-A and CWB was .27 ($K = 8, n = 1,197$). The third criterion moderator was low job performance (JP), which we defined as any work-related outcome that was directly related to the duties of an employee. Examples of JP criteria included customer service, subjectively rated performance evaluations, and objective measures of performance. The average correlation between the CRT-A and low JP was .18 ($K = 6, n = 960$; the higher the aggression score on the CRT-A, the lower the job performance). The fourth and final criterion moderator was low organizational citizenship behaviors (OCB). We defined OCB as any work-related outcome that is not directly related to the duties of an employee. Examples of OCB criteria included cooperative social behavior and dependability. The average correlation between a CRT-A and low OCB was .08 ($K = 2$, $n = 623$).

We recognize that the distinction between CWB and aggression or JP and OCB is somewhat ambiguous. Although we attempted to define and distinguish between the two sets of criteria as objectively as possible, some readers may disagree with the definitions of each criterion or the decisions we made when assigning a correlation coefficient to a criterion. We therefore provide composite estimates. We combined the two positive criteria (JP and OCB) as well as the two negative criteria (CWB and aggression). The CRT-A had average correlations of .28 with the negative criterion ($k = 16$, $n = 2,509$) and .17 with the positive criterion ($k = 6$, $n = 960$).

Overall, these results suggest that the CRT-A can serve as a valid predictor of aggression and CWB. The CRT-A does not fare as well in predicting JP or OCB, although the validity for JP is potentially useful if it provides incremental validity over established tests of ability, integrity, and personality (see Schmidt & Hunter, 1998). Most important, these results support the construct validity of the CRT-A. The fact that the CRT-A demonstrates a positive relationship with aggression and CWB and an inverse relationship with JP and OCB is consistent with the CRT-A's stated intent of predicting direct, indirect, and partial behavioral manifestations of aggression (James & Mazerolle, 2002; James et al., 2005).

A number of methodological moderators were also considered. The first to be examined was the version of the CRT-A used in each sample. The current version of the CRT-A contains 22 items presented in paper-and-pencil format. The average validity of the current form of the CRT-A is .21 ($k = 15$, $N = 2,595$). The verbal-visual version of the test contains 14 items presented using a visual medium. The average validity of the verbal-visual form of the CRT-A is .28 ($k = 2$, $N = 285$). Some of the samples included in this meta-analysis were studied prior to the creation of the current version of the CRT-A. These samples used developmental versions of the CRT-A. The average validity for developmental forms of the CRT-A is .35 ($k = 5$, $N = 763$).

The type of sample used in a study was examined as a potential moderator. Specifically, we separated student samples from applied samples (studies that examined participants in a work-related setting). The average validity for samples that used student participants was .30 ($k = 9$, $N = 1,507$), and the average validity for applied samples was .21 ($k = 12$, $N = 2,136$).

A third moderator concerned whether the criterion measures in a study were objective or subjective. Studies employing objective criteria had an average validity of .24 ($k = 13$, $N = 2,443$), whereas studies using subjective criteria had an average validity of .18 ($k = 12$, $N = 2,084$). (Some studies had both, in which case separate estimates were computed for this analysis.)

A final methodological moderator was study design. We separated studies that used predictive or experimental designs from studies that employed concurrent or postdictive designs. Predictive and experimental studies had an average validity of .31 ($k = 12$, $N = 1,758$), while concurrent and postdictive studies had an average validity of .18 ($K = 10$, $N = 1,885$).

The methodological moderators seem to imply that student samples have a higher average validity than applied samples, predictive and experimental studies yield a higher average validity than concurrent and postdictive studies, and studies employing objective criteria have a higher average validity than studies using subjective criteria. These results have a number of interesting implications. First, the CRT-A may perform better in student samples than applied samples because of the amount of control a researcher has when conducting a study at a university as opposed to a place of business. The freedom afforded by working with students may also allow the researcher to use a true experimental design as opposed to a quasi-experimental design. It may also contribute to a more careful research design overall. This explanation is consistent with the finding that the CRT-A seems to have higher validity when the researcher uses a predictive or experimental design. Additionally, objective criteria may be more reliable or easier to measure accurately than subjective criteria, which by definition are vulnerable to a number of rater biases. Reflection on these points suggests that there may be a relationship between the quality of a study and the observed validity of the CRT-A.

To determine whether the quality of the studies impacts the validities, we performed a quality-oriented analysis. Ones, Dilchert, Viswesvaran, and Judge (2007) claimed that "appropriately conducted meta-analyses are not necessarily adversely affected by low quality studies" (p. 996, footnote 2). We disagree. In fact, we believe that the quality of the studies can have a substantial impact on the results of a meta-analysis. Our quality-oriented examination consisted of a best indicator analysis. We defined best indicators as predictive studies that used objective criteria. The average validity of the CRT-A in these studies was .41 ($k = 9$, $N = 1,254$). The average validity in these studies equals the average estimate of .41 reported for Table 4.6.

## DISCUSSION OF THE CONDITIONAL REASONING TEST FOR AGGRESSION IN RELATION TO OZER'S PRINCIPLES 2 AND 3

We have presented the results of empirical tests of the CRT-A. We focused here on information relating to Ozer's (1999) second and third principles for sound psychological test development in the personality domain, which are, respectively, that the item characteristics, scale characteristics, and factor structure of the instrument should be consistent with the theory of the instrument (presented in Chapters 2 and 3), and that the instrument should possess demonstrably high validities for the most theoretically relevant inferences. More specifically, Principle 2 requests that the item characteristics, scale characteristics, and factor structure of the CR problems be consistent with the psychological theory used to build the problems. Principle 3 focuses on estimates of the validity of inferences regarding (a) the reliability of the instrument (e.g., internal consistency, stability); (b) empirical validities, namely, prediction of behavioral measures of aggression; and (c) the instrument's relationships with measures of other theoretical constructs of interest (e.g., self-report personality variables, or potential confounds such as intelligence, gender, and race). Additional validity issues pertain to the potential for faking and the establishment of critical values for interpreting various degrees of aggressiveness, or the lack thereof.

Results obtained at this point in time indicate that the factor structure of the CR problems for aggression is consistent with the theoretical foundation of CR and justification processes. Results suggest further that scores on the CRT-A are reliable and that the CRT-A predicts a range of behavioral measures of aggression. There is also evidence to show that scores on the CRT-A are not generally related to confounding variables such as intelligence, gender, and race. A general lack of susceptibility to faking is indicated when the CRT-A is administered under normal circumstances. Finally, critical values have been empirically established for determining the point at which scores on the CRT-A imply implicit aggressiveness. In Chapter 5, we report our ongoing research on tests of new models regarding interfaces between scores on the CRT-A and self-reports of aggression.

There is also much more work to be accomplished. Reliabilities need to be higher, and achieving that result will likely require the addition of problems to the CRT-A. Stand-alone measures are needed for each of the three factors, or for each of the justification mechanisms, and they will require even more problems. Research is limited to establishing reliability and validity in samples from college students and adult working populations. The efficacy of the test as a general assessment instrument outside these populations remains to be explored, as does the extent to which the CRT-A generalizes to other cultures. As a final illustration, much of the foundation on which the CRT-A rests, that is, the theory of the instrument, remains to be tested. For example, how "implicit" are justification mechanisms for aggression?

On the other hand, we believe that it is fair to say that the CR technique for measuring aggression receives passing marks on Ozer's (1999) Principles 2 and 3. In the future, the method may or may not attain Ozer's conception of an ideal personality test. For the present, it appears to have reasonably satisfied a number of the exacting standards required to build a valid and efficient indirect measurement system. This system has many uses in science (e.g., studies of implicit cognitive processes) and in the field (e.g., selection of nonaggressive employees and identification of students at risk). These uses will likely multiply as researchers and professionals conducting research on the CRT-A offer new insights into theory development and application. They may also wish to develop their own CR tests.

## EMPIRICAL RESULTS FOR RELATIVE MOTIVE STRENGTH

The first 5 years that James and his students spent developing the theory for CR and the initial CR problems focused on achievement motivation and fear of failure. Approximately 50 problems were given a trial test, and data were collected on more than 1,500 primarily academic respondents during this developmental period. Fifteen items survived this process to become elements of a provisional Conditional Reasoning Test for Relative Motive Strength (CRT-RMS). The results of two preliminary studies that were based on this CRT-RMS were reported in the first journal publication on CR (James, 1998).

The first results obtained for a nascent but promising CR measure for aggression were also reported in James (1998). At about this time, a transition occurred among most of the members of the CR research group. Investigators, including the present authors, shifted focus from relative motive strength to developing the embryonic aggression measure. The result was a concentrated focus on developing and validating a CR test that became the CRT-A. The provisional CRT-RMS received far less attention and thus remained provisional. Examinations of the test were largely left to the few graduate students who were interested in studying relative motive strength for theses and dissertations. Development of the CRT-RMS was of low priority until 2008, when the U.S. Navy provided support for a revision of the test. The initial examination of this new CRT-RMS was promising in that it significantly predicted voluntary withdrawal from U.S. Navy Seals training program (see Table 4.15).

Our objective for the development of the CRT-RMS is to build a 25- to 30-problem measure of relative motive strength. It will take several years to accumulate data analogous to what we reported in this chapter for the CRT-A. On the other hand, the initial study by James (1998) and the academic as well as field studies completed since 1998 have shown considerable promise. Indeed, like aggression, a particular strength of the CR measures for relative motive strength has been a capacity to predict behaviors in both academic and field settings. The higher the score on a version of the CRT-RMS, the greater the likelihood of students performing well in the classroom, of executives performing well in assessment centers, and of sailors successfully completing training to become members of the elite U.S. Navy Seals. Table 4.15 summarizes

## TABLE 4.15
### Uncorrected Validities for Conditional Reasoning Test for Relative Motive Strength

| Criterion | n | Sample | Research design | Uncorrected validity[a] |
|---|---|---|---|---|
| 1. Average test score over a semester | 336 | Undergraduates | Predictive | .52* |
| 2. Overall GPA | 110 | Undergraduates | Postdictive | .32* |
| 3. In-basket performance in assessment center | 263 | Middle-level managers | Predictive | .39* |
| 4. Final grade in course | 359 | Undergraduates | Predictive | .35* |
| 5. Final grade in course | 101 | Undergraduates | Predictive | .30* |
| 6. Overall GPA | 287 | 1st-year law school students | Predictive | .09 |
| 7. Overall GPA | 221 | Upper class Romanian high school students | Postdictive | .40* |
| 8. Voluntary withdrawal from U.S. Navy Seals training | 365 | Trainees | Cross-validation | .30* |

Note. GPA = grade point average.
[a]Uncorrected means not corrected for either range restriction or attenuation due to unreliability in either the predictor or the criterion.
*Statistically significant ($p < .05$).

the results of eight validation studies on a CRT-RMS. The average validity in this table is .37.

As with the CRT-A, an average validity of .37 places the CRT-RMS in the upper section of the distribution of validities for personality measures. We hope to be able to improve on this average validity as we develop and refine the CRT-RMS. At the present time, it is fair to characterize the CRT-RMS as a work in progress. Its initial psychometrics with respect to such things as reliability, distributions, factor structure, and correlations with demographics and critical reasoning skills are also promising, although different from those for the CRT-A (with the exception of reliability, which remains in the .70s). Correlations with self-reports of achievement motivation and/or fear of failure also tend to be modest, although a bit higher than those between the CRT-A and self-reports of aggression. We address this issue in the presentation of the channeling models in the next chapter.

# 5

# ADDITIONAL EXAMINATIONS OF CONDITIONAL REASONING BASED ON CHANNELING MODELS

As noted in Chapter 1, a long history of rivalry exists between people who rely on indirect assessments designed to assess aspects of the implicit personality (e.g., the Thematic Apperception Test [TAT]; Murray, 1935) and people who rely on direct assessments designed to assess aspects of the explicit personality (e.g., self-report surveys such as the California Psychological Inventory; Winter, John, Stewart, Klohnen, & Duncan, 1998). However, we believe this rivalry is coming to an end, in part because of the dissociative models we described in Chapter 4 of this volume. As we discussed, the proposed dissociation between the implicit and explicit components of personality has been supported by several recent studies (e.g., Bornstein, 1998, 2002; Brunstein & Maier, 2005; Frost et al., 2007; Wilson et al., 2000). The results support McClelland et al.'s (1989) view that the implicit personality consists of automatically activated, unconscious forces that influence thinking and behaviors without the awareness of the individual. They further support McClelland et al.'s belief that the explicit personality consists of relatively independent (in comparison to the implicit personality), self-attributed characteristics, that is, forces that a person "openly acknowledges as being characteristic of his or her day-to-day functioning and experience" (Bornstein, 1998, p. 778). Perhaps most important, results of research support McClelland et al.'s hypothesis that the implicit and explicit components of personality *predict different behaviors*.

Although important, the story does not end with dissociative models. The data often indicate that measures of the explicit and implicit components of personality do not just operate independently of one another to predict different behaviors. Rather, a much richer and psychologically informative model appears to be at work that involves an interaction between the explicit and implicit components of personality. This model suggests that we can obtain a better understanding of why people behave as they do by "integrating" information from the explicit and implicit components of personality. The theoretical foundation for integrating the explicit personality with the implicit personality is the channeling hypothesis proposed by Winter et al. (1998).

## CHANNELING HYPOTHESIS

To quote Winter et al. (1998, p. 231), "motives involve wishes, desires, or goals (often implicit or nonconscious), whereas traits channel or direct the ways in which motives are expressed in particular actions throughout the life course." The basic idea here is that a number of people could have the same implicit motive but express that motive in quite different ways because they have different traits. Moreover, the same behavior (trait) might be serving as channels for different motives for different people. Thus, to understand a person's personality, an assessment needs to be made of the person's implicit motives and of how those motives are channeled into behavior by characteristic behaviors (traits).

Winter et al. (1998) translated the channeling hypothesis into a substantive and testable system by proposing an *integrative model*. An integrative model begins with a motive and then adds a variation on a trait that should serve as a channel for the motive. Winter et al. used the affiliation motive and the trait of extraversion–introversion for illustrative purposes. They built an integrative model by looking at the confluence between high-low scores on the affiliation motive and whether a person is disposed toward extraversion or introversion. This model is described below (this description is drawn from James and Mazerolle, 2002).

### Integrative Model

The integrative model for the affiliation motive and extraversion–introversion trait is partially reproduced in Table 5.1. A person with a strong affiliation motive has needs to establish and to maintain friendships and associations with others, to experience warm, positive, friendly, or intimate

## TABLE 5.1
### Hypotheses About the Interactions of the Affiliation Motive and Extraversion–Introversion

| Motive | In combination with | |
| --- | --- | --- |
| | Introversion | Extraversion |
| High affiliation | Wants affection and friendship but ill at ease in many interpersonal situations | Unconflicted in pursuit of wide-ranging interpersonal relationships |
| Low affiliation | Comfortable and most effective when working alone; not concerned about what others think | Well regarded and adept at interpersonal relations, but not dependent on them |

*Note.* Reprinted from *Personality in Work Organizations* (p. 169), by L. R. James and M. D. Mazerolle, 2002, Thousand Oaks, CA: Sage Publications. Copyright 2002 by Sage Publications, Inc. Reprinted with permission.

relationships, and to engage in friendly, cooperative acts. Winter et al. (1998) noted also that this motive might engender a defensive or "prickly" reaction if a person is threatened or stressed. With respect to the trait, extraverts are characteristically talkative, active, outgoing, sociable, gregarious, spirited, expressive, and outspoken. Introverts are typically quiet, reserved, shy, modest, withdrawn, inhibited, and retiring.

The union of extraversion with a high need for affiliation is presented in the upper right quadrant of Table 5.1. Winter et al. (1998) suggested that individuals in this cell would pursue a wide range of relationships without conflict because of the congruity between the implicit affiliation motive and their characteristic interactive style. Congruity between motive and trait is also in evidence for the union of a low need to affiliate with introversion (lower left quadrant). Members of this cell were described as caring little for what others think and working effectively, indeed contently, by themselves.

The remaining two cells involve incongruities between implicit motives and traits. The upper left quadrant consists of affiliation-motivated introverts, whom Winter et al. (1998) described as individuals desirous of affection and friendship but uncomfortable in many interpersonal situations. These same individuals were characterized by Winter et al. as desiring a few warm and deep relationships as opposed to a large number of friendships. The authors predicted that members of this cell are likely to experience conflict in these close relationships when they become withdrawn and introspective, as introverts are prone to do.

An extravert with a low need for affiliation seems a bit far-fetched until we imagine politicians who, though charismatic, popular, and interpersonally adept, are not reliant on interpersonal relations with others for emotional sustenance. Indeed, the driving force for these individuals may be the power motive. Thus, the manifest extraversion displayed by these individuals is not driven by the affiliation motive but serves (i.e., channels) instead the need to impress and to influence people. This point underscores a caveat emphasized by Winter et al. (1998) that a two-variable model leaves much to be explained about even narrow behavioral domains. Nevertheless, even though incomplete and in rudimentary form, we believe that Winter et al.'s integrative model furnishes a creative paradigm shift for personality research.

*Test of the Integrative Model*

Winter et al. (1998) tested the integrative model presented in Table 5.1 on two samples of college women. The first sample was composed of 51 women from Mills College, whereas the second included 89 women from Radcliffe College. While students, the women in both samples were given the TAT to measure their affiliation motive and the California Psychological Inventory (CPI; Winter et al., 1998) to measure their extraversion–introversion. Approximately 25 years later, when the women were generally in their 40s, data were obtained on specific life outcomes. We focus here on one group of illustrative outcomes from this data set. These outcomes are (a) marriage and family by age 28, followed by divorce (Mills sample); (b) number of marriages and divorces (Radcliffe sample); (c) self-rated dissatisfaction with intimate relationships (Mills sample); and (d) self-described problems with intimacy (Radcliffe sample).

Results based on the integrative model are presented graphically in Figures 5.1 and 5.2. These figures denote that the joint relationship of the affiliation motive and the extraversion–introversion trait takes the form of an interaction in this case (a different form of relationship is presented later). To be specific, the direction and magnitude of the regression slope linking behavioral outcomes (marriage and divorce; Figure 5.1) and attitudinal outcomes (dissatisfaction in intimate relationships; Figure 5.2) to the affiliation motive are dependent on whether the subjects are introverts or extroverts. All interactions reached significance at acceptable levels (see Winter et al., 1998). The variables in the graphs are in standardized form with a mean of 0 and a standard deviation of 1.

Perhaps the most direct method for interpreting Figures 5.1 and 5.2 is to view them in terms of motive-trait congruence and incongruence, much as we just did with Table 5.1. The Mills sample in Figure 5.2 provides a good exemplar for all of the graphs. If we look only at the slope for introverts, we find that relationship dissatisfaction increases as the affiliation motive increases (i.e., the slope is positive). These results suggest that when intro-

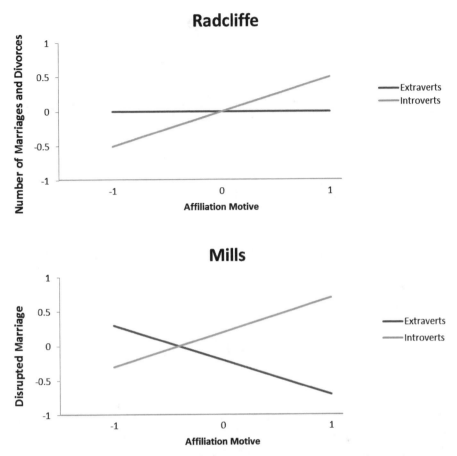

*Figure 5.1.* Joint effects of the affiliation motive and extraversion on marriage and divorce across the Radcliffe and Mills samples. Adapted from "Traits and Motives: Toward an Integration of Two Traditions in Personality Research," by D. G. Winter, O. P. John, A. J. Stewart, E. C. Klohnen, and L. E. Duncan, 1998, *Psychological Review, 105,* p. 245. Copyright 1998 by American Psychological Association.

verts have a low motive to affiliate (congruence), they are likely to be satisfied with intimate relationships (or at least not dissatisfied). In concert with Table 5.1, Winter et al. (1998) interpreted these data to indicate that intimate relationships are not particularly salient for women with low needs to affiliate.

However, when introverts have a high need to affiliate (incongruence), they are likely to experience dissatisfaction with intimate relationships (and to experience a greater frequency of divorces—see Figure 5.1). As discussed with the integrative model, affiliation-motivated introverts desire a few intimate

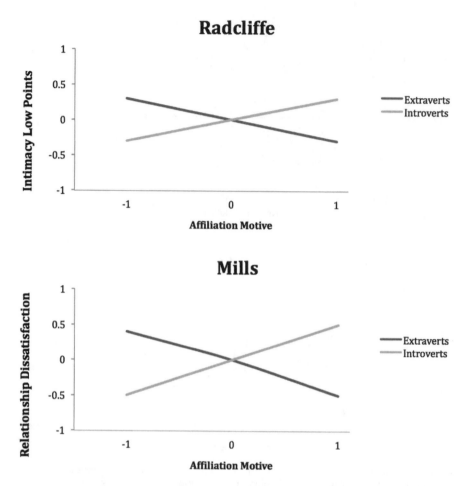

*Figure 5.2.* Joint effects of the affiliation motive and extraversion on dissatisfaction in intimate relationships across the Radcliffe and Mills samples. Adapted from "Traits and motives: Toward an Integration of Two Traditions in Personality Research," by D. G. Winter, O. P. John, A. J. Stewart, E. C. Klohnen, and L. E. Duncan, 1998, *Psychological Review, 105,* p. 245. Copyright 1998 by American Psychological Association.

relationships but then have trouble sustaining them. Winter et al. (1998) suggested that

> affiliation-motivated introverts, with their more inward focus and preferences for privacy and solitude, should find such relationships overarousing, troublesome, conflicted, and even at times aversive. . . . To a partner they may seem remote and even withholding. If they are lucky, they may find an understanding partner, with whom they develop a deep, intense relationship—perhaps after one or two false starts. On the average and over

time [however], they may tend to *establish intimate relationships that become problematic and fail.* (p. 240; italics in original)

Let us turn now to the regression slope for extraverts in Figure 5.2 for the Mills sample. This slope is negative, which means that dissatisfaction with intimate relationships begins high when the affiliation-motive is low and progressively decreases (i.e., becomes more positive or less negative) as the need to affiliate increases. This suggests that in congruent situations in which extraverts have a high affiliation motive, we tend to find people who are happy (not dissatisfied) and nonconflicted with intimate relationships (and have fewer divorces in the Mills sample—see Figure 5.1). However, in incongruent situations characterized by extraverts with a low need to affiliate, we tend to find more disrupted marriages (in the Mills sample only) and dissatisfaction with intimate relationships (both samples). Winter et al. attributed the latter results to people who simply did not care for close relationships and thus failed to derive satisfaction from them. In fact such relationships may be framed as constraining or time-consuming. A similar set of interpretations would ensue for the Radcliffe sample in Figure 5.2, and reference was made above to key aspects of the data in Figure 5.1.

As a general statement, we agree with Winter et al.'s (1998) conclusion that "traits channel the ways in which motives are expressed in behavior and life outcomes" (p. 243). A strong need for affiliation is expressed behaviorally and emotionally in different ways by introverts and extraverts. Moreover, the ease and comfort with which a motive is expressed appears to be related to whether it is congruent with characteristic ways of adapting to one's environment. Extraverts appear to have a comfortable and nonconflicted path for expressing a strong motive to affiliate. The path for affiliation-motivated introverts appears to be rocky and strewn with psychological hazards. On the other hand, introverts appear to adapt to a low need to affiliate better than do extraverts.

## INTEGRATIVE MODELS THAT INVOLVE
## CONDITIONAL REASONING

Winter et al. (1998) based their tests of the channeling hypothesis–integrative models on the use of the TAT projective technique to measure implicit motives. We now present an overview of recently published tests of the channeling hypothesis–integrative models that employed the conditional reasoning (CR) approach to measure implicit motives. Studies were conducted that involve both the Conditional Reasoning Test for Aggression (CRT-A) and the Conditional Reasoning Test for Relative Motive Strength (CRT-RMS).

We look at studies on aggression first, followed by studies on relative motive strength (often referred to as *achievement motivation*).

## Integrative Model of Assessment for Aggression

Our objective was to test a model of proposed relationships among the explicit personality, the implicit personality, and aggressive behavior. The explicit personality was assessed using self-report surveys of aggression. Scores from the CRT-A were used as indicators for the implicit personality. We build on results presented in Chapter 4, where we demonstrated a dissociation between self-reports of aggression and scores on the CRT-A, that is, scores on the Justification of Aggression Scale (JAGS). Scores from the self-report surveys and the CRT-A were essentially unrelated and tended to predict different criteria. Thus, as implied by the term *dissociation*, self-beliefs about aggressiveness and implicit measures of aggressiveness appear to operate independently and in a sense competitively. However, we have found with additional analyses that it is better to think of CR and self-beliefs about aggressiveness as operating in a complementary manner as opposed to a dissociative or competitive one (Bing, Stewart, et al., 2007; James & Mazerolle, 2002).

We use the results of a recent study on 183 college intramural basketball players (70 females, 113 males) to illustrate why this is so (Frost et al., 2007; Study 12 in Tables 4.5 and 4.6). This is the same study we employed to illustrate dissociation. To summarize, the players completed a CRT-A and a self-report of aggressiveness (i.e., the Angry Hostility Scale of the NEO-PI-R; Costa & McCrae, 1992) before the start of the basketball season. Their overt aggressiveness (e.g., fighting), passive aggressiveness (e.g., obstructiveness, such as holding onto the ball to disrupt play), and verbal hostility (e.g., loud swearing, mocking) were then tracked for the entire intramural season. We show below that students who were implicitly prepared to rationalize aggressiveness had a strong likelihood of engaging in aggressive behavior. However, which of the three aggressive behaviors this implicit preparedness to aggress was "channeled" into was dependent on self-beliefs about aggressiveness. Of particular interest was the finding that students who were implicitly prepared to rationalize harming others tended to engage in (a) overt aggression if they viewed themselves as aggressive and (b) passive aggression if they viewed themselves as nonaggressive.

The integrative model for aggression is presented in Figure 5.3. The a priori model based on hypotheses and the final model based on results differed little, with the one exception noted in the lower right quadrant of the figure. Each of the four quadrants is described briefly below.

| | | Self-reported aggression | |
|---|---|---|---|
| | | Low | High |
| Strength of justification mechanisms | High | • Do not see themselves as aggressive. However, because justification mechanisms are in place they are implicitly prepared to rationalize aggression.<br>• Tend to channel behavior toward subtle acts of aggression, such as passive-aggressiveness, that can be misrepresented as being nonaggressive.<br>• Channel aggression into obstructionism in basketball. | • See themselves as aggressive (e.g, easy to anger, confrontational, and hostile).<br>• Have justification mechanisms in place and thus are implicitly prepared to rationalize acts of aggression.<br>• Channel aggression into overt acts of hostility such as pushing, shoving, and fighting in basketball. |
| | Low | • See themselves as nonaggressive.<br>• Do not have justification mechanisms in place and thus lack the implicit capacity to justify aggression.<br>• Typically channel their behavior toward prosocial objectives. Do not engage in aggressive behaviors in basketball. | • See themselves as aggressive.<br>• Lack the justification mechanisms that would prepare them to rationalize engaging in aggression.<br>• Channel thoughts and behaviors toward inhibiting self-ascribed aggressive tendencies.<br>• Channel aggression into socially acceptable expressions that do not need to be defended, such as loud swearing and mocking in the heat of a basketball game.[a] |

*Figure 5.3.* Integrative Model for Aggression. Adapted from (a) "Implicit and Explicit Personality: A Test of a Channeling Hypothesis for Aggressive Behavior," by B. C. Frost, C. E. Ko, and L. R. James, 2007, *Journal of Applied Psychology, 92,* p. 1305. Copyright 2007 by American Psychological Association, and (b) "An Integrative Typology of Personality Assessment for Aggression: Implications for Predicting Counterproductive Workplace Behavior," by M. N. Bing, S. M. Stewart, H. K. Davison, P. D. Green, M. D. McIntyre, and L. R. James, 2007, *Journal of Applied Psychology, 92,* p. 725. Copyright 2007 by American Psychological Association. [a]Unlike other cells, this result was not predicted by Frost et al. (2007). We include it because engaging in socially acceptable aggression that does not have to be defended by justification mechanisms is now part of this cell.

## Conditions of Congruence

The upper right quadrant of this model contains the union between persons who (a) have justification mechanisms in place to help rationalize aggression and (b) perceive themselves to be aggressive. This is a case of what Winter et al. (1998) referred to as a *congruency* between the implicit and explicit personalities. Individuals in this quadrant are prepared to rationalize a desire to harm others as self-defense, righting of injustices, and the like. Basically, a strong motive to aggress is protected, and reflected, by strong justifications. Moreover, these same individuals tend to think of themselves as argumentative, easy to anger, and confrontational (but not necessarily malevolent, intentionally hostile, or deriving pleasure from harming others). The protection afforded by justification mechanisms allows them to channel their aggressiveness into all forms of aggression, especially overt hostilities, and still not think of themselves as being malicious or hostile by nature. Frost et al. (2007) thus predicted that they would channel their implicit aggression into overt acts of aggression such as pushing, shoving, and fighting in basketball.

The lower left quadrant of the model contains the other source of congruency between the explicit and implicit personalities. Individuals in this quadrant view themselves as nonaggressive. They also tend to reason in ways that promote nonaggressiveness. Their reasoning serves as a logical counterbalance to aggressive individuals' attempts to rationalize behaving aggressively. Members of this quadrant are typically prosocial, one indication being that they channel their behavior toward socially adaptive ends. For example, they are disposed to favor cooperation and harmony over vengeance and retribution (James & Mazerolle, 2002). Frost et al. predicted that they would channel their behavior toward prosocial objectives and thus not engage in aggressive behaviors in basketball.

### Conditions of Incongruence

The upper left quadrant contains individuals who report that they are nonaggressive. However, they have justification mechanisms in place to rationalize a desire to harm others. This "incongruous" pattern suggests that the desire to harm others remains latent and is not manifested in a manner that could be described as aggressive (e.g., physically abusing someone). This latent aggressiveness is channeled into behaviors that these individuals do not explicitly think of as being aggressive. Passive aggressive acts appear to be prime candidates for such misinterpretation. Examples of passive aggressive acts are giving someone the silent treatment, intentionally failing to return phone calls, passively obstructing attempts by others to attain goals, leaving when someone enters a room, and refusing to attend meetings when a particular person is present. With respect to basketball, Frost et al. (2007) predicted that individuals with strong implicit but not explicit aggression would channel their implicit aggression into the passive-aggressive expressions of obstructionism.

The lower right quadrant involves an interesting incongruity in which individuals describe themselves as easy to anger, confrontational, and argumentative, and yet they lack the justification mechanisms for aggression that would help them rationalize engaging in acts that harm others. Given the lack of implicit protective mechanisms, the explicit belief in self-aggressiveness is likely to channel thoughts and behaviors toward inhibiting or at least dampening the self-ascribed aggressive tendencies (James & Mazerolle, 2002). For example, individuals in this quadrant are likely to be self-monitors, to be highly self-critical, and to be distrustful of their basic instincts and motives (which they believe to be aggressive). Frost et al. (2007) made no predictions regarding the basketball players who fell into this quadrant. However, as shown below, the data indicated rather strongly that they were likely to channel their explicit or self-ascribed aggressiveness into socially acceptable expressions that do not need to be psychologically defended, such as loud swearing and mocking in the heat of a basketball game. This is a worthwhile, and reasonable, addition to this quadrant that we had not seen previously.

## Test of the Channeling Hypothesis–Integrative Model for Aggression

At this point the reader may wish to review the presentation of the dissociative model of personality in Chapter 4 of this volume. By way of brief summary, it was demonstrated that the scores on self-perceived aggressiveness (the Angry Hostility [A-H] Scale from the NEO-PI-R) were uncorrelated with scores on implicit preparedness to justify aggression (from the JAGS of the CRT-A). The three criterion measures of aggression were uncorrelated. Self-perceived aggressiveness was the stronger predictor of verbal hostility. Implicit preparedness to justify aggression was the stronger predictor of overt aggression and passive aggression (as assessed by obstructionism). Gender and playing time were controlled in all correlational analyses, as well as in the interaction analyses presented below.

Each of the four quadrants of the integrative model in Figure 5.3 contains expectations of how explicit beliefs about aggressiveness channel implicit preparedness to justify aggression into acts of aggression. However, the quadrants reflect pure prototypes based on extreme scores. A more realistic picture of how the implicit and explicit personalities interact is obtained by examining both self-described aggression and implicit preparedness to justify aggression in terms of their full scales (i.e., scores on both the NEO-based self-reports of aggression and the JAGS are continuously distributed). Thus, analogous to Winter et al. (1998), tests of the integrative model are based on continuous scales.

The tests of the integrative model are presented graphically in Figures 5.4, 5.5, and 5.6. One graph is presented for each of the three aggression criteria. Like Winter et al. (1998), the tests take the form of statistical interactions. This is because the direction and magnitude of the regression slopes linking type of aggression (overt aggression, obstructionism, verbal hostility) and implicit preparedness to justify aggression are dependent on the strength of an individual's self-perceived aggressiveness. That is, the higher an individual's implicit preparedness to justify aggression, the greater the force for that individual to engage in aggressive behavior. However, the channel through which this aggression is expressed is dependent on the strength of this individual's self-perceived aggressiveness.

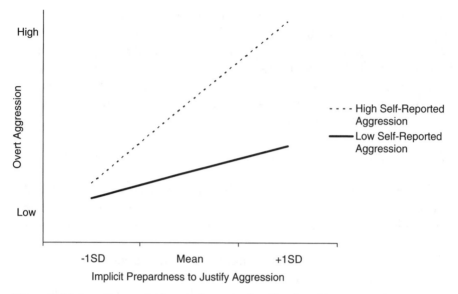

*Figure 5.4.* Integrative model for overt aggression. Reprinted from "Implicit and Explicit Personality: A Test of a Channeling Hypothesis for Aggressive Behavior," by B. C. Frost, C. E. Ko, and L. R. James, 2007, *Journal of Applied Psychology, 92,* p. 1311. Copyright 2007 by American Psychological Association.

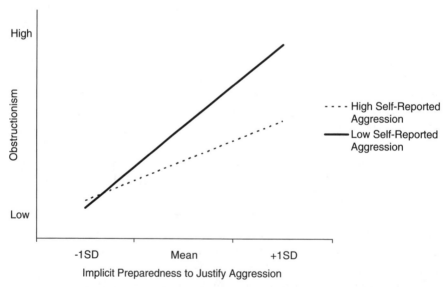

*Figure 5.5.* Integrative model for obstructionism. Reprinted from "Implicit and Explicit Personality: A Test of a Channeling Hypothesis for Aggressive Behavior," by B. C. Frost, C. E. Ko, and L. R. James, 2007, *Journal of Applied Psychology, 92,* p. 1312. Copyright 2007 by American Psychological Association.

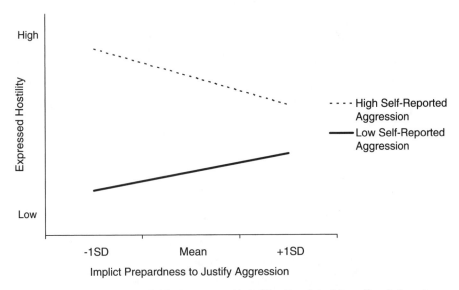

*Figure 5.6.* Integrative model for expressed hostility. Reprinted from "Implicit and Explicit Personality: A Test of a Channeling Hypothesis for Aggressive Behavior," by B. C. Frost, C. E. Ko, and L. R. James, 2007, *Journal of Applied Psychology, 92,* p. 1313. Copyright 2007 by American Psychological Association.

Of initial note is the finding of statistical significance for each of the three statistical interactions on which Figures 5.4 through 5.6 are based. Results of the interaction analyses are presented in Table 5.2. The interaction analyses were conducted via hierarchical regression using both weighted least-squares (WLS) and unweighted least-squares (ULS) estimates provided by LISREL 8.72 (Jöreskog & Sörbom, 2005). These estimation techniques were employed to address nonnormality of many of the distributions and the trichotomous, ordinal nature of the behavioral data. Both WLS and ULS give consistent estimates of parameters in such circumstances, whereas WLS provides the more consistent estimates of standard errors (see Jöreskog & Sörbom, 1996; Kaplan, 2000). Results furnished by the two estimators were essentially identical, including decisions regarding significance. Estimates furnished by ULS are reported inasmuch as this estimator is less demanding than WLS with respect to sample size.

In the first step in each analysis, the criterion variable was regressed on the proposed independent variable (i.e., the CRT-A) and the two control variables (i.e., gender and playing time). The second step added the proposed moderator (i.e., the A-H Scale) to the regression equation. The standardized regression weights closely approximated the validities for CRT-A and A-H Scale in Table 4.11, which suggests that controlling for gender and playing time had little effect on these relationships.

TABLE 5.2

Hierarchical Regression Analyses of Overt Aggression, Obstructionism, and Verbal Hostility With Playing Time and Gender Controlled

| | Overt Aggression | | | Obstructionism | | | Expressed Hostility | | |
|---|---|---|---|---|---|---|---|---|---|
| | β | $R^2$ | $\Delta R^2$ | β | $R^2$ | $\Delta R^2$ | β | $R^2$ | $\Delta R^2$ |
| Step 1 | | | | | | | | | |
| Controls + CRT-A | .53**a | .32** | | .61**a | .41** | | −.06a | .10** | |
| Step 2 | | | | | | | | | |
| A-H | .33**b | .42** | .10** | −.21** | .45** | .04** | .34** | .21** | .11** |
| Step 3 | | | | | | | | | |
| CRT-A × A-H | .26**c | .48** | .06** | −.22** | .50** | .05** | −.22** | .26** | .05** |

*Note.* CRT-A = Conditional Reasoning Test for Aggression; A-H = Angry Hostility Scale. Adapted from "Implicit and Explicit Personality: A Test of a Channeling Hypothesis for Aggressive Behavior," by B. C. Frost, C. E. Ko, and L. R. James, 2007, *Journal of Applied Psychology, 92,* p. 1312. Copyright 2007 by American Psychological Association.
aStandardized regression weight for CRT-A. bStandardized regression weight for A-H in Step 2. Regression weights for CRT-A differed only trivially from those reported for Step 1. cStandardized regression weight for CRT-A × A-H in Step 3.
** $p < .01$

The third step added the cross-product between the CRT-A and A-H Scale to the regression equation. The regression weights carrying the interaction effect were significant in all three equations. Increments in $R^2$ values produced by adding variables or cross-product terms to the equations are also reported. The magnitudes of the increments for the interaction effect were large in statistical terms (see Cohen, Cohen, West, & Aiken, 2003), as were the values of the $R^2$s produced by the interaction equations.

*Overt Aggression*

The graph in Figure 5.4 shows that the direction and magnitude of the regression slopes linking overt aggression to implicit preparedness to justify aggression (CRT-A) are dependent on self-perceived aggressiveness (A-H Scale). For illustrative purposes, the slopes in Figure 5.4 and in the subsequent figures are based on (a) players who had scores of plus one standard deviation from the mean on the A-H Scale (designated High Self-Reported Aggression in the figure) and (b) players who had scores of −1 standard deviation from the mean on the A-H Scale (designated Low Self-Reported Aggression). This is a recommended technique for reporting the results for a continuous moderator such as self-perceived aggression (see Cohen et al., 2003). (Technically, a separate slope exists for every value of self-perceived aggressiveness. One may think of these slopes as forming a fan that includes the two illustrative slopes. However, these two illustrative slopes are sufficient to show how this form of the integrative model may be employed to capture the concept of channeling.)

The steeper of the two regression slopes in Figure 5.4 suggests that when aggression is self-perceived as a characteristic component of one's behavior, the likelihood of engaging in overt aggressiveness is dependent on how strongly a player is implicitly prepared to justify aggression. At the lower end of this slope we have players whose self-perceived aggressiveness is not supported by being implicitly prepared to justify aggression. These are players in the lower right quadrant of Figure 5.3. Lack of implicit defenses presumably dampens the will to engage in overt aggressiveness. More specifically, James and Mazerolle (2002) proposed that without implicit protective mechanisms (i.e., moral disengagers, neutralizers; Bandura, 1999; Sykes & Matza, 1957), people who think of themselves as aggressive are likely to channel thoughts and behaviors toward inhibiting or at least dampening their self-ascribed aggressive tendencies. For example, these individuals are likely to be self-monitors, to be highly self-critical, and to be distrustful of their basic instincts and motives (which they believe to be aggressive). Behavior is likely to have a strong sense of self-control emanating from attempts to restrain self-attributed hostile impulses.

However, as implicit preparedness to rationalize aggression increases, players who think of themselves as aggressive become less likely to dampen their self-ascribed aggressiveness. Indeed, they become increasingly likely to channel their aggressiveness into overt acts of aggression. At the upper end of the steeper slope, we have players from the upper right quadrant of Figure 5.3. These individuals are prepared to rationalize a desire to harm others as self-defense, the righting of injustices, and the like. Moreover, they think of themselves as argumentative, easy to anger, and confrontational (but not necessarily malevolent, intentionally hostile, or taking pleasure in harming others). The implicit protection afforded by justification mechanisms allows these individuals to explicitly channel their aggressiveness into overt hostilities and still not perceive themselves as being malicious or hostile by nature.

The regression slope for players who report that they are low in aggressiveness is flatter than that for those higher in aggressiveness. These results indicate that implicit preparedness to justify aggression is not often, or at least not as often, channeled into overt aggression for people who think of themselves as nonaggressive. This includes players who are low in both the implicit and explicit components of aggression as well as players who could justify aggression but whose self-perceptions of nonaggressiveness appear to suppress their capacities to justify acting in overtly hostile manners.

*Obstructionism*

The steeper of the two slopes in Figure 5.5 shows that, for players who see themselves as nonaggressive, the lack of implicit preparedness to justify aggression denotes a lack of any form of behavioral aggression. The lower end of the slope comprises people who are typically prosocial (in the psychological sense; see Buss & Finn, 1987; Wright & Mischel, 1987), one indication being that they channel their behavior toward socially adaptive ends (see the lower left quadrant in Figure 5.3). For example, they are disposed to favor cooperation and harmony over vengeance and retribution (James & Mazerolle, 2002).

As implicit preparedness to rationalize aggression increases, perceptions of nonaggressiveness become self-delusions rather than accurate portrayals of true dispositions. Increases in implicit preparedness to justify aggression become increasingly likely to be channeled into obstructive behaviors. At the upper end of the slope, we have players who are quite likely to engage in obstructionism. The rationale for this prediction is that when aggression is not seen as a characteristic behavior, increases in the implicit capacity to justify aggression will be expressed in terms of passive-aggressive behaviors because these behaviors are easier (than overt forms of aggression) to justify as being nonaggressive (see the upper left quadrant of Figure 5.3). Simply stated, obstructive behaviors (blocking, not giving up the ball) are less obviously aggressive and therefore easier to rationalize than fighting, shoving, and pushing. With the aid of justification mechanisms, they allow the individual to maintain the self-deception that she or he is nonaggressive (Bing, Stewart, et al., 2007).

The second slope is flatter but still maintains a moderate degree of steepness, suggesting that increases in implicit preparedness to justify aggression have a modest tendency to be channeled into increases of obstructiveness for players who perceive themselves as aggressive. The key to this inference is players who have the stronger capacities to justify aggression (i.e., players who are in or approach the upper right quadrant of Figure 5.3). Although overt aggression is likely to be their preferred channel for expressing aggression, they might very well take advantage of opportunities to engage in passive forms of aggression (or passive aggression may be the only channel open to them). In contrast, players lacking the capacity to justify any form of aggression are not expected to engage in obstructive behaviors. The fear of social disapproval that would ensue if their self-ascribed hostile impulses were to surface is likely to place strong self-restraints on being obstructive.

*Verbal Expressions of Hostility*

Frost et al. (2007) offered no predictions for this criterion; they only attempted to understand the findings presented in Figure 5.6 and relate them to the integrative model. The regression slope for players who think of themselves as aggressive is negative, starting with a comparatively high number of verbal hostilities for players who lack an implicit capacity to justify aggression and decreasing to a comparatively moderate number of verbal hostilities for players who possess this implicit capacity. These findings suggest that (a) players who lack the justification mechanisms to protect themselves with rationalizations for any type of aggression, and yet think of themselves as being argumentative, easily angered, and confrontational (b) are prone to rely largely on verbal expressions of hostility as a means to express their self-attributed aggressiveness.

A possible explanation for these findings is that, lacking justification mechanisms, these individuals seek socially acceptable channels to indulge their self-attributed aggressiveness. Engaging in verbal expressions of hostility as emotions flare during the heat of competition bestows these expressions with a modest degree of social acceptability. Modest social acceptability presumably reduces the need for moral disengagement (Bandura, 1999) and neutralizers (Sykes & Matza, 1957), opening the door for explicitly aggressive but implicitly defenseless players to aggress without having to rationalize. It appears that these players are drawn to the use of verbal hostilities as a means to express, and perhaps self-validate, their beliefs that they are easy to anger, confrontational, and hostile. Consistent with this interpretation are prior results that show that these same individuals avoid channels that require implicit defenses for more seriously aggressive acts (i.e., overt hostilities, obstructionism).

The regression slope for players who think of themselves as nonaggressive is less steep than that for self-described aggressive players. Moreover, the intercept indicates a comparatively infrequent use of verbal hostilities. These results denote that increases in the implicit preparedness to justify aggression are infrequently channeled into verbal hostilities for people low in self-perceived aggression. It appears that the self-perceptions of being nonaggressive suppress verbal aggression.

*Discussion of Results*

Strong support was found for the channeling hypothesis and integrative model of aggression in the Frost et al. (2007) study. A multiplicative combination of implicit defenses and explicit self-attributions based on a channeling hypothesis from Winter et al. (1998) accounted for significant if not substantial amounts of variance in all three aggressive behaviors. More specifically, tests of the integrative model produced the following three primary results regarding the dispositional correlates of aggression.

1. Individuals who explicitly perceive themselves as aggressive and have the implicit justification mechanisms in place to rationalize behaving aggressively tend to engage in all three forms of aggression studied here. Overt aggression appears to be particularly attractive to them.

2. Individuals who do not explicitly perceive themselves as aggressive but who are implicitly prepared to justify aggression tend to channel their aggressiveness into passively aggressive behaviors.
3. Individuals who are not implicitly prepared to rationalize being aggressive but who explicitly perceive themselves as being confrontational and hostile tend to channel their self-imputed aggressiveness into verbal expressions of aggression.

The present results are consistent with the results of three additional tests of the integrative model of aggression reported in Bing, Stewart, et al. (2007). Two studies involved students and one study involved hospital employees. Each of these studies supported the hypothesis that self-described aggressiveness channels the ways in which the implicit preparedness to justify aggression finds expression in behavior. For example, Bing et al. reanalyzed the data from Study 3 in Tables 4.5 and 4.6. They showed that lying about credits deserved for participating in a college experiment was predicted by implicit preparedness to justify aggression (assessed by the Verbal/Visual Conditional Reasoning Test of Aggression). However, these relationships were significantly moderated by the self-described aggressiveness of the students. Those who described themselves as aggressive were more likely to lie about the extra credit they deserved if they had implicit mechanisms in place to rationalize a desire to aggress. (Lying was viewed as an indirect expression of aggressiveness, namely, an attempt to retaliate against powerful others [professors] without being caught; see Chapter 4.) Thus, individuals high in both the implicit and explicit components of aggression had the highest probabilities of engaging in untruthfulness.

Individuals high in self-reported aggression but lacking implicit defenses were the least likely to lie about the extra credit they deserved, a finding consistent with a proposed tendency to self-monitor and avoid socially inappropriate behavior. The remaining individuals (i.e., those low on both personality scales, and those with high implicit aggression but low self-described aggressiveness) also had low scores on the criterion. Here again we see a consistency with the integrative model of aggression. Prosocial proclivities were the order of the day for nonaggressive and passive aggressive individuals; that is, these individuals did not engage in overtly (but indirectly) aggressive behaviors. The regression slopes, when oriented as reported above, closely resemble those found for overt aggression in Figure 5.4. That the interaction was highly significant is also consistent with the Frost et al. (2007) results.

Thus, a laboratory test on students, field tests on both students and hospital employees, and a field test on intramural basketball players agree that it is the multiplicative combination of the explicit and implicit aggressive personalities that is most efficacious in predicting aggressive behaviors. We believe the results reported above are the strongest because the criteria offer the clearest manifest indicators of aggression. For the first time we were able to examine differential relationships for three different types of aggression. The consequence of this opportunity is that we appear to have gained greater insight into why people with the same justification mechanisms in place (i.e., strong defenses for aggression) behave differently; their behavior is a function of their explicit beliefs about their own aggressiveness. We also see why individuals who think of themselves as aggressive shy away from true aggressiveness; people who lack the justification mechanisms that would generate protective rationalizations tend not to engage in overtly or even passively aggressive behaviors.

### Integrative Model of Assessment for Achievement Motivation

The approach used above to test an integrative model for aggression was extended to construct and test a second integrative model. This model was based on self-reports of achievement motivation and a CR measure of relative motive strength, which many people refer to as the CR test for achievement motivation. We recently tested this model, designated the integrative model of assessment for achievement motivation (Bing, LeBreton, Migetz, Davison, & James, 2007).

The basic integrative model is summarized in Exhibit 5.1 (Bing, LeBreton, et al., 2007; James, McIntyre, & LeBreton, 2000; James & Mazerolle, 2002). The top of the model focuses on the explicit personality, that is, whether people describe themselves as high in achievement motivation (e.g., "I enjoy doing things that challenge me"; "I strive to achieve all I can") or low in achievement motivation and high in fear of failure (e.g., "I would rather do an easy job than one involving obstacles that must be overcome"; "I don't enjoy hard work"). The left side of the model describes aspects of the implicit personality; that is, a distinction between high and low relative motive strength (RMS) based on the CRT-RMS. As presented in Chapter 3, the objective of measurement on the CRT-RMS is to determine whether an individual *consistently* prefers achievement motivation (AM) alternatives or fear of failure (FF) alternatives to CR problems. Respondents who consistently select AM alternatives are believed to possess a motive structure in which the motive to achieve dominates the motive to avoid failure. These respondents have strongly positive scores on the RMS Scale and are considered to be AMs. Conversely, consistent selection of FF alternatives is indicative of a motive structure in which the motive to avoid failing dominates the motive to achieve (i.e., the respondents scored as FFs on the RMS Scale because they have strongly negative scores). Lack of a consistent pattern of favoritism suggests that neither

## EXHIBIT 5.1
### Integrative Model of Personality Assessment for Achievement Motivation

| | Self-Reported Fear of Failure | Self-Reported Achievement Motivation |
|---|---|---|
| Conditional reasoning test | "I am easygoing."<br>"I get anxious in testing situations."<br>"I am not obsessive about work."<br>"I move to another task if a problem is too difficult." | "I am driven to get ahead."<br>"I strive to achieve all I can."<br>"I am something of a workaholic."<br>"I have a strong desire to be a success." |
| *JMs for Achievement Motivation* | *Hesitant AMs* | *Congruent AMs* |
| Personal Responsibility Bias | Have conscious concerns about stress and avoiding obsessions | Approach achievement-oriented tasks |
| Opportunity Bias<br>Positive Connotation of Achievement Striving Bias | Have an underlying enthusiasm for plunging into achievement-oriented tasks | Are ambitious, aspiring, and industrious |
| Malleability of Skills Bias<br>Identification with Achievers Bias | Experience many approach-avoidance conflicts | |
| *JMs for Fear of Failure* | *Congruent FFs* | *AM Pretenders* |
| External Attribution Bias | Avoid achievement-oriented tasks | Perceive themselves as high achievers, but are disposed to reason based on FF JMs |
| Liability/Threat Bias | Are fearful, nervous, and anxious | |
| Negative Connotation of Achievement Striving Bias<br>Fixed Skills Bias<br>Indirect Compensation Bias<br>Identification With Failure Bias | | Experience conscious pressure to approach achievement-oriented tasks, but actually approach those tasks on which they can deflect responsibility for failure |

*Note.* JM = justification mechanism; FFs = people driven by a fear of failure, for whom the motive to avoid failure dominates the motive to achieve; AMs = people for whom the motive to achieve dominates the motive to avoid failure. Reprinted from *Personality in Work Organizations* (p.183), by L. R. James and M. D. Mazerolle, 2002, Thousand Oaks, CA: Sage Publications. Copyright 2002 by Sage Publications. Reprinted with permission.

type of motive dominates, and relative motive strength is regarded as "indeterminate."

Presented within the model is a typology based on attempts to integrate the self-described or explicit source of information with the CR or implicit source of information. As with aggression, the four cells in the model are based on pure types (e.g., a clear AM vs. a clear FF crossed with high vs. low self-perceived achievement motivation). In reality, a continuum exists for both relative motive strength and self-perceived achievement motivation (high fear of failure is implied). If we were to cross these two continua, we would generate a very large number of cells, each representing a degree of variation from the ideal prototypes presented in Exhibit 5.1. As before, our analyses of data relating to the model take this into account by using continuous scores for both the explicit and implicit measures of personality.

*Conditions of Congruence*

The upper right cell of the integrative models consists of persons who explicitly perceive themselves as achievement motivated and who possess the corresponding implicit justification mechanisms to enhance the logical appeal of approaching achievement-oriented behaviors. Again, this is a case of what Winter et al. (1998) referred to as a congruency between the implicit and explicit personalities. Individuals in this quadrant are prepared to justify approaching challenging tasks, frame demanding tasks as worthy of effort and commitment, persist in the face of initial failure, and to believe they can improve their skills with practice and effort. Basically, a strong achievement motive is protected, and reflected, by strong justifications. Moreover, this framing and reasoning are channeled into achievement-oriented behaviors by self-perceptions suggesting high levels of dedication, motivation, willingness to learn, and ambition.

The lower left quadrant of the model contains the other source of congruency between the explicit and implicit personalities. Individuals in this quadrant view themselves as low in achievement motivation (or high in fear of failure). They also tend to reason in ways that promote the avoidance of demanding or challenging activities (or inhibiting effort if those activities are inescapable). Stated alternatively, members of this quadrant will be avoidant when the situation permits or will rely on justification mechanisms to inhibit their applying effort in a challenging situation when such a situation is unavoidable. Basically, self-perceptions that suggest fear of failure are protected by FF justification mechanisms that serve to dampen enthusiasm for achievement and to justify avoidance of achievement activities, or withdrawal from such activities when success becomes uncertain or failure becomes likely.

Viewed in terms of channeling, a strong implicit desire to avoid humiliation by failing is channeled into avoidance of demanding tasks by self-perceptions that one is not obsessed to achieve success and an awareness of evaluation apprehension.

*Conditions of Incongruence*

The upper left quadrant contains individuals who perceive themselves as nonachievers but who, incongruously, reason in ways that enhance the rational appeal of achievement-oriented tasks, suggesting a strong latent desire to achieve. These appear to be individuals with conscious concerns for the stress and obsessiveness that can characterize some high achievers. These conscious concerns may serve to dampen if not inhibit a strong latent disposition to plunge into achievement-oriented tasks. The accompanying proclivity to reason in ways that justify approaching demanding tasks is likely to engender strong approach-avoidance conflicts with the self-perception of being cautious and stress avoidant. When reason wins out, approach of achievement-oriented tasks will occur, but it will likely be a careful, deliberate approach subject to being arrested if excessive stress is experienced.

Finally, the lower right quadrant contains individuals who see themselves as high achievers but who, incongruously, have FF justification mechanisms in place. These individuals are fearful, nervous, and anxious when faced with achievement-oriented tasks. However, these individuals' perceptions of themselves as achievers check most attempts to engage openly in avoidance/withdrawal behaviors. Instead, to remain consistent with their self-perceptions, these individual experience conscious pressure to approach achievement-oriented tasks. This incongruence between the implicit and explicit personality likely engenders strong approach-avoidance conflicts. The extant FF justification mechanisms likely play a protective, albeit subtle, role here. One means by which the FF justification mechanisms can subtly protect these individuals from the uncertainties and potential aversive consequences of achievement striving is to shield them from responsibility for failure, should failure occur.

For example, individuals in this cell may attempt only those achievement-oriented tasks for which an excuse of nonaccountability is available (e.g., failure, if it occurs, is due to uncontrollable external forces). A second example consists of what in Chapter 3 was described as "unnecessary diffusion of responsibility." Unnecessary diffusion occurs when, as an attempt to avoid complete responsibility for important decisions, an executive disperses decision-making responsibility to others, such as subordinates, committees, or teams. Such dispersion is unnecessary, even counterproductive, but is justified by the executive as a form of participative management or empowerment.

## Tests of the Integrative Model of Assessment
## for Achievement Motivation

We tested the integrative model for achievement motivation on a sample of 263 middle-level managers who participated in an assessment center (Bing, LeBreton, et al., 2007). The criterion consisted of scores on an in-basket exercise. High scores on this exercise were obtained by managers who were willing to assume personal responsibility for the outcomes of their business decisions. A correlation (empirical validity) of .39 was obtained between scores on the RMS scale and performance on the in-basket exercise. Scores from this scale correlated .32 with scores on Achievement via Independence from the California Psychological Inventory (CPI; Gough & Bradley, 1996). The CPI is the self-report measure used in this study and, like the CRT-RMS, was given to the managers during the assessment center. The self-descriptions of achievement motivation furnished by the CPI correlated .38 with in-basket performance. Both the CPI and the CRT-RMS contributed uniquely and significantly to prediction of in-basket performance in a multiple regression after controlling for cognitive ability (assessed via the Watson-Glaser Critical Thinking Inventory; Watson & Glaser, 1980).

The graph in Figure 5.7 shows that the slopes of the regression lines linking in-basket performance to relative motive strength do not differ significantly as a function of self-perceived achievement motivation. There is no interaction. The intercepts of the slopes did, however, differ significantly ($p < .01$). Statistical procedures employed to generate the slopes in this figure are based on hierarchical regression as described in Cohen et al. (2003). The illustrative slopes for high and low self-reported achievement motivation are, like self-reported aggression, based on scores of +1 and −1 standard deviation above and below the means on the CPI self-report scale.

The higher of the two regression slopes—that is, the slope with the significantly higher intercept—suggests that when achievement is perceived to be a characteristic component of personality, the likelihood of attaining successful performance in an executive selection task is dependent on how strongly a manager is implicitly prepared to achieve. At the lower end of this slope we have individuals whose self-perceived motivation is not supported by a strong implicit motive to achieve or implicit preparation to justify achievement activities. Lack of implicit defenses presumably dampens the will to engage in this achievement-oriented activity.

Note, however, that conscious desires to achieve may have had a salutary effect on the performance of these individuals. Consequently, the performance of individuals with low implicit AM and high explicit AM was better than that of individuals with a low/low pattern (see the lower end of the slope with the lower intercept). On the other hand, anxiety over possible failure likely

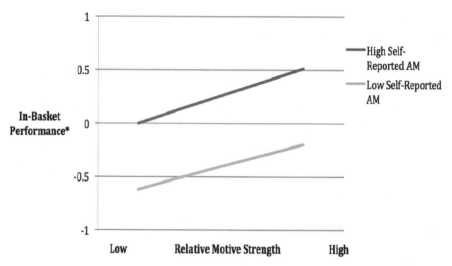

*Figure 5.7.* Integrative model for assessment centers. AM = achievement motivation. Adapted from *Personality in Work Organizations,* by L. R. James and M. D. Mazerolle, 2002. Thousand Oaks, CA: Sage Publications. Copyright 2002 by Sage Publications, Inc. Adapted with permission.
*Scored in standard deviation units.

interfered at least partially with the performance of the low/high group on the high-stress in-basket exercise. The result was comparatively lower scores on the in-basket exercise for these individuals compared to those scoring high/high (i.e., high implicit AM and high explicit AM). In other words, as indicated by the upper slope, as the implicit desire to achieve increased for people who thought of themselves as achievers, the likelihood of performing well on the in-basket exercise increased.

Turning now to the lower slope, the anxiety of being evaluated in an evocative, high-demand situation appeared to inhibit the performance of individuals in the low/low quadrant. That is, the anticipation of failure and its accompanying embarrassment likely produced "test anxiety" (cf. Sarason, 1978), which in turn interfered with performance (e.g., the managers choked under pressure). The behavioral result was that the low/low individuals had the lowest average scores of any of the managers on the in-basket exercise. As the implicit motive to achieve increased, however, performance on the in-basket exercise also increased for people who did not think of themselves as achievement oriented. Apparently, in evocative situations, the implicit personality may trump the explicit personality even for those whose self-conscious fears make them hesitant to engage.

The key to Figure 5.7 is that a highly significant difference ($p < .001$) in the intercepts, when combined with a nonsignificant interaction, argues for the use of an *additive* model on which to base the integration of CR and self-reported motivation. High/high individuals had the highest in-basket scores of all subgroups because they were high both on relative motive strength and self-ascribed achievement motivation. Low/low individuals had the lowest performance of all subgroups because they were low on both relative motive strength and self-ascribed achievement motivation. In-basket performances of the incongruent subgroups fell between those of the two congruent subgroups.

An opportunity to replicate the test of the integrative model for achievement motivation was provided by a study of 267 college undergraduates who had scores on both a CRT-RMS and a self-report measure of achievement motivation (i.e., Achievement Striving facet of the Conscientiousness factor of the NEO-PI-R). Overall grade point average (GPA) served as the criterion. Scores on the RMS scale correlated .00 with scores on self-reported Achievement Striving.

Predictions were based on the additive interpretation of the integrative model. Individuals with a high/high configuration were predicted to have the highest performance scores (GPAs) of all subgroups because they were high both on self-ascribed achievement motivation and on relative motive strength. These are individuals who see themselves as achievement oriented and who have the justification mechanisms in place to justify huge expenditures of effort to achieve. Individuals with a low/low configuration were predicted to have the lowest GPAs of all subgroups. These are individuals who did not see themselves as high in achievement motivation and are prepared to justify avoidance of high-demand situations (or to rationalize failure, should it occur). The GPAs of individuals with incongruent configurations (i.e., low/high and high/low) were hypothesized to fall between those of the two congruent subgroups.

These predictions produced two primary statistical hypotheses. First, the regression slopes relating GPA to relative motive strength for students high and low in self-described achievement motivation were both predicted to be positive. Second, the two slopes were predicted to be roughly parallel in slope and significantly varied in intercept.

We again controlled for the effects of cognitive ability using ACT scores as a proxy for general mental ability. Graphic results of the statistical analyses are presented in Figure 5.8. Both hypotheses were confirmed. An additive model fit the data. This means that the CR measure combined with the self-report measure to significantly enhance prediction over either of the personality measures taken separately. Moreover, the intercepts for the regression slopes varied significantly, whereas the slopes themselves did not (i.e., the interaction is not significant).

Most striking is the similarity in the patterns of slopes when Figure 5.8 is compared with Figure 5.7. The results displayed in Figure 5.8 appear to replicate the results presented in Figure 5.7. Thus, two field tests, one based

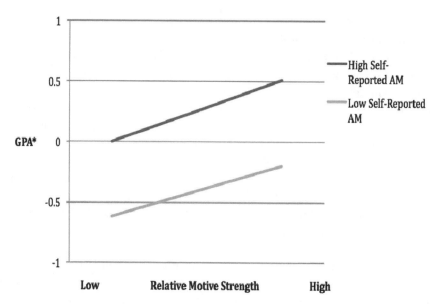

*Figure 5.8.* Integrative model for grade point average. AM = achievement motivation; GPA = grade point average. Adapted from (a) "Integrating Implicit and Explicit Social Cognitions forr Enhanced Personality Assessment: A General Framework for Choosing Measurement and Statistical Methods," by M. N. Bing, J. M. LeBreton, H. K. Davison, D. Z. Migetz, and L. R. James, 2007, *Organizational Research Methods, 10,* p. 376. Copyright 2007 by Sage Publications, Inc., and (b) *Personality in Work Organizations,* by L. R. James and M. D. Mazerolle, 2002. Thousand Oaks, CA: Sage Publications. Copyright 2002 by Sage Publications, Inc. Adapted with permission.
*Scored in standard deviation units.

on middle-level managers and one based on students, coincided in their support of an additive integrative model for achievement motivation. In addition to these additive effects, we also proposed and found evidence for additional interactions and quadratic effects. The interested reader is directed to Bing, LeBreton, et al. (2007).

## CONCLUDING COMMENTS REGARDING INTEGRATIVE MODELS

Results of multiple tests of integrative models, involving two different personality domains, indicate that Winter et al. (1998) were correct in their assumption that traits channel the ways in which latent motives are expressed in cognitive, emotional, and physical behaviors. For example, individuals with strong motives to aggress may, depending on different characteristic ways of behaving, engage in active forms of aggression, such as verbal or physical attack, or in passive forms of aggression, such as withholding effort. Or individuals with strong motives to achieve may commit themselves completely and intensely to the pursuit of excellence and mastery or they may approach achievement-oriented tasks with hesitation resulting from conflict over whether to approach a challenging task or to avoid a possible psychological hazard.

If research continues to indicate that the same motive is channeled and expressed in different ways by individuals with different explicit self-perceptions, then personality research is in for some serious changes. Theoretically, models of the form presented in Tables 5.1 and 5.2 and Figure 5.3 will need to be considered. In fact, these rather simple integrative models are likely to give way to more complex models that consider multiple implicit motives and explicitly described traits simultaneously.

Earlier, we agreed with Winter et al. that the ease and comfort with which a latent motive is expressed appears to be related to whether it is congruent with characteristic ways of adapting to one's environment. Our research on aggression and achievement motivation also indicates that congruence between latent motive and trait is less likely to engender conflict than lack of congruence. However, the motive to avoid failure and a characteristic pattern of avoidance behavior are also congruent. Yet, the justification mechanisms for fear of failure suggest that FFs are consistently engaged in a conflict between motive-driven avoidance and culturally valent achievement. So things may get a bit more complex than the simple hypothesis of congruence indicates.

Finally, the statistical form taken by the integrative relation between latent motive and explicit trait appears to depend on the personality variables under examination. Both additive and nonadditive models have been replicated. Future research may identify still other patterns (curvilinear relations with or without additivity; Bing, LeBreton, et al., 2007). And multivariate models are likely when multiple motives and/or traits are considered simultaneously.

# 6

## FUTURE DIRECTIONS:
## NEW CONSTRUCTIONS

Our objective in this "idea chapter" is to suggest possible applications of the conditional reasoning (CR) principles of assessing the implicit personality beyond aggression and achievement motivation/fear of failure. We illustrate how CR might be used to measure justification mechanisms that we believe contribute to depression, addiction proneness, and toxic leadership. These psychological constructs were chosen to represent broad domains of psychology, including but not limited to clinical psychology, counseling and educational psychology, social psychology, and industrial–organizational psychology. Our intent is to illustrate how CR principles can be applied to identify and measure potentially useful justification mechanisms in each of these broad domains.

The first illustrative justification mechanism is a *negative self-bias* (NSB). In the more extensive discussion to follow, we define an NSB as an implicit propensity to view the self through a lens of inadequacy and to reason in ways that render one personally at fault for one's perceived failures. We believe that this may be one of the myriad factors predisposing people to depression, and then reinforcing the depression, because it encourages people to infer that they are unworthy and incompetent in various life domains. The capacity to measure an NSB via CR could give therapists such as clinical psychologists an additional avenue for assessing the breadth and depth of cognitive dysfunction in regard to the self-concept. These assessments might assist in decisions regarding treatment strategy.

Assessments of the NSB could also be used in a number of ways in clinical research. In earlier chapters, we discussed dissociative models, which involved comparisons of explicit, typically self-report, measures and implicit CR tests with respect to correlations with third variables (e.g., behavioral criteria). Similar research could be conducted here. For example, scores on the Beck Depression Inventory (BDI; Beck, 2006) could be compared with NSB scores. If the pattern of prior research repeats itself, then the scores will have a low correlation. And if history is again predictive, it will be found that scores on the BDI predict criteria different from the NSB scores. Thus, we would expect to find different relationships with such things as time of onset of depression, length of depressive episodes, severity of depression, and the likelihood of committing suicide.

It might also be found that the explicit BDI has an integrative relationship with the implicit NSB. Investigators could build models in which the explicit BDI channels the implicit NSB. To illustrate, a strong implicit negative self-bias might be channeled into overt actions such as suicide if the BDI indicates severe self-ascriptions of depression. However, a strong implicit self-bias coupled with a nonsevere self-assessment of depression on the BDI could indicate indirect and subtle forms for expressing latent perceptions of inadequacy.

The second illustration involves justification mechanisms that are thought to be associated with addiction proneness. We will briefly describe five justification mechanisms that are believed to contribute to how people rationalize addictive behavior. We will also suggest that assessments of these justification mechanisms might be used along with other factors to aid in the identification of addiction-prone individuals. This information might be useful to counseling and educational psychologists, among others.

The potential application of CR measures is indicated by a recent article regarding the need for a system that assists in the identification of people with a latent propensity to engage in substance abuse (Conway et al., 2010). The authors recommended "liability to addiction" as a latent variable that predisposes certain people to addiction. They suggested that current "shortcomings" in research and clinical practice

> can be overcome through the use of new technologies to develop reliable, valid, and standardized assessment instrument(s) to measure and distinguish individual variations in the expressions of the latent trait(s) [liability to addiction] that comprise propensity to and severity of drug addiction. (Conway et al., 2010, p. 4)

We believe that the CR procedure we describe in this chapter could serve as one of the instruments that will be developed in response to this article.

Our final illustration is targeted to those who work in the field of leadership (e.g., industrial–organizational psychologists, social psychologists). Two forms of CR are introduced here. First, we discuss reasoning that distinguishes leaders from nonleaders. Second, we describe reasoning and supporting justification mechanisms that differentiate between two primary types of leaders. Type 1 is composed of people with strong needs for "instrumental influence." These leaders desire influence in order to promote cooperation, maintain order, dispense justice, avoid conflict, develop people, and enhance productivity and profits. In contrast, Type 2 is composed of people with strong needs for "egoistic dominance." These leaders seek influence in order to dominate others and to enhance their personal entitlements (e.g., their privileges, status, prestige).

Leaders motivated by egoistic dominance (Dominators) often prove to be toxic to organizations. These leaders seek and use influence in ways that are counterproductive or harmful to organizations, to those around them, or even to themselves (i.e., they are self-destructive). Unfortunately, Dominators are seldom aware of the full extent of their toxic capacity. This is because, like most leaders, Dominators tend to solve problems in much the same way as expert decision makers do, like grand chess masters who simply look at a chessboard and see potential winning strategies (see Kahneman & Klein, 2009). We believe these leaders think of problem solving and decision making as reflecting their intuition (Klein, 1998). What Dominators do not understand is that they are predisposed to intuitively arrive at strategies that confer control and status to themselves. To them, this is simply good leadership.

But their leadership is actually being shaped by justification mechanisms that threaten their capacity to engage in rational analyses. Their strategic decision making is thereby compromised. What they think of as effective leadership ultimately dooms them and their organizations because their tacit knowledge structure and strategic decision making lead to decisions that frustrate and hinder the performance, development, and advancement of qualified and motivated individuals and cause short- or long-term harm to their organizations. We believe that there are many ways for psychologists to attempt to address this problem. For example, once potential Dominators are identified, one could follow Kahneman and Klein's (2009) general recommendation and develop artificial intelligence programs to aid Dominators develop more effective and less toxic strategic decisions. These or other forms of decision aids could be included in the techniques executive coaches use to counsel leaders. We proceed now to our illustrations of possible new CR tests, beginning with depression.

# DEPRESSION

Depression is one of the major mental health concerns in the United States (Beck & Alford, 2009; Weissman, 1987), affecting 17% of adults at some point in their lifetime (Kessler et al., 2005). Depression represents a major concern in part because it has been linked to a number of serious mental and physical health outcomes, including increased risk for suicide (Dumais et al., 2005; Fergusson, Horwood, Ridder, & Beautrias, 2005; Guze & Robins, 1970), alcohol abuse/dependence (Swendsen & Merikangas, 2000), diabetes (Anderson, Freedland, Clouse, & Lustman, 2001), cardiovascular disease (Glassman, 2007; Van der Kooy et al., 2007), anxiety (Assano, Rossi, & Pini, 1994), and nicotine dependence, educational underachievement, unemployment, and early parenthood (Fergusson & Woodward, 2002). Given such serious mental and physical health consequences, the early identification of individuals who are at risk for developing depression would make an important contribution to research and practice involving depression.

We suggest it might be possible to assist in the identification of individuals who are at risk for developing depression by focusing on a key depression-linked justification mechanism, the NSB. People with an NSB are implicitly disposed to view themselves through a lens of inadequacy and to reason in ways that render them personally at fault for all or at least most of their perceived inadequacies (see Baumeister et al., 2003; Crocker & Park, 2004; DuBois & Flay, 2004). This bias further engenders expectancies of failure in future endeavors (see James, 1998). People with NSBs typically have low self-esteem because they unconsciously filter information and reason in manners that foster, at the conscious level, negative self-perceptions. Self-perceptions and inferences that would be self-enhancing are overlooked or discounted by being attributed to unstable or external factors (e.g., luck, external assistance). Unfavorable information is magnified and given comparatively greater weight than it deserves. Basically, an NSB works to promote a generalized feeling of unworthiness and incompetence in various life domains. Although perception and thinking are negatively distorted by an NSB, people with NSBs accept their perceptions as veridical and their analyses as impartial and rational. They have no knowledge of their NSB, and introspection will not shed light on its presence in the unconscious.

Our concern is the distortions that people with NSBs unknowingly engage in to channel analyses toward casting the self in a negative light. Several of the more salient of these biases are

- a tendency to overestimate personal factors (e.g., lack of motivation and/or skills) and to underestimate external factors (e.g., lack of resources, insufficient training) when making attributions about the causes of failure;

- a propensity to assume that problem-solving skills are fixed and cannot be enhanced through experience, training, or dedication to learning;
- a proclivity to attend selectively to information that confirms an expectancy of failure on even moderately demanding tasks; and
- a disposition to be overly critical when comparing abilities, assets, skills, and knowledge to those of others, which is a cornerstone to feelings of inadequacy.

We illustrate the assessment of the NSB justification mechanism using the CR item format. Please consider the following logical premises:

Promotion at Company A is based on a set of standards. To be promoted, people must have performed successfully on their present job, be liked by their coworkers, be acceptable to management, and be prepared to take on more responsibilities. It has been found that the people in Company A who meet these standards tend to do well after being promoted.

People with an NSB are predisposed to feel threatened by this logical set of premises. That is, the reasoning proclivities of people with NSBs are likely to engender considerable skepticism that they, if working at Company A, would be able to meet the standards for promotion. Ways in which they might find the premises threatening are illustrated by the following:

- the promotion standards would highlight their preexisting (i.e., fixed) deficits in their abilities and skills for performing their present jobs;
- their inadequacies to deal with others, including their coworkers, would be exposed;
- it is most unlikely that management would think of them as acceptable for promotion; and
- holding more responsibility would likely engender even greater threat.

Thus, the request for a logical analysis of the standards for promotion at Company A draws out the same types of distortions that NSBs engage in to promote their own inadequacies. Similarity of distortion occurs because the premises are inconsistent with the self-depreciating reasoning that is characteristic of NSBs, as illustrated earlier. This suggests that it is possible to prime the use of the NSB by asking people with NSBs to analyze logical premises that conflict with (or support) reasoning known to be engendered by their bias. In the resulting attempts to furnish logical and impartial analyses, respondents who are NSBs will unknowingly reveal the types of distorted reasoning that is characteristic of their NSBs. Using our knowledge of this reasoning bias, we adopted the premises above and used them to build the CR problem presented in Exhibit 6.1.

## Straightforward, Logical Answer

In attempting to find a logical answer, many respondents will identify the following unstated assumption: People who are promoted according to the standards tend to be successful because the standards are based on important factors for success. Alternative C is thus a logically correct answer to the problem—"The standards for promotion at Company A appear to be based on important factors for success." Alternative C is not shaped by the NSB and thus represents a straightforward, logical answer.

## NSB Answer

Alternative B is based on an inference that people with NSBs are likely to be logically attracted to, given the threatening nature of the premises to the problem. This inference is given in alternative B: "The bar for promotion at Company A is rather high." As discussed already, NSBs unconsciously seek out information that indicates that they are inadequate. Alternative B offers the type of self-deprecating reasoning that NSBs seek. The reasoning is designed to project an image of not being up to meeting the standards for promotion. Such reasoning is intended to be logically appealing to NSBs because

---

EXHIBIT 6.1
Sample Conditional Reasoning Problem Designed
to Measure Negative Self-Bias

---

Promotion at Company A is based on a set of standards. To be promoted, people must have performed successfully on their present job, be liked by their coworkers, be acceptable to management, and be prepared to take on more responsibilities. It has been found that the people in Company A who meet these standards tend to do well after being promoted.

Based on the above, we might reasonably conclude that

- A. Only the relatives of the managers at Company A are given the upper level positions.
- B. The bar for promotion at Company A is rather high.
- C. The standards for promotion at Company A appear to be based on important factors for success.
- D. People who work at Company A tend to be unhappy with the fairness of the promotion process.

---

it offers them the opportunity to think of the self (i.e., the typical applicant) as less worthy than outstanding others (i.e., employees of Company A who do meet the standards).

Alternative B thus projects an image designed to trigger the NSB and to offer reasoning that is logically appealing to those who are unconsciously disposed to seek out negative information about the self. The decision to solve the problem with alternative B reveals the likely presence of an NSB in the unconscious personality. There is a high probability, therefore, that many of these respondents are people with NSBs.

As we have stated previously, a probabilistic statement is necessary because some respondents might select alternative B for reasons other than possessing a latent NSB. For example, a respondent may have had a recent negative experience with promotion that affects his or her reasoning on this problem. What is important for measurement is whether a respondent consistently selects NSB forms of reasoning across a set of problems that vary in terms of assertion and subject matter. It is the consistent selection of NSB alternatives that most reliably reveals the unconscious personality.

Respondents who lack an implicit NSB will determine that the NSB alternative is less logically appealing than alternative C. Although they may not be able to reject the NSB alternative on purely logical grounds, they are unlikely to be receptive to the image of self-depreciation projected by this alternative.

### Illogical Answers

Alternatives A and D are illogical and designed to be selected by no or very few respondents.

In sum, we believe that a number of important justification mechanisms can serve as precursors to depression. In our example, we focused on a justification mechanism that we believe may play a significant role in the development of depression—the NSB. This bias may be revealed by engaging individuals in CR problems. The key is to include item content in the stem of the item that will trigger the NSB. In our example, we sought to activate this bias by asking individuals to analyze a premise centered on the evocative subject of promotion. These premises are likely to trigger the basic implicit belief structure of NSBs and thus served as content for constructing our item.

It is noteworthy that we suggest testing an NSB to see if it adds incrementally in both a statistical sense and a substantive sense to the myriad factors already in use to assess the propensity to develop different forms of depression. We suggest further that, in testing the efficacy of an NSB, investigators consider the use of the dissociative models and channeling models we mentioned earlier in this chapter and described in prior chapters.

# ADDICTION PRONENESS

Like depression, substance abuse occurs frequently in the United States (Substance Abuse and Mental Health Services Administration, 2007) and carries with it a host of negative consequences for not only the individual but also for society at large. For example, at the personal level, excessive alcohol consumption has been linked to increased risk of heart failure (Djoussé & Gaziano, 2008) and stroke (Saremi & Arora, 2008). At the societal level, substance abuse and addiction have been linked to criminal behavior (Center for Substance Abuse Prevention, 1995; Fendrich, Goldstein, Spunt, Brownstein, & Mackesy-Amiti, 1995) as well as to injuries, illness, and absenteeism in the workplace (Cohen, 1984; Frone, 2004; Martin, Kraft, & Roman, 1994). Given such relationships, the early identification of individuals who are prone to becoming addicted to drugs, alcohol, and tobacco would make an important contribution to research and practice involving substance abuse.

Bowler, Bowler, and James (in press) suggested that it is possible to assist in the identification of at-risk individuals because these individuals often rely on a unique set of addiction-related justification mechanisms. That is, addiction-prone individuals frame and reason about the world (and more specifically, their addictive activities) in a manner that is qualitatively different than used by individuals who are not addiction prone. These authors were quick to note that addiction-prone individuals are likely not a homogenous group and not all addiction-prone individuals rely on the identical justification mechanisms. Instead, they argued that it was possible to isolate a unique family of justification mechanisms that addiction-prone individuals may call on to rationalize their continued engagement in a behavior that is dysfunctional to the point of being life-threatening. Not all addiction-prone individuals are presumed to rely equally on all justification mechanisms for their rationalizations. Some individuals may rely on all justification mechanisms, and others may invoke only one or two. Whatever the case, what is critical is the identification of the reasoning processes (i.e., justification mechanisms) individuals use to facilitate (i.e., justify) their participation in the addictive activity.

Bowler et al. (in press) identified five justification mechanisms that they believe contribute strongly to the rationalization of addictive behavior and thus represent a possible basis for aiding in the identification of addiction-prone individuals. The first justification mechanism is the NSB just described. The second justification mechanism is the *evasion of discomfort bias*, which represents an implicit tendency to overestimate the distress and anxiety associated with adverse circumstances. Individuals with this bias tend to frame minor nuisances as major irritants. As such, any activity that removes or reduces the distressing experience is justifiable. As Bowler et al. noted, the addictive activity (e.g., drugs, alcohol) serves the dual purposes of temporarily distracting the individual from the source of stress and offering a mechanism for relieving the stress. Thus, individuals rely on this justification mechanism to rationalize engaging in the addictive activity because it facilitates relief from the overwhelming distress they are experiencing.

The third justification mechanism is the *immediate gratification bias*. This bias involves an implicit framing of pleasurable acts as most important, irrespective of the consequences of those acts. This is a fairly hedonistic bias, with individuals being predisposed to rationalize the selection of activities that serve as temporally proximal sources of satisfaction over activities that might serve as temporally distal sources of satisfaction. In addition, individuals with this bias tend to discount the negative long-term consequences and implications of these pleasurable acts, such as the long-term negative toll that alcohol, drugs, and smoking can take on one's body. Bowler et al. (in press) suggested that both the evasion of discomfort bias and the immediate gratification bias involve rationalizations for behavior designed to reduce or relieve stress. However, the primary difference is that the former bias is activated by the perception of overwhelming environmental stressors, whereas the latter bias is focused on the euphoric effect associated with engaging in the addictive behavior.

The fourth justification mechanism is the *self-revision bias*, which refers to an implicit tendency to frame certain addiction-related behaviors as having personally relevant transformative consequences. These transforming behaviors are justified because they help overcome some form of inadequacy or shortcoming. Individuals with this bias typically have low self-esteem (hence the NSB) and thus are predisposed toward seeing the need for transforming one or more aspects of their self-concept. The addictive activity is thus justified because it serves as a mechanism for redressing various shortcomings or inadequacies in the self. Bowler et al. (in press) provided a specific example of an individual who rationalizes the use of alcohol because it relaxes his or her social inhibitions, thus permitting the individual to change from being a shy, reserved person (negative quality) into someone who is outgoing and social (positive quality). In short, addictive and dysfunctional behaviors are rationalized because they facilitate implicitly needed changes in the self.

The fifth and final justification mechanism is the *displacement of responsibility bias*. This bias refers to a tendency to deflect responsibility for one's behavior—to frame behavior as beyond one's control. One is not responsible for one's behavior but is instead the victim of circumstances beyond one's control. Within the context of addiction proneness, a common way to deflect responsibility for the addictive activity is to frame addictive behaviors as being biologically rooted, that is, to reason from the perspective that individuals are genetically hard-wired to engage in the addictive activity and are thus victims of genetic circumstance. Bowler et al. (in press) noted that this bias is further bolstered when an individual has firsthand knowledge that a relative has also struggled with the addictive activity. In such instances, individuals with this bias tend to frame the addictive activity as being 100% biologically hard-wired and thus irrepressible and immutable.

Taken collectively, these justification mechanisms emphasize the distortions that addiction-prone individuals engage in to channel analyses toward rationalizing the continued involvement in addictive activity. Such justification mechanisms may elicit specific biases in perception, encoding, analysis, and inference, including

- the tendency to underestimate the potential impact of self-control, willpower, and self-regulation on addictive behaviors and overestimate the potential impact of genetic or biological factors on these behaviors;
- the tendency to discount or ignore information suggesting that the addictive behavior is dangerous or unhealthy while selectively attending to information that confirms that the behavior is likely to be pleasurable or reduce the subjective experience of distress; and
- the tendency to frame even minor sources of stress or anxiety as psychologically overwhelming, thus setting the stage for a reduction in that stress/anxiety via the addictive activity.

Using such cognitive biases, Bowler et al. (in press) developed a pilot test of addiction proneness using the CR item format. A sample item from this test is presented Exhibit 6.2. This item is designed to measure the displacement of responsibility bias. Like the CR problems discussed in Chapter 3, this item asks individuals to analyze a set of logical assertions and draw an inference. The stem of this item asserts that smoking can engender health problems that in turn may shorten one's life. It is also noted that many of these health problems may be reversed if one abstains from smoking. Nevertheless, many individuals continue to smoke. The respondent is asked to explain why someone would continue to engage in potentially life-threatening behavior. To answer this question, the reader must identify one or more unstated assumptions in the item.

## Nonaddiction-Prone Answer

In attempting to answer this question some respondents may identify the following unstated assumption: Overcoming addictive habits is possible with sufficient self-discipline and self-control. It follows that if individuals continue to engage in unhealthy addictive behaviors, they likely lack the willpower to change. Alternative C is thus an answer that should be attractive to individuals who do not rely on the justification mechanisms associated with addiction

Cigarette smoking contributes to lung cancer, which can shorten one's life by as much as 10 years. However, research suggests that these health risks can be reversed after several years of abstaining from smoking. Although this evidence has encouraged many smokers to quit, others are actually smoking more than ever before.

Which of the following is the most logical explanation for why people continue to smoke?

    A. Most people are unaware of the risks of cigarette smoking.
    B. Long-term smoking creates a physical dependency that is impossible to reverse.
    C. Abstaining from smoking requires intense self-discipline, which many smokers lack.
    D. Workplaces are now allowing more smoking breaks.

proneness: "Abstaining from smoking requires intense self-discipline, which many smokers lack."

### Addiction-Prone Answer

Other individuals may identify a different unstated assumption: Habitual smoking leads to a physical dependency on nicotine; one's body craves and needs the drug. It follows that no matter how much one tries to quit smoking, the body cannot function without nicotine. This dependency worsens over time and becomes increasingly difficult to change. This leads to a belief that the needs of the body trump the wishes of the mind. Such an assumption is rooted in the displacement of responsibility bias and was used as the basis for developing alternative B: "Long-term smoking creates a physical dependency that is impossible to reverse."

### Illogical Answers

As noted in Chapter 3 of this volume, CR problems also contain illogical responses. Alternatives A and D do not flow inductively from the stem of the item (i.e., to explain why smokers continue to smoke despite the health risk) and are, moreover, contrary to common knowledge. Companies have actually cut down on the prevalence of smoking breaks (contra alternative D) and the national ad campaigns and warning labels printed on every pack of cigarettes have resulted in most people being acutely aware of the health risks associated with smoking (contra alternative A). Thus, both of these alternatives are illogical solutions to the problem.

Using the justification mechanisms described earlier, Bowler et al. (in press) developed a CR test of addiction proneness. They conducted an initial feasibility study designed to test whether such a test might prove useful for identifying individuals at risk of developing substance abuse addictions. In their initial feasibility study, these authors found that scores on their CR test of addiction proneness were internally consistent and successfully discriminated between a random sample of undergraduate students and a known sample of individuals in treatment for addiction. This test is still undergoing revisions and additional validation studies. However, the initial results suggest that there may be merit in examining the implicit justifications that some individuals use to facilitate their involvement in addictive activities.

## POWER AND TOXIC LEADERSHIP

Our final example discusses how the principles of CR can be applied to the assessment of power and leadership, notably toxic or abusive leadership. Throughout human evolution, leaders have been responsible for strategic decisions that affect the survival of their social collective (e.g., family, clan, kingdom, government, military organization, social institution, business; see Finkelstein & Hambrick, 1996; Van Vugt, Hogan, & Kaiser, 2008). This broad mission is dependent on leaders' abilities to reason and solve problems in ways that engender the safety and security of the collective (e.g., protect the collective from enemies), assist the collective in acquiring resources (e.g., food, donations, raw materials, financing), promote efficient coordination and cooperation among components of the collective (e.g., design an organizational structure), and provide for effective delivery of a product (e.g., knowledge dissemination, art, health care, warfare, transportation, investments).

To identify effective leaders, we measure two types of CR. The first type focuses on differences in reasoning between leaders and nonleaders. The primary psychological factor separating leaders from nonleaders is a motivational force or desire to influence others via a position of significance in a leadership hierarchy. Leaders have a strong desire to have influence and impact, that is, to attain positions in which they can affect courses of events by influencing how people think (e.g., decisions they make), feel (e.g., how stressed they are), and act (e.g., how they perform) (Foti & Hauenstein, 2007; House et al., 1991; Judge et al., 2002; McClelland & Boyatzis, 1982; Winter, 1973). Nonleaders have only a weak to very modest desire to influence others (Stricker & Rock, 1998), seeking neither impact nor power over others (Winter, 1992).

The second type of CR focuses on differences between people who desire to be leaders. The question here is *why* people seek to attain leadership positions and affect others. Forty or so years of research suggest that two primary personality types seek to lead (McClelland & Boyatzis, 1982; Winter, 1973, 1992: Winter, John, Stewart, Klohnen, & Duncan, 1998). People with what we shall refer to as strong needs for *instrumental influence* want to advance the common good of the organization and society (see Collins, 2001). They exercise their influence instrumentally—that is, they use influence to promote cooperation, maintain order, dispense justice, avoid conflict, develop people, and enhance productivity and profits. In contrast, people with strong needs for *egoistic dominance* seek power (i.e., to exert their will) and personal entitlements (e.g., privileges, status, prestige; Veroff, 1992; Winter, 1973).

We believe that leaders motivated by instrumental influence (Influencers) have the highest probability of producing effective organizations. For example, a review by Judge et al. (2002) determined that the most effective leaders were high in both dominance and socialization. House et al. (1991) showed that the more effective United States presidents were high in need for socialized power and used transformational leadership styles. The dominance and power components of these studies indicate a will to lead. The socialization components of these studies indicate that the will to lead is channeled through a leadership style that is instrumental in benefiting both the organizations and those who work in them.

In contrast, leaders motivated by egoistic dominance (Dominators) often prove to be toxic to organizations, and organizational effectiveness suffers accordingly (Kellerman, 2004). These leaders seek and use power in ways that are counterproductive or harmful to organizations, to those around them, or even to themselves (i.e., they are self-destructive; Hogan & Kaiser, 2005; Kaiser et al., 2008). These are leaders who abuse their authority and engage in illegitimate uses of vested powers, often for self-aggrandizing reasons, such as the seeking of status and privilege (Bargh & Alvarez, 2001). Their organizations become toxic when their abuses of power unfairly frustrate and hinder the performance, development, and advancement of qualified and motivated individuals and cause short- or long-term harm to the organization (Resick et al., 2009; Van Vugt et al., 2008).

We argue that the manner in which these two types of leaders frame and reason about the world is qualitatively different. Specifically, Dominators tend to rely on the justification mechanisms for aggression discussed in Chapter 2 (especially the potency and hostile attribution biases). Basically, these individuals are driven by a desire for personal power or potency. Their reasoning is shaped by these biases to justify engaging in toxic behaviors to enhance the self-perception that they are not weak but in fact are dominant and in control. These individuals also tend to see themselves as playing by their own rules (or no rules at all). Their toxicity often takes the form of various unethical leader behaviors, including corruption, callousness, evil, and insularity (Kellerman, 2004).

In contrast, Influencers still seek to have the power to make decisions. However, their motive toward power is not driven by egoistic dominance but by a genuine desire to help people accomplish the collective's objectives. Such individuals experience a sense of accomplishment and take pride not so much in their personal achievements as in the achievements of the collectives whose success they have taken responsibility for engineering (McClelland & Boyatzis, 1982). Thus, for these individuals, the exercise of power and influence is intrinsically rewarding because they enjoy making decisions that are instrumental in shaping the behavior of companies, military divisions, government agencies, schools and universities, religious institutions, extended families, and so forth (Yukl, 2009).

When reasoning about strategic decisions, Influencers tend to rely on their own ideas, visions, solutions, and strategies. By "their own," we mean ideas, visions, solutions, and strategies that they developed themselves, accepted little assistance in developing, or adopted as their own. They consistently reason that the chance of success is greater if they personally define problems, build visions, and make, or at least have strong influence on, final strategies (Eden, 1992). It is this sense of the efficacy of their own reasoning and strategic problem-solving that motivates such individuals to take on leadership responsibilities, seek out leadership opportunities, and attempt to persuade others that their visions and goals will be effective (Bass, 1985; House et al., 1991). Basically, Influencers design strategies to benefit their collectives as opposed to enhancing their personal power and status. The result is that their collectives tend to be more effective than collectives led by those motivated by egoistic dominance (Kellerman, 2004; Resick et al., 2009).

We recently developed a new CR test designed to measure power and toxic leadership on the basis of the reasoning proclivities of Influencers vs. Dominators vs. Nonleaders. Next, we describe an illustrative item that is presented in Exhibit 6.3.

### Instrumental Influence Alternative

Alternative B is based on the CR of Influencers. This alternative comes directly from the findings that such individuals tend to have visions (e.g., ideas, strategies, points of view, solutions) that are effective. Moreover, these individuals believe that they can persuade subordinates to support their visions because these visions promote the subordinates' own needs, values, and goals. As a result, this type of leader believes he or she will be instrumental in enhancing subordinates' effectiveness and commitment to the goals of the collective.

EXHIBIT 6.3.
## Sample Conditional Reasoning Problem Designed
## to Measure Power and Toxic Leadership

---

Participative leadership involves inviting subordinates to share in discussions and decision making with their leader. Together, the leader and subordinates generate and evaluate ideas, and then attempt to reach a consensus about what should be done. Subordinates are often more committed to a course of action when they have had a chance to participate in deciding what it will be.

Based on the above, which one of the following provides the most logical inference regarding participative leadership?

    A. It works well when subordinates are independent and prefer to work alone.
    B. It is useful to leaders with visions who want their subordinates' support.
    C. It works best when subordinates are well informed about the problem at hand.
    D. It is a strategy used by weak leaders who need to tap into their subordinates' ideas.

---

Our intent is that this alternative will appeal logically to Influencers because these are people who (a) place themselves in the role of leader in thinking about the question, (b) possess a sense of the efficacy of their own reasoning and strategic problem-solving, and (c) are prone to conclude that they can be persuasive to subordinates because they want to be instrumental in seeing that the subordinates are effective and motivated. Selection of alternative B is thus scored as one indicator of the presence of a strong need for instrumental influence.

### Egoistic Dominance Alternative

Alternative D is based on the CR of Dominators. This alternative projects Dominators' fear of weakness as a leader and willingness to rationalize the use of unethical methods to enhance their power. This statement is intended to appeal logically to Dominators because it captures their proclivities (a) to think of themselves as leaders, (b) to fixate on not being seen as weak, impotent, timid, fearful, or not in control, and (c) to infer that it is acceptable to appropriate the ideas of their subordinates in order to increase their personal potency. Selection of alternative D is thus scored as one indicator of the presence of a strong need for egoistic dominance.

### Nonleader Alternative

Alternative C is designed to appear as logically plausible and psychologically persuasive to respondents whose reasoning is not guided by a motivational force or desire to influence others via a position of significance in a leadership hierarchy. These individuals do not naturally place themselves in the role of leader when they reason. (Indeed, they often reason from the perspective of those who will be affected by the decisions and actions of leaders.) Alternative C is logically neutral with respect to leadership and is intended to appeal to those whose reasoning is not conditioned to analyze ideas and events in terms of their implications for either influence or egoistic dominance. Selection of alternative C is thus scored as one indicator of the presence of low aspirations to leadership positions.

**Illogical Alternative**

Because CR problems are meant to appear to respondents as traditional reasoning problems, it is necessary to include clearly illogical responses in the problems to accomplish this objective. The clearly illogical alternative in this problem is alternative A. Our intent, and the usual result, is that almost no respondents attempt to solve the problems using the clearly incorrect alternative.

In sum, we believe it is possible to invoke the principles of CR to guide inferences concerning leaders versus nonleaders, and, more important, toxic leaders (i.e., Dominators) from effective leaders (i.e., Influencers). We recently completed a test to achieve these goals and are in the process of securing field research sites for conducting future validation efforts.

When the test for power and toxic leadership is finished, there will be a tendency for many to use it for selection. For example, it could be adopted by companies that conduct assessment centers to identify individuals who have leadership potential and then used as one of the factors to find Influencers and to screen out Dominators. However, we noted earlier that leaders with propensities toward egoistic dominance often operate from a tacit knowledge structure that their dominance behaviors constitute "good leadership" (e.g., they project an aura of potency and strength). Moreover, they are often unaware that their strategic decision making is implicitly biased toward choices that enhance their status, prestige, and power. We proposed that there is room for decision aids and counseling (coaching) here, in addition to or in place of selection. The example we offered is based on a recent article by Kahneman and Klein (2009) and involves the development of artificial intelligence programs to aid Dominators in constructing more effective and less toxic strategic decisions. This is one of many techniques that executive coaches could use to counsel leaders who score moderately to highly on egoistic dominance. The objective here would not be to change personality but to direct decisions away from strategies that unknowingly toxify organizational environments.

## CONCLUSION

The purpose of this chapter was to illustrate how the principles of CR could be adapted and extended to new construct domains. A theme that permeates the application of CR to new construct domains is the role that implicit cognitive biases play in justifying behavior. In our final chapter, we described how CR could be used to aid in the assessment of depression, addiction proneness, and power and toxic leadership. Most of these characteristics are socially undesirable. Normatively, with the exception of Instrumental Influence in the domain of power, all of these characteristics could be regarded as undesirable. Nevertheless, individuals find ways to justify engaging in these behaviors. Those justifications (many of which we believe occur implicitly) provide the foundation for developing CR tests. We encourage researchers interested in applying the principles of CR to their areas of interest to begin by cataloguing the justifications and rationalizations that individuals use for their behavior.

# REFERENCES

Aiken, L. R. (1994). *Psychological testing and assessment* (8th ed.). Needham Heights, MA: Allyn & Bacon.

Allen, M. J., & Yen, W. M. (1979). *Introduction to measurement theory*. Prospect Heights, IL: Waveland Press.

Allport, G. W. (1961). *Pattern and growth in personality*. New York, NY: Holt, Rinehart, and Winston.

Ambrose, M. L., Seabright, M. A., & Schminke, M. (2002). Sabotage in the workplace: The role of organizational injustice. *Organizational Behavior and Human Decision Processes, 89*, 947–965. doi:10.1016/S0749-5978(02)00037-7

American Educational Research Association, American Psychological Association, & National Council on Measurement in Education. (1999). *Standards for Educational and Psychological Testing*. Washington, DC: Author.

Anastasi, A. (1982). *Psychological testing* (5th ed.). New York, NY: Macmillan.

Anderson, C. A., & Bushman, B. J. (2002). Human aggression. *Annual Review of Psychology, 53*, 27–51. doi:10.1146/annurev.psych.53.100901.135231

Anderson, E. (1994, May). The code of the streets. *Atlantic Monthly, 273*, 81–94.

Anderson, R. J., Freedland, K. E., Clouse, R. E., & Lustman, P. J. (2001). The prevalence of comorbid depression in adults with diabetes: A meta-analysis. *Diabetes Care, 24*, 1069–1078. doi:10.2337/diacare.24.6.1069

Arkes, H. R., & Tetlock, P. E. (2004). Attributions of implicit prejudice, or "Would Jesse Jackson 'fail' the implicit association test?" *Psychological Inquiry, 15*, 257–278. doi:10.1207/s15327965pli1504_01

Assano, G. B., Rossi, N. B., & Pini, S. (1994). Comorbidity of depression and anxiety. In S. Kasper, J. A. den Boer, & J. M. Sitsen (Eds.), *Handbook of depression and anxiety* (pp. 69–90). New York, NY: Dekker.

Atkinson, J. W. (1957). Motivational determinants of risk-taking behavior. *Psychological Review, 64*, 359–372. doi:10.1037/h0043445

Atkinson, J. W. (1964). *An introduction to motivation*. Princeton, NJ: Van Nostrand.

Atkinson, J. W. (1978). The mainsprings of achievement-oriented activity. In J. W. Atkinson & J. O. Raynor (Eds.), *Personality, motivation, and achievement* (pp. 11–39). Washington, DC: Hemisphere.

Averill, J. R. (1993). Illusions of anger. In R. B. Felson & J. T. Tedeschi (Eds.), *Aggression and violence: A social interactionist perspective* (pp. 171–192). Washington, DC: American Psychological Association. doi:10.1037/10123-007

Bandura, A. (1973). *Aggression: A social learning analysis*. Englewood Cliffs, NJ: Prentice Hall.

Bandura, A. (1986). *Social foundations of thought and action: A social cognitive theory*. Englewood Cliffs, NJ: Prentice Hall.

Bandura, A. (1999). Moral disengagement in the perpetration of inhumanities. *Personality and Social Psychology Review, 3*, 193–209. doi:10.1207/s15327957pspr0303_3

Bandura, A., Barbaranelli, C., Caprara, G. V., & Pastorelli, C. (1996). Mechanisms of moral disengagement in the exercise of moral agency. *Journal of Personality and Social Psychology, 71*, 364–374. doi:10.1037/0022-3514.71.2.364

Bandura, A., Caprara, G. V., Barbaranelli, C., Pastorelli, C., & Regalia, C. (2001). Sociocognitive self-regulatory mechanisms governing transgressive behavior. *Journal of Personality and Social Psychology, 80*, 125–135. doi:10.1037/0022-3514.80.1.125

Bargh, J. A., & Alvarez, J. (2001). The road to hell: Good intentions in the face of nonconscious tendencies to misuse power. In A. Lee-Chai & J. A. Bargh (Eds.), *The use and abuse of power: Multiple perspectives on the causes of corruption* (pp. 41–55). New York, NY: Psychology Press.

Baron, R. A., & Richardson, D. R. (1994). *Human aggression* (2nd ed.). New York, NY: Plenum.

Barrick, M. R., & Mount, M. K. (1991). The Big Five personality dimensions and job performance: A meta-analysis. *Personnel Psychology, 44*, 1–26.

Barrick, M. R., & Mount, M. K. (1996). Effects of impression management and self-deception on the predictive validity of personality constructs. *Journal of Applied Psychology, 81*, 261–272. doi:10.1037/0021-9010.81.3.261

Bass, B. M. (1985). Leadership: Good, better, best. *Organizational Dynamics, 13*, 26–40. doi:10.1016/0090-2616(85)90028-2

Baumeister, R. F., Campbell, J. D., Krueger, J. I., & Vohs, K. D. (2003). Does high self-esteem cause better performance, interpersonal success, happiness, or healthier lifestyles? *Psychological Science in the Public Interest, 4*, 1–44. doi:10.1111/1529-1006.01431

Baumeister, R. F., Dale, K., & Sommer, K. L. (1998). Freudian defense mechanisms and empirical findings in modern social psychology: Reaction formation, projection, displacement, undoing isolation, sublimation, and denial. *Journal of Personality, 66*, 1082–1124. doi:10.1111/1467-6494.00043

Baumeister, R. F., & Scher, S. J. (1988). Self-defeating behavior patterns among normal individuals: Review and analysis of common self-destructive tendencies. *Psychological Bulletin, 104*, 3–22. doi:10.1037/0033-2909.104.1.3

Baumeister, R. F., Smart, L., & Boden, J. M. (1996). Relation of threatened egotism to violence and aggression: The dark side of high self-esteem. *Psychological Review, 103*, 5–33. doi:10.1037/0033-295X.103.1.5

Beck, A. T. (2006). *Depression: Causes and treatment.* Philadelphia: University of Pennsylvania Press.

Beck, A. T., & Alford, B. A. (2009). *Depression: Causes and treatment.* Philadelphia: University of Pennsylvania Press.

Berglas, S., & Jones, E. E. (1978). Drug choice as a self-handicapping strategy in response to noncontingent success. *Journal of Personality and Social Psychology, 36*, 405–417. doi:10.1037/0022-3514.36.4.405

Berkowitz, L. (1993). *Aggression: Its causes, consequences, and control*. New York, NY: McGraw-Hill.

Bersoff, D. M. (1999). Why good people sometimes do bad things: Motivated reasoning and unethical behavior. *Personality and Social Psychology Bulletin, 25*, 28–39. doi:10.1177/0146167299025001003

Bettencourt, B. A., Talley, A., Benjamin, A. J., & Valentine, J. (2006). Personality and aggressive behavior under provoking and neutral conditions: A meta-analytic review. *Psychological Bulletin, 132*, 751–777. doi:10.1037/0033-2909.132.5.751

Bing, M. N., LeBreton, J. M., Davison, H. K., Migetz, D. Z., & James, L. R. (2007). Integrating implicit and explicit social cognitions for enhanced personality assessment: A general framework for choosing measurement and statistical methods. *Organizational Research Methods, 10*, 136–179. doi:10.1177/1094428106289396

Bing, M. N., Stewart, S. M., Davison, H. K., Green, P. D., McIntyre, M. D., & James, L. R. (2007). An integrative typology of personality assessment for aggression: Implications for predicting counterproductive workplace behavior. *Journal of Applied Psychology, 92*, 722–744. doi:10.1037/0021-9010.92.3.722

Binning, J. F., & Barrett, G. V. (1989). Validity of personnel decisions: A conceptual analysis of the inferential and evidential bases. *Journal of Applied Psychology, 74*, 478–494. doi:10.1037/0021-9010.74.3.478

Blanton, H., & Jaccard, J. (2006). Arbitrary metrics in psychology. *American Psychologist, 61*, 27–41. doi:10.1037/0003-066X.61.1.27

Blanton, H., Jaccard, J., Christie, C., & Gonzales, P. M. (2007). Plausible assumptions, questionable assumptions and post hoc rationalizations: Will the real IAT, please stand up? *Journal of Experimental Social Psychology, 43*, 399–409. doi:10.1016/j.jesp.2006.10.019

Blanton, H., Jaccard, J., Klick, J., Mellers, B., Mitchell, G., & Tetlock, P. E. (2009). Strong claims and weak evidence: Reassessing the predictive validity of the IAT. *Journal of Applied Psychology, 94*, 567–582. doi:10.1037/a0014665

Block, J. (1995). A contrarian view of the five-factor approach to personality description. *Psychological Bulletin, 117*, 187–215. doi:10.1037/0033-2909.117.2.187

Blum, M.L., & Naylor, J. C. (1968). *Industrial psychology: Its theoretical and social foundations* (3rd ed.). New York, NY: Harper and Row.

Bornstein, R. F. (1998). Implicit and self-attributed dependency strivings: Differential relationships to laboratory and field measures of help seeking. *Journal of Personality and Social Psychology, 75*, 778–787. doi:10.1037/0022-3514.75.3.778

Bornstein, R. F. (2002). A process dissociation approach to objective-projective test score interrelationships. *Journal of Personality Assessment, 78*, 47–68. doi:10.1207/S15327752JPA7801_04

Borum, R. (1996). Improving the clinical practice of violence risk assessment: Technology, guidelines, and training. *American Psychologist, 51*, 945–956. doi:10.1037/0003-066X.51.9.945

Bowler, J. L., Bowler, M. C., & James, L. R. (in press). The cognitive underpinnings of addiction. *Substance Use & Misuse*.

Bradbury, T. N., & Fincham, F. D. (1990). Attributions in marriage: Review and critique. *Psychological Bulletin, 107,* 3–33. doi:10.1037/0033-2909.107.1.3

Brehmer, B. (1976). Social judgment theory and the analysis of interpersonal conflict. *Psychological Bulletin, 83,* 985–1003. doi:10.1037/0033-2909.83.6.985

Brewin, C. R. (1989). Cognitive change processes in psychotherapy. *Psychological Review, 96,* 379–394. doi:10.1037/0033-295X.96.3.379

Brunstein, J. C., & Maier, G. W. (2005). Implicit and self-attributed motives to achieve: Two separate but interacting needs. *Journal of Personality and Social Psychology, 89,* 205–222. doi:10.1037/0022-3514.89.2.205

Bushman, B. J., & Anderson, C. A. (2001). Is it time to pull the plug on hostile versus instrumental aggression dichotomy? *Psychological Review, 108,* 273–279. doi:10.1037/0033-295X.108.1.273

Buss, A. H. (1961). *The psychology of aggression.* New York, NY: Wiley. doi:10.1037/11160-000

Buss, A. H., & Finn, S. E. (1987). Classification of personality traits. *Journal of Personality and Social Psychology, 52,* 432–444. doi:10.1037/0022-3514.52.2.432

Buss, A. H., & Perry, M. (1992). The Aggression Questionnaire. *Journal of Personality and Social Psychology, 63,* 452–459. doi:10.1037/0022-3514.63.3.452

Cattell, R. B. (1957). *Personality and motivation: Structure and measurement.* Yonkers-on-Hudson, NY: World Book Company.

Center for Substance Abuse Prevention (1995, Spring). *Making the link: Violence and crime and alcohol and other drugs* (Prevention Works Publication ML002). Rockville, MD: Author.

Cohen, A. (1984). Drugs in the workplace. *The Journal of Clinical Psychiatry, 45,* 4–8.

Cohen, J., Cohen, P., West, S. G., & Aiken, L. S. (2003). *Applied multiple regression/correlation analysis for the behavioral sciences* (3rd ed.). Mahwah, NJ: Erlbaum.

Collins, J. (2001). *Good to great: Why some companies make the leap . . . and others don't.* New York, NY: HarperCollins.

Conway, K. P., Levy, J., Vanyukov, M., Chandler, R., Ritter, J., Swan, G. E., & Neale, M. (2010). Measuring addiction propensity and severity: The need for a new instrument. *Drug and Alcohol Dependence, 111,* 4–12. doi:10.1016/j.drugalcdep.2010.03.011

Cooper, W. H. (1981). Ubiquitous halo. *Psychological Bulletin, 90,* 218–244. doi:10.1037/0033-2909.90.2.218

Costa, P. T., Jr., & McCrae, R. R. (1992). *Revised NEO personality inventory (NEO-PI-R) and NEO five-factor inventory (NEO-FFI): Professional manual.* Odessa, FL: Psychological Assessment Resources.

Cramer, P. (1998). Defensiveness and defense mechanisms. *Journal of Personality, 66,* 880–894. doi:10.1111/1467-6494.00035

Cramer, P. (2000). Defense mechanisms in psychology today: Further processes for adaptation. *American Psychologist, 55,* 637–646. doi:10.1037/0003-066X.55.6.637

Cramer, P. (2006). *Protecting the self: defense mechanisms in action.* New York, NY: Guilford Press.

Crick, N. R., & Dodge, K. A. (1994). A review and reformulation of social information-processing mechanisms in children's social adjustment. *Psychological Bulletin, 115,* 74–101. doi:10.1037/0033-2909.115.1.74

Crocker, J. (1981). Judgment of covariation by social perceivers. *Psychological Bulletin, 90,* 272–292. doi:10.1037/0033-2909.90.2.272

Crocker, J., & Major, B. (1989). Social stigma and self-esteem: The self-protective properties of stigma. *Psychological Review, 96,* 608–630. doi:10.1037/0033-295X.96.4.608

Crocker, J., & Park, L. E. (2004). The costly pursuit of self-esteem. *Psychological Bulletin, 130,* 392–414.

De Houwer, J., Teige-Mocigemba, S., Spruyt, A., & Moors, A. (2009). Implicit measures: A normative analysis and review. *Psychological Bulletin, 135,* 347–368. doi:10.1037/a0014211

Diefendorff, J. M., & Mehta, K. (2007). The relations of motivational traits with workplace deviance. *Journal of Applied Psychology, 92,* 967–977. doi:10.1037/0021-9010.92.4.967

Djoussé, L., & Gaziano, J. M. (2008). Alcohol consumption and heart failure: A systematic review. *Current Atherosclerosis Reports, 10,* 117–120. doi:10.1007/s11883-008-0017-z

Dodge, K. A. (1986). A social information processing model of social competence in children. In M. Perlmutter (Ed.), *Cognitive perspectives on children's social and behavioral development: Vol. 18* (pp. 77–125). Hillsdale, NJ: Erlbaum.

Dodge, K. A., & Coie, J. D. (1987). Social-information-processing factors in reactive and proactive aggression in children's peer groups. *Journal of Personality and Social Psychology, 53,* 1146–1158. doi:10.1037/0022-3514.53.6.1146

Dodge, K. A., & Crick, N. R. (1990). Social information-processing bases of aggressive behavior in children. *Personality and Social Psychology Bulletin, 16,* 8–22. doi:10.1177/0146167290161002

Douglas, S. C., & Martinko, M. J. (2001.) Exploring the role of individual differences in the prediction of workplace aggression. *Journal of Applied Psychology, 86,* 547–559.

DuBois, D. L., & Flay, B. R. (2004). The healthy pursuit of self-esteem: Comment and alternative to the Crocker & Park (2004) formulation. *Psychological Bulletin, 130,* 415–420. doi:10.1037/0033-2909.130.3.415

Dumais, A., Lesage, A. D., Alda, M., Rouleau, G., Dumont, M., Chawky, N., . . . Turecki, G. (2005). Risk factors for suicide completion in major depression:

A case-control study of impulsive and aggressive behaviors in men. *The American Journal of Psychiatry, 162*, 2116–2124. doi:10.1176/appi.ajp.162. 11.2116

Dweck, C. S., & Leggett, E. L. (1988). A social-cognitive approach to motivation and personality. *Psychological Review, 95*, 256–273. doi:10.1037/0033-295X. 95.2.256

Eden, D. (1992). Leadership and expectations: Pygmalion effects and other self-fulfilling prophecies. *The Leadership Quarterly, 3*, 271–305. doi:10.1016/1048-9843(92)90018-B

Edwards, A. L. (1959). *Manual for the Edwards personal preference schedule*. New York, NY: Psychological Corporation.

Einhorn, H. J., & Hogarth, R. M. (1978). Confidence in judgment: Persistence of the illusion of validity. *Psychological Review, 85*, 395–416. doi:10.1037/0033-295X.85.5.395

Ellingson, J. E., Sackett, P. R., & Connelly, B. S. (2007). Personality assessment across selection and development contexts: Insights into response distortion. *Journal of Applied Psychology, 92*, 386–395.

Ellingson, J. E., Smith, D. B., & Sackett, P. R. (2001). Investigating the influence of social desirability on personality factor structure. *Journal of Applied Psychology, 86*, 122–133.

Epstein, S. (1979). The stability of behavior: I. On predicting most of the people much of the time. *Journal of Personality and Social Psychology, 37*, 1097–1126. doi:10.1037/0022-3514.37.7.1097

Epstein, S. (1994). Integration of the cognitive and the psychodynamic unconscious. *American Psychologist, 49*, 709–724. doi:10.1037/0003-066X.49.8.709

Exner, J. E., Jr. (1986). *The Rorschach: A comprehensive system: Vol. 1. Basic foundations* (2nd ed.). New York, NY: Wiley.

Fazio, R. H., & Olson, M. A. (2003). Implicit measures in social cognition research: Their meaning and uses. *Annual Review of Psychology, 54*, 297–327. doi:10.1146/annurev.psych.54.101601.145225

Feldman, J. M. (1981). Beyond attribution theory: Cognitive processes in performance appraisal. *Journal of Applied Psychology, 66*, 127–148. doi:10.1037/0021-9010.66.2.127

Feldman, J. M., & Lindell, M. K. (1989). On rationality. In I. Horowitz (Ed.), *Organization and decision theory* (pp. 83–164). Boston, MA: Kluwer.

Felson, R. B., & Tedeschi, J. T. (Eds.). (1993). *Aggression and violence: Social interactionist perspectives*. Washington, DC: American Psychological Association. doi:10.1037/10123-000

Fendrich, M., Goldstein, P. J., Spunt, B., Brownstein, H. H., & Mackesy-Amiti, M. E. (1995). Substance involvement among juvenile murderers: Comparisons with older offenders based on interviews with prison inmates. *International Journal of the Addictions, 30*, 1363–1382.

Fergusson, D. M., Horwood, J. L., Ridder, E. M., & Beautrias, A. L. (2005). Sub-threshold depression in adolescence and mental health outcomes in adulthood. *Archives of General Psychiatry, 62*, 66–72. doi:10.1001/archpsyc.62.1.66

Fergusson, D. M., & Woodward, L. J. (2002). Mental health, educational and social role outcomes for adolescents with depression. *Archives of General Psychiatry, 59*, 225–231. doi:10.1001/archpsyc.59.3.225

Finkelsten, S., & Hambrick, D. C. (1996). *Strategic leadership: Top executives and their effects on organizations*. Minneapolis/St. Paul, MN: West.

Finnegan, W. (1997, December). 1. The unwanted. *The New Yorker, 73*, 61–78.

Fiske, S. T., & Taylor, S. E. (1984). *Social cognition*. Reading, MA: Addison-Wesley.

Fiske, S. T., & Taylor, S. E. (1991). *Social cognition* (2nd ed.). New York, NY: McGraw-Hill.

Folger, R., & Baron, R. A. (1996). Violence and hostility at work: A model of reactions to perceived injustice. In G. R. VandenBos & E. Q. Bulatao (Eds.), *Violence on the job: Identifying risks and developing solutions* (pp. 51–85). Washington, DC: American Psychological Association. doi:10.1037/10215-002

Foti, R. J., & Hauenstein, N. M. (2007). Pattern and variable approaches in leadership emergence and effectiveness. *Journal of Applied Psychology, 92*, 347–355. doi:10.1037/0021-9010.92.2.347

Freud, S. (1936). *The ego and the mechanisms of defense*. New York, NY: Hogarth Press.

Freud, S. (1959). *An outline of psychoanalysis*. New York, NY: Norton.

Frone, M. R. (2004). Alcohol, drugs, and workplace safety outcomes: A view from a general model of employee substance use and productivity. In J. Barling & M. R. Frone (Eds.), *The psychology of workplace safety* (pp. 127–156). Washington, DC: American Psychological Association. doi:10.1037/10662-007

Frost, B. C., Ko, C. E., & James, L. R. (2007). Implicit and explicit personality: A test of a channeling hypothesis for aggressive behavior. *Journal of Applied Psychology, 92*, 1299–1319. doi:10.1037/0021-9010.92.5.1299

Funder, D. C. (1987). Errors and mistakes: Evaluating the accuracy of social judgment. *Psychological Bulletin, 101*, 75–90. doi:10.1037/0033-2909.101.1.75

Galotti, K. M. (1989). Approaches to studying formal and everyday reasoning. *Psychological Bulletin, 105*, 331–351. doi:10.1037/0033-2909.105.3.331

Ganellen, R. J., Wasyliw, O. E., Haywood, T. W., & Grossman, L. S. (1996). Can psychosis be malingered on the Rorschach? An empirical study. *Journal of Personality Assessment, 66*, 65–80. doi:10.1207/s15327752jpa6601_5

Garb, H. N., Florio, C. M., & Grove, W. M. (1998). The validity of the Rorschach and the Minnesota Multiphasic Personality Inventory: Results from meta-analyses. *Psychological Science, 9*, 402–404. doi:10.1111/1467-9280.00075

Gawronski, B. (2009). Ten frequently asked questions about implicit measures and their frequently supposed, but not entirely correct answers. *Canadian Psychology, 50*, 141–150. doi:10.1037/a0013848

Gay, P. (1993). *The cultivation of hatred*. New York, NY: Norton.

Glassman, A. H. (2007). Depression and cardiovascular comorbidity. *Dialogues in Clinical Neuroscience, 9*, 9–17.

Goldberg, L. R. (1993). The structure of phenotypic personality traits. *American Psychologist, 48*, 26–34. doi:10.1037/0003-066X.48.1.26

Gough, H.G., & Bradley P. (1996). *CPI manual* (3rd ed.). Palo Alto, CA: Consulting Psychologists Press.

Green, P. D., & James, L. R. (1999, May). The use of conditional reasoning to predict deceptive behavior. In L. J. Williams & S. M. Burroughs (Chairs), *New developments using conditional reasoning to measure employee reliability*. Symposium conducted at the annual meeting of the Society for Industrial and Organizational Psychology, Atlanta, GA.

Greenberg, J. (1990). Employee theft as a reaction to underpayment inequity: The hidden cost of pay cuts. *Journal of Applied Psychology, 75*, 561–568. doi:10.1037/0021-9010.75.5.561

Greenberg, J. (1996). *The quest for justice on the job: Essays and experiments*. Thousand Oaks, CA: Sage.

Greenberg, J. (2002). Who stole the money, and when? Individual and situational determinants of employee theft. *Organizational Behavior and Human Decision Processes, 89*, 985–1003. doi:10.1016/S0749-5978(02)00039-0

Greenwald, A. G., & Banaji, M. R. (1995). Implicit social cognition: Attitudes, self-esteem, and stereotypes. *Psychological Review, 102*, 4–27. doi:10.1037/0033-295X.102.1.4

Greenwald, A. G., & Farnham, S. D. (2000). Using the implicit association test to measure self-esteem and self-concept. *Journal of Personality and Social Psychology, 79*, 1022–1038. doi:10.1037/0022-3514.79.6.1022

Greenwald, A. G., McGhee, D. E., & Schwartz, J. L. K. (1998). Measuring individual differences in implicit cognition: The implicit association test. *Journal of Personality and Social Psychology, 74*, 1464–1480. doi:10.1037/0022-3514.74.6.1464

Greenwald, A. G., Poehlman, T. A., Uhlmann, E. L., & Banaji, M. R. (2009). Understanding and using the Implicit Association Test: III. Meta-analysis of predictive validity. *Journal of Personality and Social Psychology, 97*, 17–41. doi:10.1037/a0015575

Grumm, M., & von Collani, G. (2007). Measuring Big-Five personality dimensions with the implicit association test—Implicit personality traits or self-esteem? *Personality and Individual Differences, 43*, 2205–2217. doi:10.1016/j.paid.2007.06.032

Guilford, J. P. (1954). *Psychometric methods* (2nd ed.). New York, NY: McGraw-Hill.

Guilford, J. P., & Fruchter, B. (1973). *Fundamental statistics in psychology and education*. New York, NY: McGraw-Hill.

Gulliksen, H. O. (1950). *Theory of mental tests*. New York, NY: Wiley.

Guze, S. B., & Robins, E. (1970). Suicide and affective disorders. *The British Journal of Psychiatry, 117,* 437–438. doi:10.1192/bjp.117.539.437

Hafer, C. L., & Begue, L. (2005). Experimental research on just-world theory: Problems, developments, and future challenges. *Psychological Bulletin, 131,* 128–167. doi:10.1037/0033-2909.131.1.128

Hahn, U., & Oaksford, M. (2007). The rationality of informal argumentation: A Bayesian approach to reasoning fallacies. *Psychological Review, 114,* 704–732. doi:10.1037/0033-295X.114.3.704

Haidt, J. (2001). The emotional dog and its rational tail: A social intuitionist approach to moral judgment. *Psychological Review, 108,* 814–834. doi:10.1037/0033-295X.108.4.814

Haley, A. (1976). *Roots: The saga of an American family.* New York, NY: Doubleday.

Hall, D. T. (1971). A theoretical model of career subidentity development in organizational settings. *Organizational Behavior and Human Performance, 6,* 50–76. doi:10.1016/0030-5073(71)90005-5

Harris, D. B. (1963). *Children's drawings as measures of intellectual maturity.* New York, NY: Harcourt, Brace & World.

Hinshaw, S. P. (1992). Externalizing behavior problems and academic underachievement in childhood and adolescence: Causal relationships and underlying mechanisms. *Psychological Bulletin, 111,* 127–155.

Hogan J., Barrett, P., & Hogan, R., (2007). Personality measurement, faking, and employment selection. *Journal of Applied Psychology, 92,* 1270–1285.

Hogan, J., & Hogan, R. (1989). How to measure employee reliability. *Journal of Applied Psychology, 74,* 273–279. doi:10.1037/0021-9010.74.2.273

Hogan, R. (1991). Personality and personality measurement. In L. M. Hough & M. D. Dunnette (Eds.), *Handbook of industrial and organizational psychology: Vol 2* (2nd ed.). Palo Alto, CA: Consulting Psychologist Press.

Hogan, R. (2006). Who wants to be a psychologist? *Journal of Personality Assessment, 86,* 119–130.

Hogan, R., & Hogan, J. (1995). *Hogan personality inventory manual* (2nd ed.). Tulsa, OK: Hogan Assessment Systems.

Hogan, R., Hogan, J., & Roberts, B. W. (1996). Personality measurement and employment decisions: Questions and answers. *American Psychologist, 51,* 469–477. doi:10.1037/0003-066X.51.5.469

Hogan, R., & Kaiser, R. B. (2005). What we know about leadership. *Review of General Psychology, 9,* 169–180. doi:10.1037/1089-2680.9.2.169

Hogarth, R. M. (1987). *Judgement and choice* (2nd ed.). Chichester, England: Wiley.

Holmes, D. S. (1974). The conscious control of thematic projection. *Journal of Consulting and Clinical Psychology, 42,* 323–329. doi:10.1037/h0036671

Hough, L. M., Eaton, N. K., Dunnette, M. D., Kamp, J. D., & McCloy, R. A. (1990). Criterion-related validities of personality constructs and the effect of response distortion on those validities [Monograph]. *Journal of Applied Psychology, 75,* 581–595. doi:10.1037/0021-9010.75.5.581

House, R. J., Spangler, W. D., & Woycke, J. (1991). Personality and charisma in the U.S. presidency: A psychological theory of leader effectiveness. *Administrative Science Quarterly, 36,* 364–396. doi:10.2307/2393201

Huesmann, L. R. (1988). An information processing model for the development of aggression. *Aggressive Behavior, 14,* 13–24. doi:10.1002/1098-2337(1988)14:1<13::AID-AB2480140104>3.0.CO;2-J

Hurtz, G. M., and Donovan, J. J. (2000). Personality and job performance: The Big Five revisited. *Journal of Applied Psychology, 85,* 869–879.

Hyde, J. S. (2005). The gender similarities hypothesis. *American Psychologist, 60,* 581–592. doi:10.1037/0003-066X.60.6.581

Ilgen, D. R., Barnes-Farrell, J. L., & McKellin, D. B. (1993). Performance appraisal process research in the 1980s: What has it contributed to appraisals in use? *Organizational Behavior and Human Decision Processes, 54,* 321–368. doi:10.1006/obhd.1993.1015

Iverson, R. D., & Deery, S. J. (2001). Understanding the "personological" basis of employee withdrawal: The influence of affective disposition on employee tardiness, early departure, and absenteeism. *Journal of Applied Psychology, 86,* 856–866. doi:10.1037/0021-9010.86.5.856

Jackson, D. N. (1967). *Personality Research Form Manual.* Goshen, NY: Research Psychologists Press.

Jackson, D. N. (1984). *Personality research form.* Port Huron, MI: Sigma Assessment Systems.

James, L. R. (1998). Measurement of personality via conditional reasoning. *Organizational Research Methods, 1,* 131–163. doi:10.1177/109442819812001

James, L. R., & LeBreton, J. M. (2010). Assessing aggression using conditional reasoning. *Current Directions in Psychological Science, 19*(1), 30–35. doi:10.1177/0963721409359279

James, L. R., & Mazerolle, M. D. (2002). *Personality in work organizations: An integrative approach.* Thousand Oaks, CA: Sage.

James, L. R., & McIntyre, M. D. (2000). *Conditional Reasoning Test of Aggression test manual.* Knoxville, TN: Innovative Assessment Technology.

James, L. R., McIntyre, M. D., Glisson, C. A., Bowler, J. L., & Mitchell, T. R. (2004). The conditional reasoning measurement system for aggression: An overview. *Human Performance, 17,* 271–295. doi:10.1207/s15327043hup1703_2

James, L. R., McIntyre, M. D., Glisson, C. A., Green, P. D., Patton, T. W., LeBreton, J. M., . . . Williams, L. J. (2005). A conditional reasoning measure for aggression. *Organizational Research Methods, 8,* 69–99. doi:10.1177/1094428104272182

James, L. R., McIntyre, M. D., & LeBreton, J. M. (2000, April). *Innovations in selection: Use of conditional reasoning to identify reliable and achievement-motivated employees*. Workshop presented at the Society of Industrial and Organizational Psychology, New Orleans, LA.

Jones, A. P. (1973, August). *Functioning of organizational units related to differences in perceived climate and habitability*. Paper presented at the convention of the American Psychological Association, Montreal, Quebec, Canada.

Jöreskog, K. G., & Sörbom, D. (1996). *LISREL 8: User's reference guide*. Chicago, IL: Scientific Software International.

Jöreskog, K. G., & Sörbom, D. (1999). *PRELIS 2: User's reference guide*. Chicago, IL: Scientific Software International.

Jöreskog, K. G., & Sörbom, D. (2005). *LISREL 8.72 for Windows* [Computer software]. Chicago, IL: Scientific Software International.

Judge, T. A., Bono, J. E., Ilies, R., & Gerhardt, M. W. (2002). Personality and leadership: A qualitative and quantitative review. *Journal of Applied Psychology, 87*, 765–780. doi:10.1037/0021-9010.87.4.765

Judge, T. A., Scott, B. A., & Ilies, R. (2006). Hostility, job attitudes, and workplace deviance: Test of a multilevel model. *Journal of Applied Psychology, 91*, 126–138. doi:10.1037/0021-9010.91.1.126

Kahneman, D., & Klein, G. (2009). Conditions for intuitive expertise. *American Psychologist, 64*, 515–526. doi:10.1037/a0016755

Kahneman, D., & Tversky, A. (1973). On the psychology of prediction. *Psychological Review, 80*, 237–251. doi:10.1037/h0034747

Kahneman, D., & Tversky, A. (1984). Choices, values, and frames. *American Psychologist, 39*, 341–350. doi:10.1037/0003-066X.39.4.341

Kaiser, R. B., Hogan, R., & Craig, S. B. (2008). Leadership and the fate of organizations. *American Psychologist, 63*, 96–110. doi:10.1037/0003-066X.63.2.96

Kaplan, D. (2000). *Structural equation modeling: Foundations and extensions*. Thousand Oaks, CA: Sage.

Kaplan, M. F., & Eron, L. D. (1965). Test sophistication and faking in the TAT situation. *Journal of Projective Techniques & Personality Assessment, 29*, 498–503.

Kaplan, R. M. (1982). *Psychological testing*. Belmont, CA: Brooks/Cole.

Kellerman, B. (2004). *Bad leadership: What it is, how it happens, why it matters*. Boston, MA: Harvard Business School Press.

Kelly, G. A. (1963). *A theory of personality: The psychology of personal constructs*. New York, NY: Norton.

Kenrick, D. T., & Funder, D. C. (1988). Profiting from controversy: Lessons from the person-situation debate. *American Psychologist, 43*, 23–34. doi:10.1037/0003-066X.43.1.23

Kessler, R. C., Berglund, P., Demler, O., Jin, R., Merikangas, K. R., & Walters, E. E. (2005). Lifetime prevalence and age-of-onset distributions of *DSM-IV* disorders in the National Comorbidity Survey Replication. *Archives of General Psychiatry, 62*, 593–602.

Kihlstrom, J. F. (1987, September 18). The cognitive unconscious. *Science, 237,* 1445–1452. doi:10.1126/science.3629249

Kihlstrom, J. F. (1999). The psychological unconscious. In L. A. Pervin & O. P. John (Eds.), *Handbook of personality: Theory and research* (2nd ed., pp. 424–442). New York, NY: Guilford Press.

Kihlstrom, J. F., Mulvaney, S., Tobias, B. A., & Tobis, I. P. (2000). The emotional unconscious. In E. Eich, J. F. Kilhstrom, G. H. Bower, J. P. Forgas, & P. M. Niedenthal (Eds.), *Cognition and emotion* (pp. 30–86). New York, NY: Oxford University Press.

Klein, G. (1998). *Sources of power: How people make decisions.* Cambridge, MA: MIT Press.

Ko, C. E., Shim, H. S., & Roberts, J. S. (2008, April). The conditional reasoning test for aggression: Assessment of differential item functioning on gender. In J. LeBreton (Chair), *Psychometric properties of conditional reasoning tests.* Symposium conducted at the 23rd Annual Conference of the Society of Industrial and Organizational Psychology, San Francisco, CA.

Ko, C. E., Thompson, V. M., Shim, H. S., Roberts, J. S., & McIntyre, H. (2008, April). Alternative scoring strategies for the conditional reasoning test of aggression. In J. LeBreton (Chair), *Psychometric properties of conditional reasoning tests.* Symposium conducted at the 23rd Annual Conference of the Society of Industrial and Organizational Psychology, San Francisco, CA.

Koestner, R., & McClelland, D. C. (1990). Perspectives on competence motivation. In L. A. Pervin (Ed.), *Handbook of personality: Theory and research* (pp. 527–548). New York, NY: Guilford Press.

Koestner, R., Weinberger, J., & McClelland, D. C. (1991). Task-intrinsic and social-extrinsic sources of arousal for motives assessed in fantasy and self-report. *Journal of Personality, 59,* 57–82. doi:10.1111/j.1467-6494.1991.tb00768.x

Kruglanski, A. W. (1989). The psychology of being "right": The problem of accuracy in social perception and cognition. *Psychological Bulletin, 106,* 395–409. doi:10.1037/0033-2909.106.3.395

Kruglanski, A. W., & Ajzen, I. (1983). Bias and error in human judgment. *European Journal of Social Psychology, 13,* 1–44. doi:10.1016/0022-1031(83)90022-7

Kruglanski, A. W., & Klar, Y. (1987). A view from a bridge: Synthesizing the consistency and attribution paradigms from a lay epistemic perspective. *European Journal of Social Psychology, 17,* 211–241. doi:10.1002/ejsp.2420170208

Kuhl, J. J. (1978). Standard setting and risk preference: An elaboration of the theory of achievement motivation and an empirical test. *Psychological Review, 85,* 239–248. doi:10.1037/0033-295X.85.3.239

Kuhn, D. (1991). *The skills of argument.* New York, NY: Cambridge University Press.

Kunda, Z. (1990). The case for motivated reasoning. *Psychological Bulletin, 108,* 480–498. doi:10.1037/0033-2909.108.3.480

Landy, F. J., & Farr, J. L. (1980). Performance ratings. *Psychological Bulletin, 87,* 72–107. doi:10.1037/0033-2909.87.1.72

Langan-Fox, J., Canty, J. M., & Sankey, M. J. (2010). Motive congruence moderation: The effects of dependence and locus of control on implicit and self-attributed affiliation motive congruency and life satisfaction. *Personality and Individual Differences, 48,* 664–669. doi:10.1016/j.paid.2010.01.009

Lanyon, R. I., & Goodstein, L. D. (1997). *Personality assessment* (3rd ed.). New York, NY: Wiley.

Laursen, B., & Collins, W. A. (1994). Interpersonal conflict during adolescence. *Psychological Bulletin, 115,* 197–209. doi:10.1037/0033-2909.115.2.197

LeBreton, J. M., Barksdale, C. D., Robin, J. D., & James, L. R. (2007). Measurement issues associated with conditional reasoning tests: Deception and faking. *Journal of Applied Psychology, 92,* 1–16. doi:10.1037/0021-9010.92.1.1

LeBreton, J. M., Binning, J. F., & Adorno, A. J. (2006). Subclinical psychopaths. In J. C. Thomas & D. Segal (Eds.), *Comprehensive handbook of personality and psychopathology: Vol. I, Personality and everyday functioning* (pp. 388–411). New York, NY: Wiley.

Lilienfeld, S. O., Wood, J. M., & Garb, H. M. (2000). The scientific status of projective techniques. *Psychological Science in the Public Interest, 1,* 27–66.

Loeber, R., & Stouthamer-Loeber, M. (1998). Development of juvenile aggression and violence: Some misconceptions and controversies. *American Psychologist, 53,* 242–259. doi:10.1037/0003-066X.53.2.242

Loewenstein, G. F., Weber, E. U., Hsee, C. K., & Welch, N. (2001). Risk as feelings. *Psychological Bulletin, 127,* 267–286. doi:10.1037/0033-2909.127.2.267

Lord, F. M., & Novick, M. R. (1968). *Statistical theories of mental tests.* Reading, MA: Addison-Wesley.

Martin, J. K., Kraft, J. M., & Roman, P. M. (1994). Extent and impact of alcohol and drug use problems in the workplace: A review of the empirical evidence. In S. Macdonald & P. M. Roman (Eds.), *Drug testing in the workplace: Research advances in alcohol and drug problems* (pp. 3–31). New York, NY: Plenum Press.

Masling, J. (2002). How do I score thee? Let me count the ways. Or some different methods of categorizing Rorschach responses. *Journal of Personality Assessment, 79,* 399–421. doi:10.1207/S15327752JPA7903_02

McClelland, D. C. (1985). *Human motivation.* Glenview, IL: Scott, Foresman and Company.

McClelland, D. C., & Boyatzis, R. E. (1982). Leadership motive pattern and long-term success in management. *Journal of Applied Psychology, 67,* 737–743. doi:10.1037/0021-9010.67.6.737

McClelland, D. C., Koestner, R., & Weinberger, J. (1989). How do self-attributed and implicit motives differ? *Psychological Review, 96,* 690–702. doi:10.1037/0033-295X.96.4.690

McConnell, A. R., & Leibold, J. M. (2009). Weak criticisms and selective evidence: Reply to Blanton et al. (2009). *Journal of Applied Psychology, 94,* 583–589. doi:10.1037/a0014649

McCrae, R. R., & Costa, P. T., Jr. (1997). Personality trait structure as a human universal. *American Psychologist, 52,* 509–516. doi:10.1037/0003-066X.52.5.509

McFarland, L. A., & Ryan, A. M. (2000). Variance in faking across noncognitive measures. *Journal of Applied Psychology, 85,* 812–821.

Meehl, P. E. (1972). Reactions, reflections, projections. In J. N. Butcher (Ed.), *Objective personality assessment: Changing perspectives.* New York, NY: Academic Press.

Meisner, S. (1988). Susceptibility of Rorschach distress correlates to malingering. *Journal of Personality Assessment, 52,* 564–571. doi:10.1207/s15327752jpa5203_19

Meites, T. M., Deveney, C. M., Steele, K. T., Holmes, A. J., & Pizzagalli, D. A. (2008). Implicit depression and hopelessness in remitted depressed individuals. *Behaviour Research and Therapy, 46,* 1078–1084. doi:10.1016/j.brat.2008.05.008

Meyer, G. J., Finn, S. E., Eyde, L. D., Kay, G. G., Moreland, K. L., Dies, R. R.,... Read, G. M. (2001). Psychological testing and psychological assessment: A review of evidence and issues. *American Psychologist, 56,* 128–165. doi:10.1037/0003-066X.56.2.128

Miller, S. M. (1987). Monitoring and blunting: Validation of a questionnaire to assess styles of information seeking under threat. *Journal of Personality and Social Psychology, 52,* 345–353. doi:10.1037/0022-3514.52.2.345

Millon, T. (1990). The disorders of personality. In L. A. Pervin (Ed.), *Handbook of personality theory and research* (pp. 339–370). New York, NY: Guilford Press.

Mischel, W. (1968). *Personality and assessment.* New York, NY: Wiley.

Mischel, W., & Shoda, Y. (1995). A cognitive-affective system theory of personality: Reconceptualizing situations, dispositions, dynamics, and invariance in personality structure. *Psychological Review, 102,* 246–268. doi:10.1037/0033-295X.102.2.246

Morgeson, F. P., Campion, M. A., Dipboye, R. L., Hollenbeck, J. R., Murphy, K., & Schmitt, N. (2007). Reconsidering the use of personality tests in personnel selection contexts. *Personnel Psychology, 60,* 683–729. doi:10.1111/j.1744-6570.2007.00089.x

Murphy, K. R., & Anhalt, R. L. (1992). Is halo error a property of the rater, ratees, or the specific behaviors observed. *Journal of Applied Psychology, 77,* 494–500. doi:10.1037/0021-9010.77.4.494

Murray, H. A. (1935). *Thematic Apperception Test.* Cambridge, MA: Harvard University Press.

Murray, H. A. (1938). *Explorations in personality.* New York, NY: Oxford University Press.

Neter, J., Wasserman, W., & Kutner, M. H. (1990). *Applied linear statistical models.* Homewood, IL: Irwin.

Neuman, J. H., & Baron, R. A. (1998). Workplace violence and workplace aggression: Evidence concerning specific forms, potential causes, and preferred targets. *Journal of Management, 24,* 391–419. doi:10.1016/S0149-2063(99)80066-X

Nicholls, J. C. (1984). Achievement motivation: Conceptions of ability, subjective experience, task choice, and performance. *Psychological Review, 91*, 328–346. doi:10.1037/0033-295X.91.3.328

Nisbett, R. E. (1993). Violence and U.S. regional culture. *American Psychologist, 48*, 441–449. doi:10.1037/0003-066X.48.4.441

Nisbett, R. E., & Wilson, T. D. (1977). Telling more than we can know: Verbal reports on mental processes. *Psychological Review, 84*, 231–259. doi:10.1037/0033-295X.84.3.231

Nosek, B. A., Greenwald, A. G., & Banaji, M. R. (2007). The Implicit Association Test at age 7: A methodological and conceptual review. In J. A. Bargh (Ed.), *Automatic processes in social thinking and behavior* (pp. 265–292). New York, NY: Psychology Press.

Nunnally, J. C., & Bernstein, I. H. (1994). *Psychometric theory* (3rd ed.). New York, NY: McGraw-Hill.

O'Leary-Kelly, A. M., Griffin, R. W., & Glew, D. J. (1996). Organization-motivated aggression: A research framework. *Academy of Management Review, 21*, 225–253. doi:10.2307/258635

Olsson, U., Drasgow, F., & Dorans, N. J. (1982). The polyserial correlation coefficient. *Psychometrika, 47*, 337–347. doi:10.1007/BF02294164

Ones, D. S., Dilchert, S., Viswesvaran, C., & Judge, T. A. (2007). In support of personality assessment in organizational settings. *Personnel Psychology, 60*, 995–1027. doi:10.1111/j.1744-6570.2007.00099.x

Ones, D. S., & Viswesvaran, C. (1998). Gender, age, and race differences in overt integrity tests: Results across four large-scale job applicant data sets. *Journal of Applied Psychology, 83*, 35–42.

Ones, D. S., Viswesvaran, C., & Reiss, R. D. (1996). Role of social desirability in personality testing for personnel selection: The red herring. *Journal of Applied Psychology, 81*, 660–679. doi:10.1037/0021-9010.81.6.660

Orpen, C. (1978). Conscious control of projection in the Thematic Apperception Test. *Psychology: A Journal of Human Behavior, 15*, 67–75.

Ozer, D. J. (1999). Four principles of personality assessment. In L. A. Pervin & O. P. John (Eds.), *Handbook of personality: Theory and research* (2nd ed., pp. 671–688). New York, NY: Guilford Press.

Paulhus, D. L., & Williams, K. (2002). The Dark Triad of personality: Narcissism, Machiavellianism, and psychopathy. *Journal of Research in Personality, 36*, 556–568.

Pearson, C. M. (1998). Organizations as targets and triggers of aggression and violence: Framing rational explanations for dramatic organizational deviance. *Research in the Sociology of Organizations, 15*, 197–223.

Pyszczynski, T., & Greenberg, J. (1987). Toward an integration of cognitive and motivational perspectives on social inference: A biased hypothesis-testing model. In L. Berkowitz (Ed.), *Advances in experimental social psychology: Vol. 20* (pp. 297–340). New York, NY: Academic Press. doi:10.1016/S0065-2601(08)60417-7

Raynor, J. O. (1978). Motivation and career striving. In J. W. Atkinson & J. O. Raynor (Eds.), *Personality, motivation, and achievement* (pp. 199–242). Washington, DC: Hemisphere.

Resick, C. J., Whitman, D. S., Weingarden, S. M., & Hiller, N. J. (2009). The bright-side and the dark-side of CEO personality: Examining core self-evaluations, narcissism, transformational leadership, and strategic influence. *Journal of Applied Psychology, 94*, 1365–1381. doi:10.1037/a0016238

Revelle, W., & Michaels, E. J. (1976). The theory of achievement motivation revisited: The implications of inertial tendencies. *Psychological Review, 83*, 394–404. doi:10.1037/0033-295X.83.5.394

Richetin, J., Richardson, D. S., & Mason, G. D. (2010). Predictive validity of IAT aggressiveness in the context of provocation. *Social Psychology, 41*, 27–34. doi:10.1027/1864-9335/a000005

Roberts, B. W., Harms, P. D., Caspi, A., & Moffitt, T. E. (2007). Predicting the counterproductive employee in a child-to-adult prospective study. *Journal of Applied Psychology, 92*, 1427–1436. doi:10.1037/0021-9010.92.5.1427

Robinson, S. L., & Bennett, R. J. (1995). A typology of deviant workplace behaviors: A multi-dimensional scaling study. *Academy of Management Journal, 38*, 555–572. doi:10.2307/256693

Rorschach, H. (1942). *Psychodiagnostics*. New York, NY: Grune & Stratton.

Ross, L. (1977). The intuitive psychologist and his shortcomings: Distortion in the attribution process. In L. Berkowitz (Ed.), *Advances in experimental social psychology* (Vol. 10, pp. 87–116). New York, NY: Academic Press.

Rosse, J. G., Stecher, M. D., Miller, J. L., & Levin, R. A. (1998). The impact of response distortion on preemployment personality testing and hiring decisions. *Journal of Applied Psychology, 83*, 634–644. doi:10.1037/0021-9010.83.4.634

Rothbaum, F., Weisz, J. R., & Snyder, S. S. (1982). Changing the world and changing the self: A two-process model of perceived control. *Journal of Personality and Social Psychology, 42*, 5–37. doi:10.1037/0022-3514.42.1.5

Rotundo, M., & Sackett, P. R. (2002). The relative importance of task, citizenship, and counterproductive performance to global ratings of job performance: A policy-capturing approach. *Journal of Applied Psychology, 87*, 66–80. doi:10.1037/0021-9010.87.1.66

Russell, S. M., & James, L. R. (2008). Recording lying, cheating, and defiance in an Internet based simulated environment. *Computers in Human Behavior, 24*, 2014–2025. doi:10.1016/j.chb.2007.09.003

Sarason, I. G. (1978). *Test anxiety: Concept and measurement*. In I. G. Sarason & C. D. Spielberger (Eds.), *Stress and anxiety*. New York, NY: Wiley.

Saremi, A., & Arora, R. (2008). The cardiovascular implications of alcohol and red wine. *American Journal of Therapeutics*, *15*, 265–277. doi:10.1097/MJT.0b013e3180a5e61a

Schlenker, B. R., & Leary, M. R. (1982). Social anxiety and self-presentation: A conceptualization and model. *Psychological Bulletin*, *92*, 641–669. doi:10.1037/0033-2909.92.3.641

Schmidt, F. L., & Hunter, J. E. (1998). The validity and utility of selection methods in personnel psychology: Practical and theoretical implications of 85 years of research findings. *Psychological Bulletin*, *124*, 262–274. doi:10.1037/0033-2909.124.2.262

Schmit, M. J., & Ryan, A. M. (1993). The Big Five in personnel selection: Factor structure in applicant and nonapplicant populations. *Journal of Applied Psychology*, *78*, 966–974. doi:10.1037/0021-9010.78.6.966

Schneider, D. J. (1991). Social cognition. *Annual Review of Psychology*, *42*, 527–561. doi:10.1146/annurev.ps.42.020191.002523

Schneider, W., & Shiffrin, R. M. (1977). Controlled and automatic human information processing: I. Detection, search, and attention. *Psychological Review*, *84*, 1–66. doi:10.1037/0033-295X.84.1.1

Schultheiss, O. C. (2008). Implicit motives. In O. P. John, R. W. Robins, & L. A. Pervin (Eds.), *Handbook of personality: Theory and research* (pp. 603–633). New York, NY: Guilford Press.

Skarlicki, D. P., & Folger, R. (1997). Retaliation in the workplace: The roles of distributive, procedural, and interaction justice. *Journal of Applied Psychology*, *82*, 434–443. doi:10.1037/0021-9010.82.3.434

Smith, B. S., & Ellingson, J. E. (2002). Substance versus style: A new look at social desirability in motivating contexts. *Journal of Applied Psychology*, *87*, 211–219.

Smith, D. B., Hanges, P. J., & Dickson, M. W. (2001). Personnel selection and the five-factor model: Reexamining the effects of applicant's frame of reference. *Journal of Applied Psychology*, *86*, 304–315.

Snell, A. F., Sydell, E. J., & Lueke, S. B. (1999). Toward a theory of applicant faking: Integrating studies of deception. *Human Resources Management Review*, *9*, 119–242.

Sorrentino, R. M., & Short, J.-A. C. (1986). Uncertainty orientation, motivation, and cognition. In R. M. Sorrentino & E. T. Higgins (Eds.), *Handbook of motivation and cognition: Foundations of social behavior* (pp. 379–403). New York, NY: Guilford Press.

Spangler, W. D. (1992). Validity of questionnaire and TAT measures of need for achievement: Two meta-analyses. *Psychological Bulletin*, *112*, 140–154. doi:10.1037/0033-2909.112.1.140

Spence, J. T., & Helmreich, R. L. (1983). Achievement-related motives and behaviors. In J. T. Spence (Ed.), *Achievement and motives* (pp. 7–74). San Francisco, CA: Freeman.

Stark, S., Chernyshenko, O., Chan, K.-Y., Lee, W., & Drasgow, F. (2001). Effects of the testing situation on item responding: Cause for concern. *Journal of Applied Psychology, 86*, 943–953.

Sternberg, R. J. (1982). In R. J. Sternberg (Ed.), *Handbook of human intelligence* (pp. 227–295). Cambridge, England: Cambridge University Press.

Stricker, L. J., & Rock, D. A. (1998). Assessing leadership potential with a biographical measure of personality traits. *International Journal of Selection and Assessment, 6*, 164–184. doi:10.1111/1468-2389.00087

Sturman, M. C. (1999). Multiple approaches to analyzing count data in studies of individual differences: The propensity for type I errors, illustrated with the case of absenteeism prediction. *Educational and Psychology Measurement, 59*, 414–430.

Substance Abuse and Mental Health Services Administration. (2007). *Results from the 2006 National Survey on Drug Use and Health: National Findings*. Office of Applied Studies, NSDUH Series H-32, DHHS Publication No. SMA 07-4293, Rockville, MD.

Swendsen, J. D., & Merikangas, K. R. (2000). The comorbidity of depression and substance abuse disorders. *Clinical Psychology Review, 20*, 173–189. doi:10.1016/S0272-7358(99)00026-4

Sykes, G. M., & Matza, D. (1957). Techniques of neutralization: A theory of delinquency. *American Sociological Review, 22*, 664–670. doi:10.2307/2089195

Taylor, S. E. (1991). Asymmetrical effects of positive and negative events: The mobilization minimization hypothesis. *Psychological Bulletin, 110*, 67–85. doi:10.1037/0033-2909.110.1.67

Taylor, S. E., & Brown, J. D. (1988). Illusion and well-being: A social psychological perspective on mental health. *Psychological Bulletin, 103*, 193–210. doi:10.1037/0033-2909.103.2.193

Taylor, S. E., & Lobel, M. (1989). Social comparison activity under threat: Downward evaluation and upward contacts. *Psychological Review, 96*, 569–575. doi:10.1037/0033-295X.96.4.569

Tedeschi, J. T., & Nesler, M. S. (1993). Grievances: Development and reactions. In R. B. Felson & J. T. Tedeschi (Eds.), *Aggression and violence: Social interactionist perspectives* (pp. 13–46). Washington, DC: American Psychological Association. doi:10.1037/10123-001

Tepper, B. J., Duffy, M. K., & Shaw, J. D. (2001). Personality moderators of the relationship between abusive supervision and subordinates' resistance. *Journal of Applied Psychology, 86*, 974–983. doi:10.1037/0021-9010.86.5.974

Toch, H. H. (1993). Good violence and bad violence: Self-presentations of aggressors through accounts and war stories. In R. B. Felson & J. T. Tedeschi (Eds.), *Aggression and violence: Social interactionist perspectives* (pp. 193–208). Washington, DC: American Psychological Association. doi:10.1037/10123-008

Todorov, T., & Bargh, J. A. (2002). Automatic sources of aggression. *Aggression and Violent Behavior, 7*, 53–68. doi:10.1016/S1359-1789(00)00036-7

Tversky, A., & Kahneman, D. (1973). Availability: A heuristic for judging frequency and probability. *Cognitive Psychology, 5,* 207–232. doi:10.1016/0010-0285(73)90033-9

Tversky, A., & Kahneman, D. (1974, September 27). Judgment under uncertainty: Heuristics and biases. *Science, 185,* 1124–1131. doi:10.1126/science.185.4157.1124

Tversky, A., & Kahneman, D. (1981, January 30). The framing of decisions and the psychology of choice. *Science, 211,* 453–458. doi:10.1126/science.7455683

Tversky, A., & Kahneman, D. (1983). Extensional versus intuitive reasoning: The conjunction fallacy in probability judgment. *Psychological Review, 90,* 293–315. doi:10.1037/0033-295X.90.4.293

U.S. Department of Justice, Federal Bureau of Investigation, Criminal Justice Information Division. (2009). *Uniform crime reports: Crime in the United States.* Retrieved from http://www2.fbi.gov/ucr/cius2009/index.html

Van der Kooy, K., Van Hout, H., Marwijk, H., Marten, H., Stehouwer, C., & Beekman, A. (2007). Depression and the risk for cardiovascular diseases: Systematic review and meta-analysis. *International Journal of Geriatric Psychiatry, 22,* 613–626. doi:10.1002/gps.1723

Vane, J. R. (1981). The thematic apperception test: A review. *Clinical Psychology Review, 1,* 319–336. doi:10.1016/0272-7358(81)90009-X

Van Vugt, M., Hogan, R., & Kaiser, R. B. (2008). Leadership, followership, and evolution: Some lessons from the past. *American Psychologist, 63,* 182–196. doi:10.1037/0003-066X.63.3.182

Veroff, J. (1992). Power motivation. In C. P. Smith (Ed.), *Motivation and personality: Handbook of thematic content analysis* (pp. 278–285). New York, NY: Cambridge University Press. doi:10.1017/CBO9780511527937.020

Viswesvaran, C., & Ones, D. S. (1999). Meta-analyses of fakability estimates: Implications for personality measurement. *Educational & Psychological Measurement, 59,* 197–210. doi:10.1177/00131649921969802

Watson, G., & Glaser, E. M. (1980). Watson-Glaser Critical Thinking Appraisal: Forms A and B. San Antonio, TX: PsychCorp.

Wegner, D. M., & Vallacher, R. R. (1977). *Implicit psychology: An introduction to social cognition.* New York, NY: Oxford University Press.

Weiner, B. (1979). A theory of motivation of some classroom experiences. *Journal of Educational Psychology, 71,* 3–25. doi:10.1037/0022-0663.71.1.3

Weiner, B. (1990). Attribution in personality psychology. In L. A. Pervin (Ed.), *Handbook of personality: Theory and research* (pp. 465–485). New York, NY: Guilford Press.

Weiner, B. (1991). Metaphors in motivation and attribution. *American Psychologist, 46,* 921–930. doi:10.1037/0003-066X.46.9.921

Weissman, M. M. (1987). Advances in psychiatric epidemiology: Rates and risks for major depression. *American Journal of Public Health, 77,* 445–451. doi:10.2105/AJPH.77.4.445

Westen, D. (1991). Social cognition and object relations. *Psychological Bulletin, 109,* 429–455. doi:10.1037/0033-2909.109.3.429

Westen, D. (1998). The scientific legacy of Sigmund Freud: Toward a psycho-dynamically informed psychological science. *Psychological Bulletin, 124,* 333–371. doi:10.1037/0033-2909.124.3.333

Westen, D., & Gabbard, G. O. (1999). Psychoanalytic approaches to personality. In L. A. Pervin & O. P. John (Eds.), *Handbook of personality: Theory and research* (2nd ed.; pp. 57–101). New York, NY: Guilford Press.

Wilson, T. D., & Brekke, N. (1994). Mental contamination and mental correction: Unwanted influences on judgments and evaluations. *Psychological Bulletin, 116,* 117–142. doi:10.1037/0033-2909.116.1.117

Wilson, T. D., Lindsey, S., & Schooler, T. Y. (2000). A model of dual attitudes. *Psychological Review, 107,* 101–126. doi:10.1037/0033-295X.107.1.101

Winter, D. G. (1973). *The power motive.* New York, NY: Free Press.

Winter, D. G. (1992). Power motivation revisited. In C. P. Smith, J. W. Atkinson, D. C. McClelland, and J. Veroff (Eds.), *Motivation and personality: Handbook of thematic content analysis* (pp. 301–310). New York, NY: Cambridge University Press.

Winter, D. G., John, O. P., Stewart, A. J., Klohnen, E. C., & Duncan, L. E. (1998). Traits and motives: Toward an integration of two traditions in personality research. *Psychological Review, 105,* 230–250. doi:10.1037/0033-295X.105.2.230

Wood, J. V. (1989). Theory and research concerning social comparisons of personal attributes. *Psychological Bulletin, 106,* 231–248. doi:10.1037/0033-2909.106.2.231

Wright, J. C., & Mischel, W. (1987). A conditional approach to dispositional constructs: The local predictability of social behavior. *Journal of Personality and Social Psychology, 53,* 1159–1177. doi:10.1037/0022-3514.53.6.1159

Yukl, G. (2009). *Leadership in organizations* (7th ed.). Upper Saddle River, NJ: Prentice Hall.

Zickar, M. J., & Robie, C. (1999). Modeling faking good on personality items: an item-level analysis. *Journal of Applied Psychology, 84(4),* 551–563.

Ziegert, J. C., & Hanges, P. J. (2009). Strong rebuttal for weak criticism: Reply to Blanton et al. (2009). *Journal of Applied Psychology, 94,* 590–597. doi:10.1037/a0014661

# INDEX

Dilchert, S., 161
Dimensions, 118–119
Direct assessment, 165
Discounting, 65–66
Displacement of responsibility bias, 201–202
Dissociation, 172
Dissociative model of personality
    in CRT-A, 142–148
    and implicit personality assessment, 165–166
    and integrative model for aggression, 175
Distortion, response, 9, 152–157
Distractors, 100–101
Distributions of scores, 115–118
Dominance
    in aggression conditional reasoning problems, 105
    egoistic, 195, 205–207
    justification mechanisms for, 59–60
    in leadership, 205–206
    in potency bias, 32
Draw-A-Person Test, 7–8
Drift, 28

Efficacy of persistence bias, 53–54, 93
Egoistic dominance, 195, 205–207
Empirical validity (CRT-A), 123–137
Employment context, 156–157
Encoding, 76
Environmental stimuli, 3–4
Evaluation of evidence, 73, 105–106
Evasion of discomfort bias, 200–201
Everyday reasoning, 83
Evocative stimulus, 13, 71, 72
Excitatory tendency, 46
Exner, J. E., Jr., 7
Exner's Comprehensive System, 7
Expectations
    with achievement motivation, 90
    in fear of failure, 79
    halo effect on, 64–65
    with negative self-bias, 196
    of outcomes, 74, 103
Experimental design, 161
Explicit measures, 141–142
Explicit personality, 4
    in achievement motivation, 183
    assessment of, 5

congruency with implicit personality, 174, 185–186
    in CRT-A, 148–149
    incongruency with implicit personality, 186
    and overt aggression, 146–148
    and passive aggression, 146–147
    self-report measures of, 140–142
External attribution bias, 56–57, 64, 71, 79
External threats, 56–57, 119–120
Extraversion, 166–171

Factor structure, 21, 113–114, 161–162
Failure. *See also* Fear of failure
    concentration of attention on, 57
    motive to avoid, 18, 45–47, 73
Faking, 9, 152–157
Farnham, S. D., 10
Fear of failure, 70–84
    conditional reasoning in, 55–58, 82–84
    congruence of personality in, 191
    conditional reasoning problem design for, 73–79, 88–89, 91–94
    defined, 40
    and demanding tasks, 53
    in development of CRT-RMS, 163
    implicit biases in, 65, 66
    incongruency of personality in, 186
    inductive reasoning in, 82–84
    informal reasoning in, 81–84
    justification mechanisms for, 48–49, 54–58
    logical assertions associated with, 70
    mental processes underlying, 70–73
    motive structure in, 183–185
    overestimation of, 47
    reasoning for, 85–86
    relative motive strength in, 89
    stimulus for motive to avoid failure, 73
Finnegan, W., 29
Fixed skills bias, 56, 57, 71, 73, 79, 94
Folger, R., 131–132
Framing
    with achievement motivation, 62–63
    with addiction proneness, 200
    with aggression, 21–26
    in behavioral adjustments, 38–39

Leniency, 66
Leveling bias, 56, 66, 71, 88–89
Liability inclination bias, 56, 71, 91
Lilienfeld, S. O., 8–9
Limitations of traditional implicit
measures, 9–12
Logic
in achievement motivation, 49
in conditional reasoning problem
design, 73–77
in conditional reasoning problems,
20
in encoding information, 76
in fear of failure, 55–58
illusory, 19–20
in implicit biases, 69–70
in justification mechanisms, 17, 61
with negative self-bias, 197–199
with nonaggression, 36
Logical assertions
in assumptions, 82–84
in conditional reasoning problem
development, 69–70
with fear of failure, 79–80
unstated assumptions in, 80–82
Lord, F. M., 117
Lying, 182

Maier, G. W., 143
Males, 139–140, 145
Malleability of skills bias, 53, 54, 93
Matza, D., 28
Mazerolle, M. D., 37, 39n1, 42, 49, 179
McClelland, D. C., 8, 27, 142, 143, 147,
165, 166
Measurement
of aggression, 19, 96
arbitrary metrics in, 149–150
based on multiple responses, 8
of biases, 18
with implicit association tests, 10–12
of implicit biases, in CRT-A,
119–121
of implicit personality, 4–5, 13–14
indirect, 6–8
of justification mechanisms, 69–70
limitations of traditional implicit
measures, 9–12
of negative self-bias, 198–199
Ozer's principles for, 20–21

of personality, 18
of potency bias, 120–121
with projective tests, 6–10
with response latency tests, 10–12
of retribution bias, 120–121
of social discounting bias, 121
Measures
for implicit and explicit personality,
148–149, 166
implicit vs. explicit, 141–142
of self-report, 140–142
of single vs. multiple dimensions,
118–119
standards for assessing implicit
personality, 13–14
Meehl, P. E., 20, 21
Meta-analyses, 136
Metrics
arbitrary, 149
nonarbitrary, 149–152
Mischel, W., 9
Moral standards, 26, 28, 33–34
Motivated reasoning, 83
Motivation
for aggression, 148
to approach vs. avoid, 44–48
for leaders, 204
self-reported, 187–190
Motives
behavior based on, 60–61, 81–82
in channeling hypothesis, 166
in conditional reasoning, 44–48
congruence of, with personality
traits, 167–171
implicit components of, 47–48
triggers for, 73
as unconscious, 27
Motive to achieve
in approach–avoidance conflicts,
44–45
justification mechanisms of, 49–54
and motive to avoid failure, 46–47
in personality assessment, 18
Motive to aggress, 25–27
Motive to avoid failure
in approach–avoidance conflicts,
45–46
identification of stimulus for, 73
and motive to achieve, 46–47
in personality assessment, 18

# ABOUT THE AUTHORS

**Lawrence R. James, PhD,** is a professor of psychology and management at the Georgia Institute of Technology. He is a fellow of Divisions 5 (Evaluation, Measurement, and Statistics) and 14 (Society for Industrial and Organizational Psychology) of the American Psychological Association, a founding fellow of the American Psychological Society (now the Association for Psychological Science), and a fellow of the Academy of Management. In 2003, Dr. James won the Distinguished Career Award from the Academy of Management Research Methods Division. He has been active in building new measurement systems for personality and in studying the effects of organizational environments on individual adaptation, motivation, and productivity. His statistical contributions have been designed to make possible tests of new models in areas such as organizational climate, leadership, and personnel selection.

**James M. LeBreton, PhD,** is an associate professor of psychological sciences at Purdue University. In 2009, he won the Early Career Award, cosponsored by the Academy of Management Research Methods Division and the Center for the Advancement of Research Methods and Analysis. Dr. LeBreton studies how toxic personality traits (e.g., aggression, psychopathy) are related to variables such as decision making, team interactions, counterproductive workplace behaviors, and sexual aggression. His methodological work focuses on issues related to multilevel measurement, multilevel analysis, and tests for moderation and mediation.